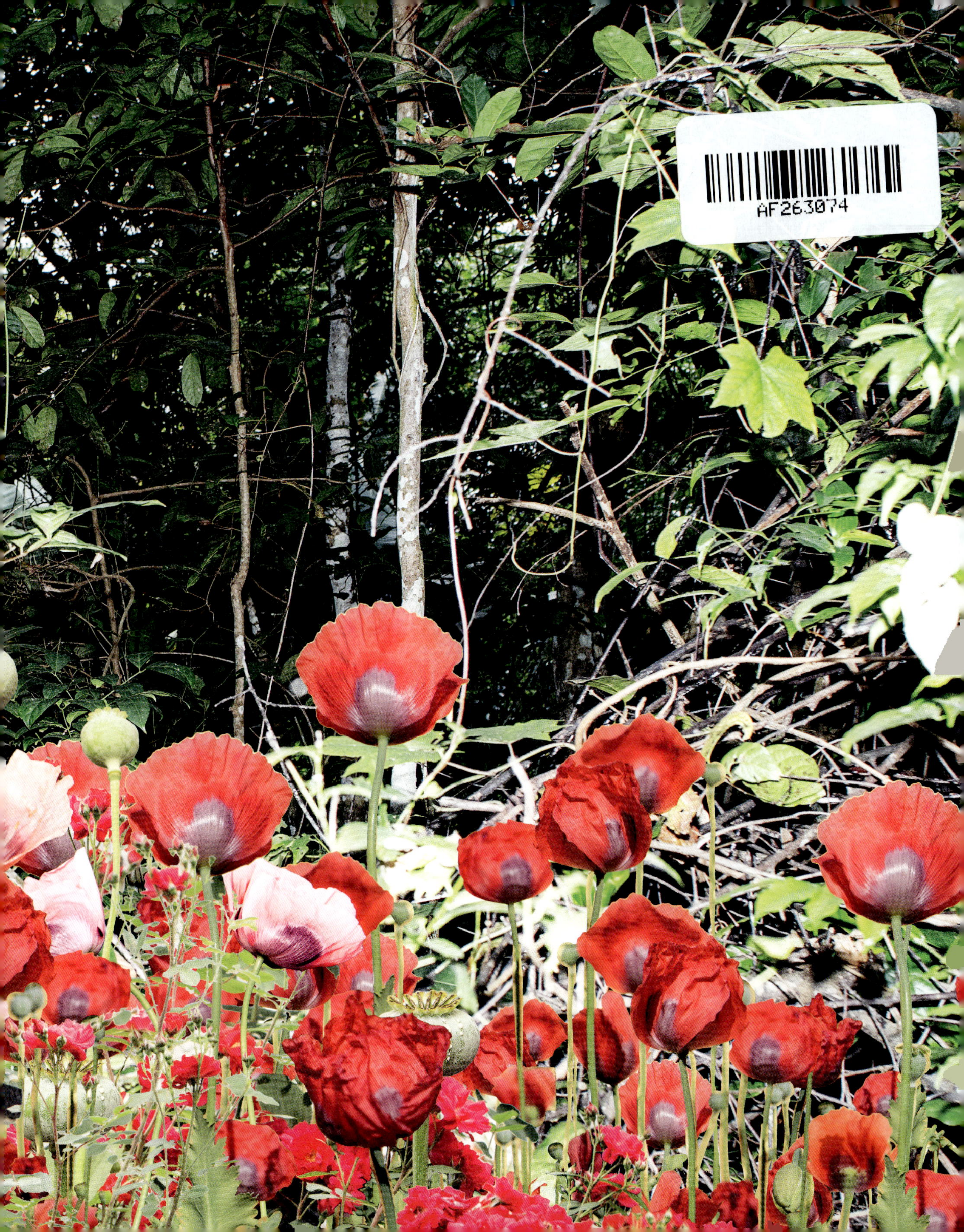
AF263074

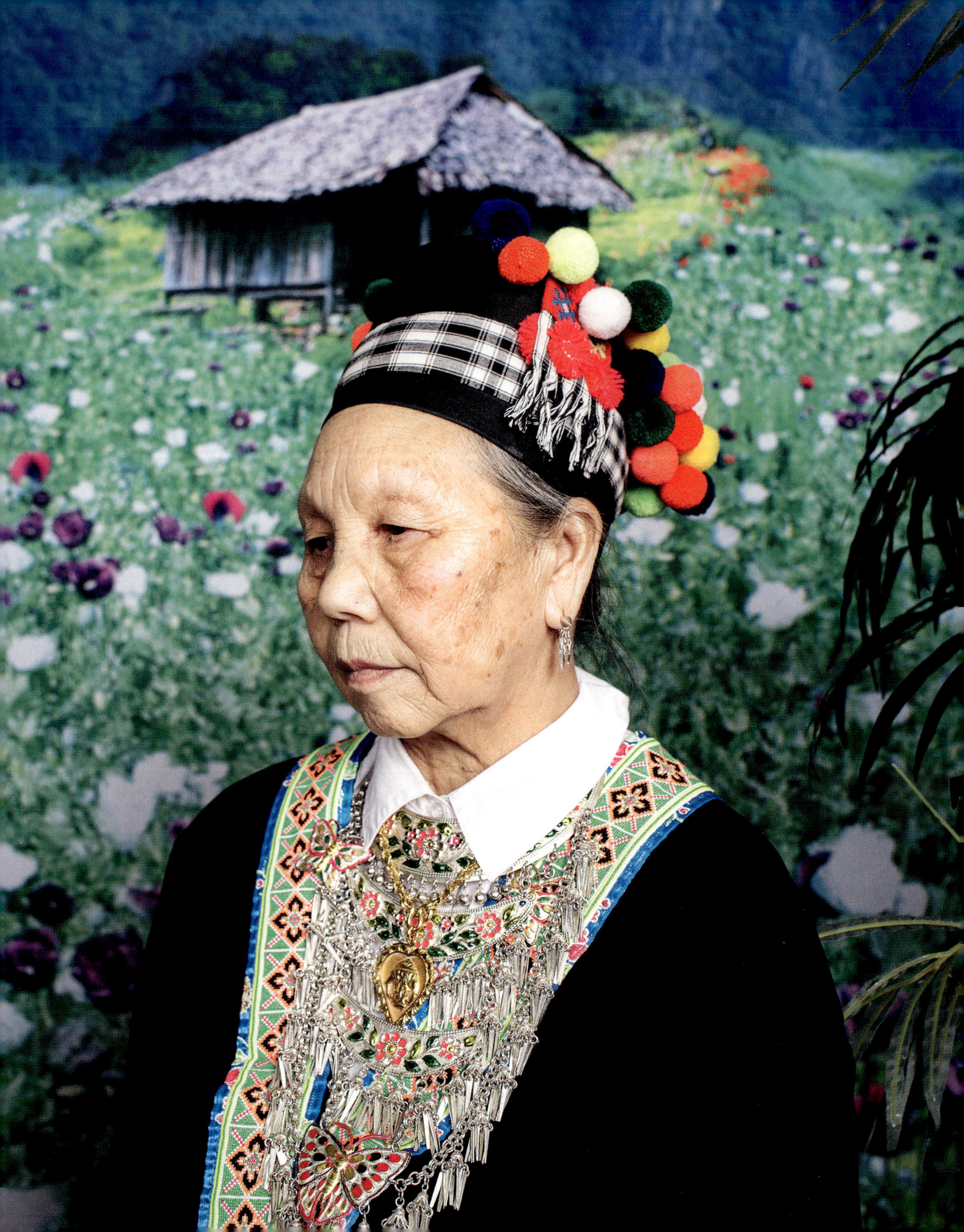

PAO HOUA HER

THE IMAGINATIVE LANDSCAPE

JOHN MICHAEL KOHLER ARTS CENTER   SAN JOSÉ MUSEUM OF ART

FOREWORD

S. SAYRE BATTON *and* AMY HORST

How do we capture the multifaceted, deeply personal, community-minded, and nationally engaging work of Pao Houa Her in a single exhibition? The answer is we don't—at least, not in a conventional way. *Pao Houa Her: The Imaginative Landscape* is envisioned as multisited and simultaneous—at the John Michael Kohler Arts Center (JMKAC) and San José Museum of Art (SJMA), and in public and community spaces in Sheboygan and San José. The exhibition is not merely a presentation of Her's work, it is an extension of her practice, a testament to her commitment to embedding art in the everyday lives of Hmong communities while also representing and exploring Hmong American constructions of homeland.

JMKAC and SJMA are honored to co-organize the first major exhibition of work by Pao Houa Her, one of the most important artists of the Hmong diaspora working today. Her's work is collected by major museums and she's well recognized by the art establishment with an MFA from Yale University, inclusion in the 2022 Whitney Biennial exhibition, a Guggenheim Fellowship, and recipient of Aperture's Next Step Award, yet the focus of her practice has been unwavering in capturing the experiences and stories of her Hmong community and making space for Hmong representation.

Co-organized by institutions in California and Wisconsin, states with the first and third-largest Hmong populations in the country, and launched during the fiftieth anniversary of Hmong resettlement in the United States, this exhibition structurally embraces diverse contexts in which Hmong people have adapted and fabricated homelands in this country. The exhibition acknowledges the specificities of Hmong American experience in different geographic contexts—experiences that are distinct, yet collaboratively longing for an elsewhere homeland.

Sheboygan, a town of roughly 50,000 (predominantly white) people, is in the top ten United States cities with the largest Hmong population. In 1985, in response to the settlement of the first wave of Hmong refugees in Wisconsin, JMKAC initiated its collection of traditional Hmong art—one of the earliest of its kind in the US—and presented an exhibition and publication, *Hmong Art: Tradition and Change*, the very next year. Pao Houa Her's work was first shown at JMKAC in the 2023 exhibition *Cloth as Land: Hmong Indigeneity*, organized by California-based curator Pachia Vang.

Within the racially, ethnically, and linguistically diverse California Bay Area, Hmong people live among large Asian American and Hispanic populations. SJMA has a core commitment to nurturing a sense of belonging and through "borderless" programming, has longstanding relationships with a variety of diasporic communities whose own experiences, while distinct, resonate with Hmong Americans, opening up larger conversations about immigrant and refugee experiences.

The vast geography of this project comes together in this book. Lauren Schell Dickens's opening essay explores the aesthetics and materiality of Pao Houa Her's work within a contemporary, art historical context, followed by an in-depth conversation between Jodi Throckmorton and the artist, who shares personal insights into her creative practice and behind-the-scenes developments of the community-rooted installation in Sheboygan. The book concludes with historian Alexander Supartono's essay, which traces the rich and complex history of Southeast Asian photography and situates Her's work within this broader cultural lineage. In addition, the catalogue features a special section of Her's recently realized *Seeds of History* portraits of the Wisconsin Hmong community. Together, these contributions frame the artist's powerful images within both community and art contexts, inviting readers to consider Her's work from multiple perspectives.

This expansive project was collaboratively envisioned by Jodi Throckmorton, chief curator at JMKAC, and Lauren Schell Dickens, chief curator at SJMA, to whom we are deeply grateful, and would not be possible without the support of many people. Thanks go to those in Sheboygan who welcomed Her's work into their spaces, especially Robert Ziegelbauer (Ziggy), Choua and Kou Lee, Thai Café; Shelia Yang; M. Chang; Board of Directors of the Hmong Mutual Assistance Association; Natasha Torry, Sheboygan County Circuit Court Judge; Kate Krause, Paradigm Coffee and Music; Grant Pauly, 3 Sheeps Brewing; and Yeng Yang, Union Asian Market. In downtown San José, thanks to Robin Treen, Adolfo Gomez,

Mezcal Restaurant; Lesley Seacrist, SJSU King Library; Julie Carlson, Lou Jimenez, Lauren Nuttell, San José Downtown Association; and Laura Chmielewski, Kaitlyn Joe, Carla Morla, Frances Wong; Team San José. We also thank the staff at both institutions. To install an exhibition within museum walls is a feat; to expand it into coffee shops, restaurants, public spaces, and even a courtroom required resourcefulness, creativity, and care. Their work allowed this project to truly live beyond the museum.

No project of this complexity comes together without major financial support, and we are grateful to the funders who made the exhibition and publication possible, including lead support from Teiger Foundation and The Andy Warhol Foundation for the Visual Arts. The JMKAC presentation is also made possible by the Kohler Trust for Arts and Education, Ruth Foundation for the Arts, the Mellon Foundation, the Frederic Cornell Kohler Charitable Trust, Kohler Foundation, Inc., the Wisconsin Arts Board with funds from the State of Wisconsin and the National Endowment for the Arts, and from the generous support of our members and donors. We are also honored to thank Steve Westphal, President, and Laura Kohler, Treasurer of JMKAC's Board of Directors—without their belief and advice this project would not be as expansive as it is today. We are deeply grateful to Vue Yang, whose decades of service on JMKAC's Board of Directors, and role as a key advisor, helped shape the Arts Center as a place of belonging for the Hmong community. Together with his wife, Pa Yang, they guided how *The Imaginative Landscape* could be rooted in Sheboygan's own landscape today. The SJMA presentation was also made possible by the SJMA Exhibitions Fund, with generous support from the E. Rhodes and Leona B. Carpenter Foundation, Brook Hartzell and Tad Freese, Wanda Kownacki, and Mary Mocas and Marv Tseu.

And, most importantly, our profound gratitude goes to Pao Houa Her, who bravely embraced this complicated project with good humor and trust. We are so grateful to her for sharing her work with us and our communities.

S. Sayre Batton
Oshman Executive Director, San José Museum of Art

Amy Horst
Executive Director, John Michael Kohler Arts Center

NEW GROUND

LAUREN SCHELL DICKENS

Photography is full of fictions, both material and conceptual. Subjects perform and pose for the camera, while the frame's imposed border omits some wider context. A photograph is a flattened representation, which is itself a material object that exists in a particular place and time, or abstracted into the digital everywhere all at once sphere. A search for origins, a pinpointing of identity, is, of course, a fiction of a different sort. Terms like "authenticity" have been weaponized to exclude and essentialize within the racist melting pot of the United States. Immigrants and refugees cut off from roots in other lands are expected to either disappear like chameleons or justify their difference. Within diasporic communities, urgencies of cultural preservation and critique animate intergenerational dialogues as the stakes of living in the States grow ever higher.

Pao Houa Her is the most well-known Hmong American artist working in the United States today, whose portraits and landscapes of her community have done much to bring their representation into the guarded, historically whitewashed walls of museums. In her first project after graduate school, Her made a series of portraits of Hmong soldiers who were enlisted to aid the CIA's covert military operations against the Northern Vietnamese Communists during the war in Vietnam. Officially recognized as allies in the so-called Secret War, but not veterans, Her photographed them in the style of American generals and civil war soldiers. The men pose in store-bought uniforms decorated with medals and military decorations either handmade or purchased on eBay, performing their own rituals of honor and self-recognition despite their egregious historical erasure. Recognition and representation matter, and are important for the Hmong community, but the radicality of Her's conceptual photo-based practice is in exceeding the confines of American identity politics into which Hmong have been thrust.

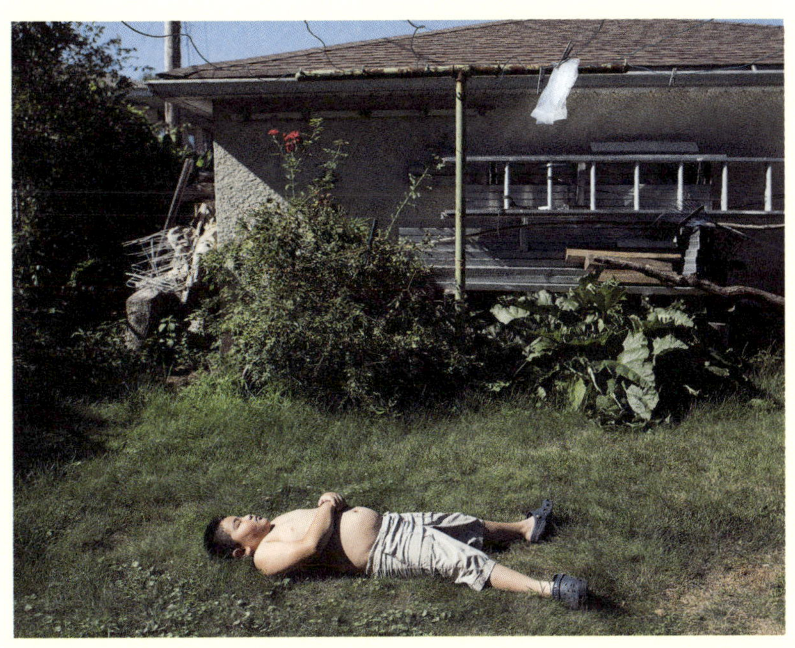

untitled (Erik laying outside with ziplock bags), 2018, from *The Imaginative Landscape* series, archival pigment print

One of Her's earliest memories is of a screening of the 1982 film *Rambo: First Blood*, projected onto a white sheet hung in one of the Thai refugee camps where her family stayed until 1985. She recalls her parents and elders later discussing and citing the heroics of John Rambo as justification for their support of American troops during the war. It was more than a decade before Her learned that Rambo was not a documentary film, as her family had surmised, but Hollywood mythmaking. But why quibble with details? Some stories are truer than fact.

The Hmong tradition of oral storytelling stretches back centuries before the rupture and dislocation caused by the American war in Vietnam, Laos, and Cambodia. Her was reared on such stories—folktales her father recorded on cassette tapes for nights when he worked past bedtime, the family legend of her grandfather reincarnated as a tiger, histories of Hmong people written in the land, of the Laotian jungle, of California's Mount Shasta region, and of opium poppy fields in Minnesota. Her's work embodies these stories. Photography "is a truth if you want it to be a truth," she has said.[1] More than pictures *of* anything, her fictious realism explores the ideological function of image-making in the construction of homeland for the Hmong diaspora.

1   Paul Schmelzer, "Homelands Lost, Constructed, Reimagined; An Interview with Pao Houa Her," Bockley Gallery, September 12, 2022, https://bockley-gallery.com/pao-houa-her-interview.

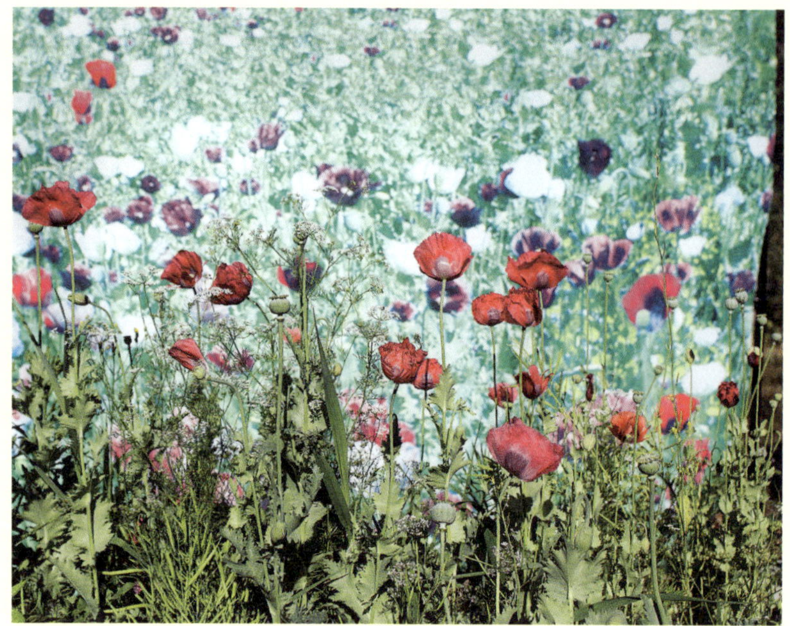

The loss of land is core to contemporary Hmong identity, the absent ground against which belonging is built in relief. Sometimes identified as an Indigenous group, the Hmong people lived in the mountainous regions of southern China as early as the third century, before being driven into the highland areas of Laos, Vietnam, and Thailand as a result of Chinese land expansion in the 1800s. There they farmed and prospered due to colonial demand for the opium poppies they cultivated. After aiding the CIA in the Laotian front of the war in Vietnam, many Hmong were forced to flee when American troops withdrew, or risk persecution or death at the hands of the incoming northern Vietnamese army. After sheltering in refugee camps in Thailand, between the 1980s and 1990s Hmong families were relocated to European and Western countries including Australia, France, Canada, French Guiana, and the United States, with the largest numbers settling in Minnesota, Wisconsin, and California's Central Valley. Her's biography on her website reads like a poetic travelogue: "She was born somewhere in the northern jungles of Laos. She fled Laos with her family when she was a baby, crossed the Mekong on her mother's back, was fed opium to keep from crying, lived in the refugee camps in

2   "About," artist's website,
www.paohher.com.

Thailand and landed in America on a silver metal bird in the mid 1980s."[2]

Perhaps because of this history of dislocation, the chimera of the lost Hmong homeland is ever present. There is a Hmong word, *teb chaw*—literally "land-place"—for this core longing, a desire so profound as to be world-shaping. In 2016, a Hmong man peddling fraudulent investments in a new homeland swindled $1.7 million out of Hmong seniors, mostly in the St. Paul, Minnesota, area. Her's series *After the Fall of Hmong Teb Chaw* (2017), made the year the con man was convicted, is comprised of portraits taken at the Hmong Elders Center in St. Paul, one of the daycare centers most heavily targeted by the scheme (and also where the artist's mother works). In the black-and-white images, seniors sit resolutely, nearly enveloped by potted tropical plants and silk flowers cascading from above. Despite the lush surroundings there is an austere unreality to the scenes; a plastic sheen betrays some of the greenery, barely perceptible threads hang from fabric leaves, the excessive blossoms too pristine. They are all fake. These portraits are interspersed with images of dense tropical foliage. Details like botanical name plates or partially visible architectural elements reveal it to be a nature conservancy, also in St. Paul, where Hmong families pass time on snowy days, relishing the comfort of a displaced yet thriving Southeast Asian jungle. Even after the swindler was exposed and forced to compensate his victims, some Hmong pledged their restitution toward his legal fees, a gesture of support for his continued work. They are not (or are no longer) duped, but willing participants in a collaborative fiction, conjuring land from sheer desire.

Traditional Hmong studio portraiture is formulaic: an artificial, pastoral backdrop of Laos, with silk flowers, frequently poppies, and plants in the foreground. The body between these elements is enveloped by landscape, wrapped in heavily embellished fabrics—the finest heirloom treasures brought out only at new year celebrations—itself a Hmong tradition of cloth as a proxy for land. The first story cloths—embroidered pictorial textiles for which the Hmong are now well known—were thought to have been made in Ban Vinai refugee camp in the late 1970s.[3] Born of the flower cloth tradition, these textiles tell narratives about wartime and migrant experiences, as well as folktales and histories, binding oral traditions into material heirlooms.

3   Joshua Kueh, "Asia, Texts and
Textiles at the Library of Congress,
Hmong Story Cloths," 4 Corners of
the World, Library of Congress, July
23, 2020, https://blogs.loc.gov/
international-collections/2020/07/
asia-texts-and-textiles-at-the-
library-of-congress-part-ii-hmong-
story-cloths.

Her grew up seeing one such traditional photographic portrait in her grandmother's home. Taken of her cousin Pao Sao, it was made not to celebrate a birthday or new year, but as the rest of the family prepared to depart for the US, leaving Pao Sao behind. The fact that portrait studios were erected in refugee camps in Thailand to produce souvenirs for families soon-to-be-separated is gut-wrenching. For a population who fled on foot, leaving belongings behind, these formal images are the beginning of a photographic history borne of loss; records of kin, culture, and homeland left behind. In some sense, photography is always entangled with death, a past time, embalmed in light-sensitive emulsion. Artificial florals and vinyl landscapes heighten this stand against mortality, a sort of immortalized nostalgia protected from wilting: poppies in perpetual bloom. To the Hmong, the opium poppy recalls not just the land where they thrived, but a prewar era of prosperity and self-reliance, an independence, a culture, all tied up in a land now lost. Whereas historically, pictures from portrait studios were opportunities to frame oneself as modern, perhaps posing with a motorbike or urban backdrop, contemporary Hmong styling favors more nostalgic framings.

Her's grandmother treasured this portrait of Pao Sao, bringing it to the US and rehanging it each time she moved house. For Her, this image became a point of study, of dissection, as she began to understand the construction of the photograph itself as an embodied act of creating homeland. The scenic backdrops, rolled out for Hmong new year and other important events, literally set the stage. In *untitled (backdrop of plain of jars and poppy field)* (2019), Her frames a close up of two overlapping vinyl backdrops in a vertical portrait style, a sort of obviation of the figure-ground distinction. One backdrop shows a verdant valley of blooming opium poppies with a wedge of cliffs behind; the other, lifted along the bottom corner to reveal its blank back and grommeted edge, a stone jar on a famous archeological mountain plateau in northeast Laos once surrounded by Hmong villages (and a heavily bombed crossroads between North and South Vietnam). In both backdrops, low perspectives ground the viewer in the landscape, among the ancient pots and blooming poppies. Yet any such immersion is interrupted by the skillfully captured glare and grommets, emphasizing the artifice of the image.

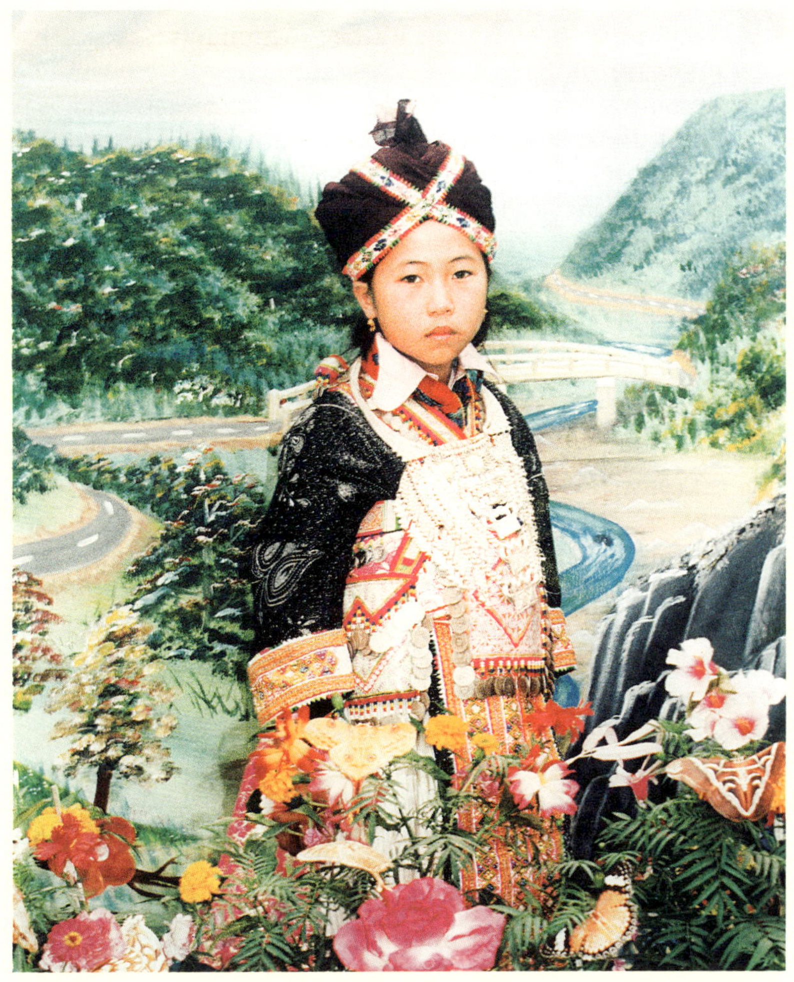

This artificial image of landscape, an approximate geography, unrealizable, is the backdrop against which nearly all Hmong portraiture plays out. It is one of several vernacular forms—along with profile pictures of Hmong Laotian girls from dating websites, fake floral bouquets, tourist souvenir photographs, and traditional *kwv txhiaj* song poetry circulated as music videos—whose aesthetic stylings inform Her's practice. In images for *Laos via Google*, for example, without concern for finesse or subtlety, Her Photoshops "travel" images for Hmong seniors, inserting their snapshots into stock imagery of Laotian landscapes. This colloquial technique echoes green screen technology available at portrait studios in St. Paul's Hmong Village, which have setups for patrons to pose in traditional village settings, with *qeej* musical instruments as props. The obvious artifice of such images is irrelevant, for the participatory visioning they enact is genuine. At other times, Her lifts vernacular images from her Hmong community directly, appropriating dating profile pictures or vacation keepsakes taken for Hmong tourists. Like many artists, she is drawing from and responding to source material from a living archive.

At Yale, Her studied under Richard Prince, whose flamboyant appropriations blew holes into notions of authorship and authenticity in contemporary art. She considers closely the staged reenactments of An-My Lê, the mythologizing family album aesthetics of Deana Lawson, and is captivated by the self-portraits taken by escaping Taliban soldiers collected by Magnum photographer Thomas Dworzak. It is a cliché to note the ingenuity of immigrants in unintendedly transforming culture, but Her takes what she needs from existing photographic discourse and skillfully chooses a different orientation. Her's most recent series, *Pictures of paradise*, is titled in direct response to Thomas Struth's *New Pictures from Paradise* (1998–99), for which the German photographer depicted aboriginal forests in Australia, Japan, and China that he considered unaltered by human intervention. Her's series, by contrast, showing dense Laotian jungle, traces the route by which Her's family hid while fleeing their home country: sleeping, cooking, giving birth, and surviving in the undergrowth. The locations were pointed out to Her and her siblings on their first family trip back to Laos, nearly forty years later. Produced as lenticular prints, the landscape shifts continually under the viewers gaze, roiling the Western logic of surveilled land almost teasingly. For Her, the thick junglescapes embody both sanctuary and beauty, as well as the violence of survival and displacement. They hide stories of wartime atrocities held in silence, to avoid passing traumas onto younger generations, and they're the backdrop of the artist's own birth. The images guard these stories closely, metaphors for the layered depths of history, of homeland, that shift and morph.

During the COVID-19 pandemic lockdown, Her began looking through old work, incorporating new images, revising and reframing a history unfolding in the present tense. Pulling from across series, from images made in the US and Laos,

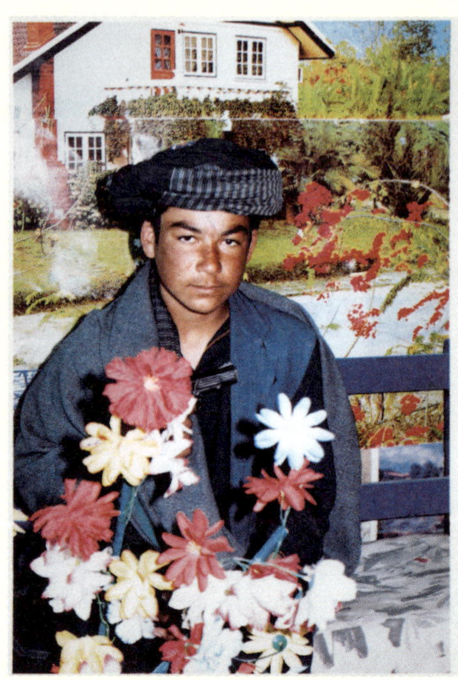

Taliban portrait, Afghanistan, Kandahar, 2002, Collection T. Dworzak/Magnum Photos

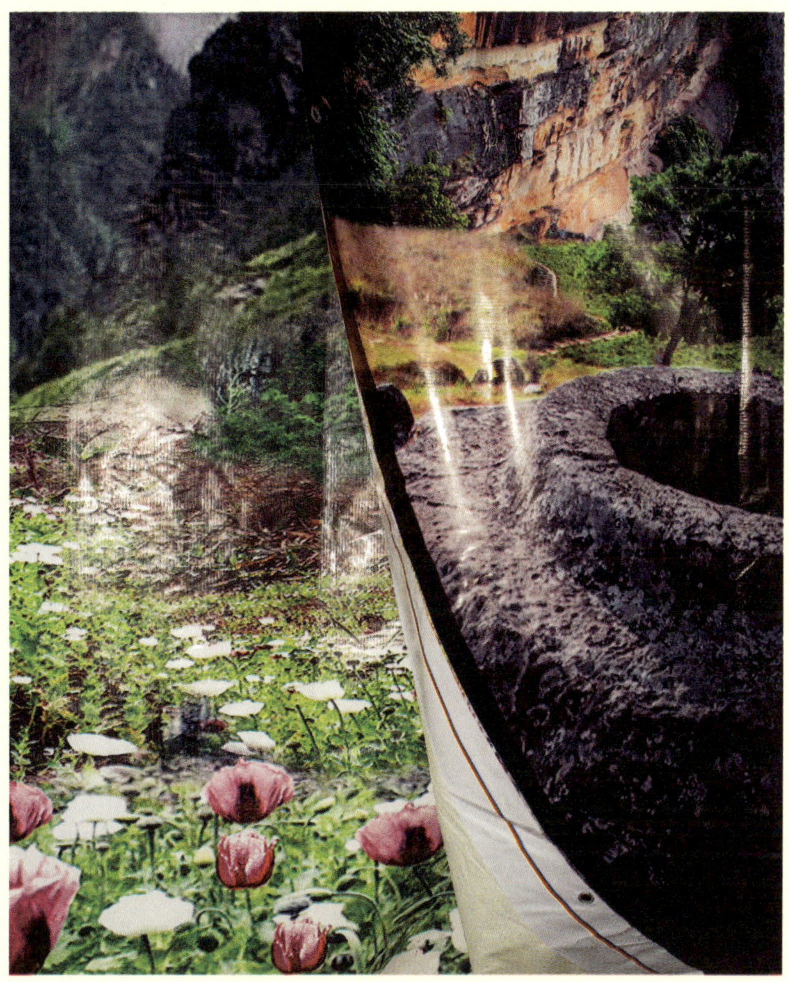

untitled (backdrop of plain of jars and poppy field), 2019, from *The Imaginative Landscape* series, archival pigment print

Her stitched together a reimagining of her grandmother's ideal of Laos, blurring geographies and temporalities, in an exploration of the power of desire to shape vision. *The Imaginative Landscape* series takes its title from Valerie Flint's study of Christopher Columbus, in which the British medievalist suggested that the explorer's understanding of the so-called new world was colored by mythology and medieval beliefs of Europe's old world, which though fanciful, "was so real ... that it had a decisive impact upon the eventual establishment of 'objective reality.' Here fact and fantasy become so hard to distinguish that the word fantasy loses its usual meaning, and fantasy of a certain sort becomes proper, indeed

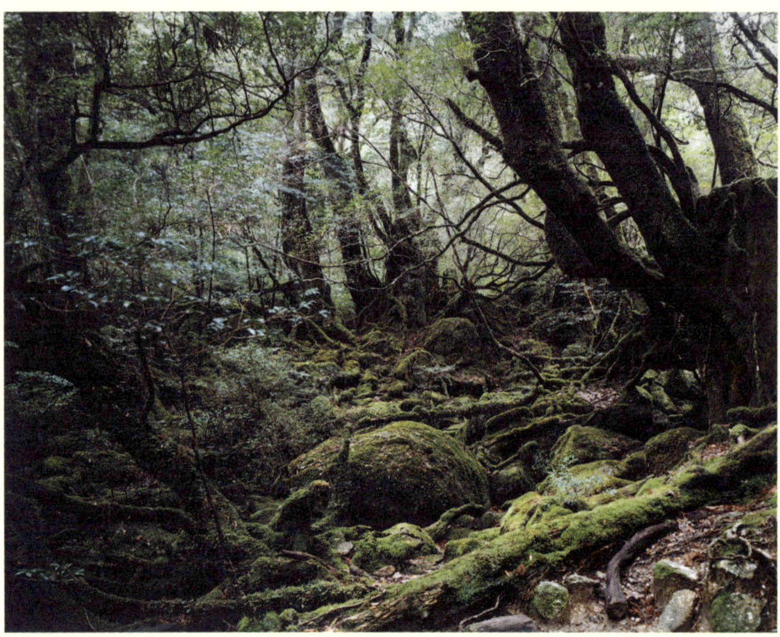

vital, to the complete understanding of fact itself."[4] Stories, family folklore, and animal transmutation, in other words, are inextricable from and indeed necessary for understanding the experience of reality. Interwoven truths and artifice are a new grounding from which to construct homeland.

We all carry stories and beliefs that implicate our vision, and photography also shapes our understanding of what we see. Nineteenth-century photography was closely linked with fantasies of exploration, European travel, and the colonial habit of fixing and organizing with a Cartesian logic of seeing (and therefore understanding). Her's moody, sweeping images of California's Mount Shasta region draw on American landscape photography traditions of the West established by Carleton Watkins and Timothy O'Sullivan, whose geographical surveys and depictions of Yosemite Valley helped cultivate a mythology of untouched wilderness that drove westward expansion. In majestic black-and-white images, Her focuses her camera on this rocky volcanic terrain where Hmong communities have migrated, putting their highland farming skills to use growing illegal cannabis, and for the lucky few, recreating the economic prosperity of prewar opium cultivation. Rather than focusing on the labor and resilience of

4   Valerie I. J. Flint, *The Imaginative Landscape of Christopher Columbus*, "Introduction" (Princeton University Press, 1992), xii.

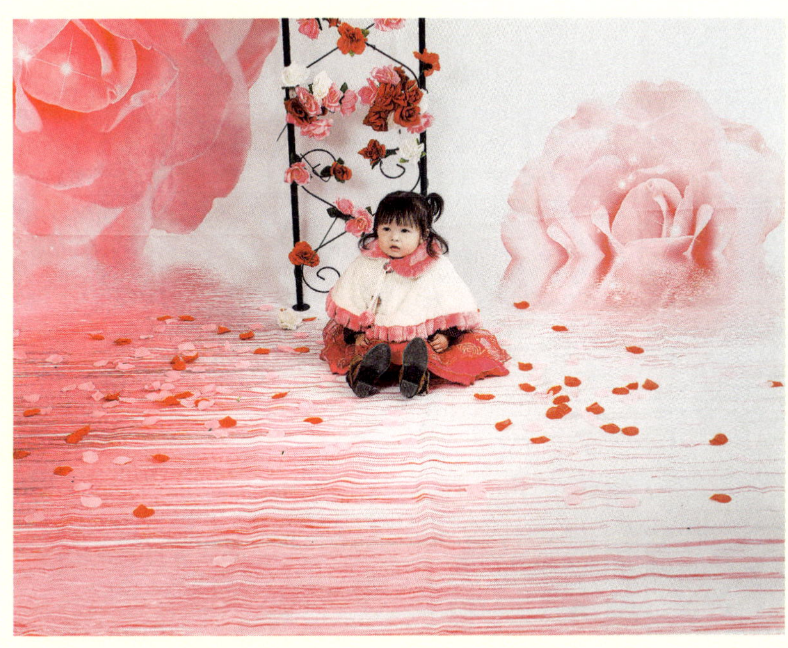

untitled, 2015, archival pigment print

these unpictured Hmong farmers, Her's Mount Shasta images are devoid of people, their presence marked only by snaking hoses, a floating plastic bag, or snow covered tools of agricultural work. But what we see in the specific geography—whether lands of manifest destiny or gardens of Indigenous caretakers, the American Dream as desirable or a trap—is up to our imaginative lens. This alluring glow is made literal as a backlit lightbox, of the type used to advertise exotic vacation destinations in airports and malls. The artifice of sublime light is decoded as desire, which hawked the American Dream during the nineteenth century and continues to sell dreams of prosperity to lure Hmong from Asia even today.

As a fiction, images hold great power in shaping the future. Her herself has no recollection of Laos. The mental image of her birthplace was assembled through familial stories, photographs, movies, and tape-recorded folktales, a collectively built imaginary filtered through diasporic experience. She first learned to use a camera to help her father record the family, a gesture of communal care that carries through her work today. In a global image economy where there is no distinction between public and private, collective and individual use, Her's vernacular embrace of Hmong image-making challenges the photographic archive on which

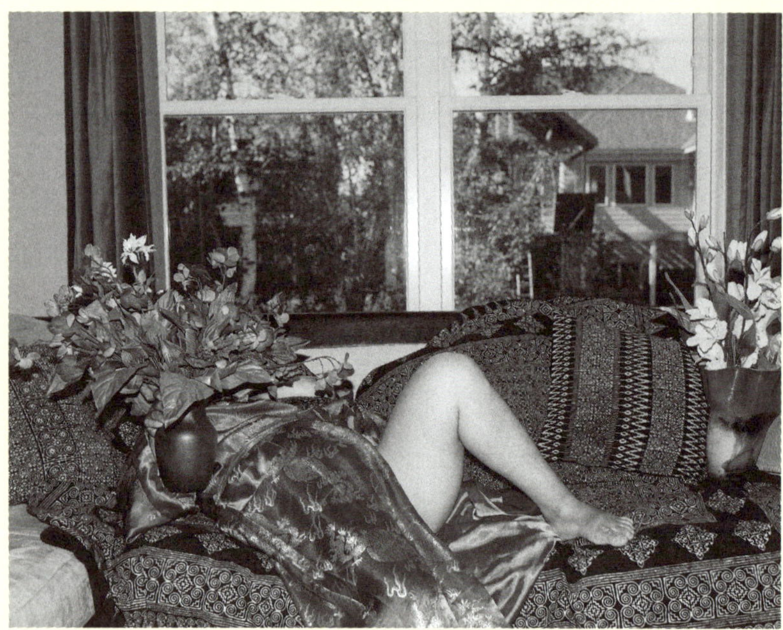

history and memory rest. For Hmong people, whose relatively recent use of written language, combined with material losses from fleeing as refugees, has meant that their story has been largely told by others, this is ground-shifting, history-writing work. It is a responsibility Her feels heavily. Yet, while uplifting she also analyzes: defamiliarizing framings of diasporic longing for return, and with it, challenging Hmong patriarchy to tell new stories on new ground.

History is often told as a sequence of male-centered military conflicts, and from Her's perspective, Hmong diasporic narratives similarly revolve around war and men. It's not surprising that the military-focused *Attention* series was Her's entry into national recognition and the work by which she is still best known. But in the decade since, Her has subtly challenged such patriarchal narratives by centering an alternate, era-defining symbol in contemporary Hmong memory, that of the opium poppy. In some ways a surrogate for the Hmong people themselves, the flower recalls a period when Hmong culture and life flourished in Laos. In diaspora, it is now only the women who plant poppies—the artist, her mother, and her mother-in-law all cultivate gardens in Minnesota, tending their seedlings and so much more. Flowers resonate across

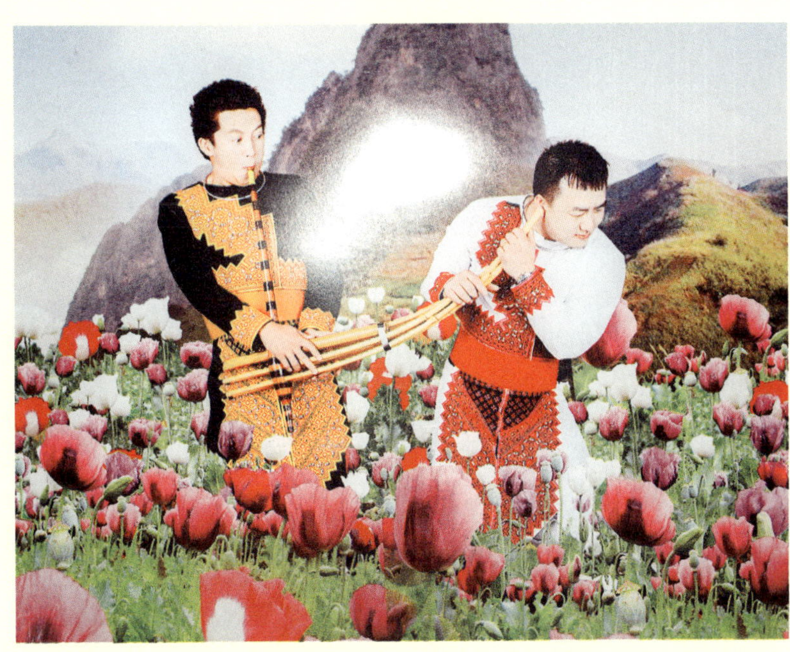

untitled (photograph of two men with instrument), 2019, from *The Imaginative Landscape* series, archival pigment print

cultures as symbols of fertility and womanhood, and take center stage in another early series. In *My Mother's Flowers* (2016), Her made formal still life images of her mother's collection of fake floral bouquets, which she'd made based on designs in *Martha Stewart Living Magazine*, founded by the matriarch of American domestic housekeeping. These floral arrangements are interspersed with profile pictures from Hmong Laotian dating websites, both appropriated and made, which scrutinize the symbols by which womanhood is advertised. In Her's most recent work, *A Conversation between 4 Hmong Women* (2025), she returns to the aesthetic format of *kwv txhiaj*, one of the only Hmong traditions in which men and women have equal standing, and omits the male voice entirely. The work functions as both an archive and reclamation. It preserves the complex musical and storytelling genre of improvisational call-and-response that serves a vital role in intergenerational knowledge sharing—while questioning the societal structures that affect Hmong women's lives. Across four screens, four women sing of the duties and sorrows of marriage. Though cinematically isolated, their narratives intertwine in a shared story of struggle, resilience, and intimacy. Women are harbingers of the future, shaping new stories.

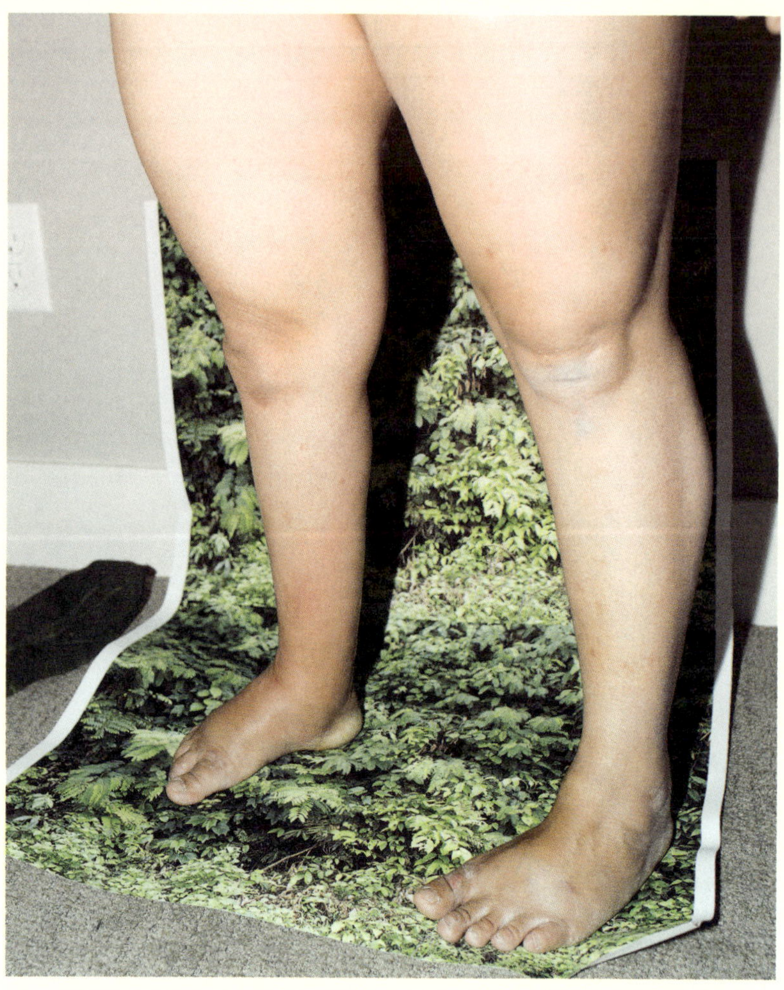

Feet on print, 2017, from the *My grandfather turned into a tiger* series, archival pigment print

The Imaginative Landscape stretches between the Midwest and California, bridging the two largest geographic centers of the Hmong diaspora. For the exhibition, Her's images are situated in institutional and public spaces—libraries, a courthouse, restaurants, a community center, disused storefronts, and public streets—different cultural contexts, and take on the vernacular forms of advertising lightboxes, billboards, wheat-pasted posters, lawn signs, and even as a community calendar. This malleability to context, agility in adaptation even while resolutely maintaining their own image and aesthetic, echoes immigrant tenacity across the US. Within the museum, the photograph's treatment and

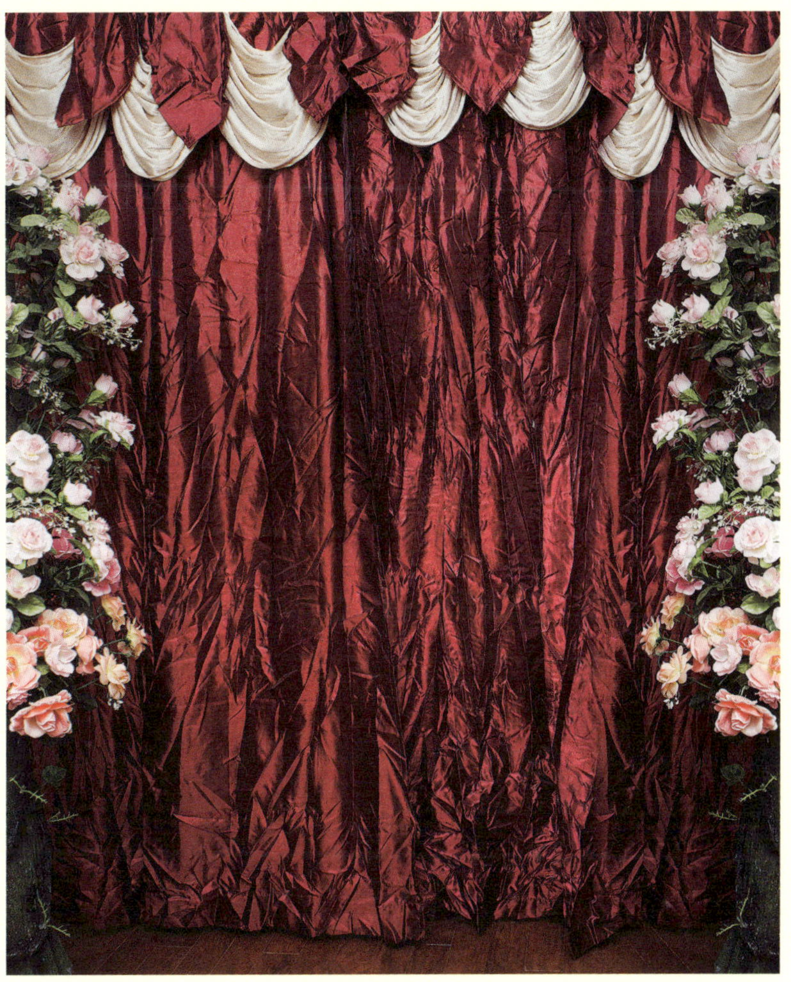

Maroon backdrop, 2017, from the *My grandfather turned into a tiger* series, archival pigment print

framing conforms to institutional norms of canon-writing, but in public space, any prescribed system of standardization is discarded as the images are adopted into various informal formats. This bridging of formal and colloquial, history-minded and community-centered, opens up to new forms of storytelling. It's a dazzling display of Hmong spirit, a community vernacular twisting the institution to work for its own purposes, honing fact with fiction to point to new possibilities for grounding, for homeland.

Despite the material flexibility Her embraces for her work, the physicality of the images as objects matter. Even digitally appropriated images are printed and rendered as objects, an intriguing corollary to our gravity-bound bodies, which stubbornly inhabit terra firma, in spite of our digital present. In Hmong culture, elaborate funeral rituals guide a person's spirit back across the ocean, unwinding a geographic migration through refugee camps and jungles to their birthplace in Laos. Yet this historical foreshortening that frames Laos as original homeland is itself a partial fiction, just one layer of the dancing lenticular, a pastoral backdrop that turns out to be vinyl, a clumsy Photoshop edit. The artifice is always present, and in embracing it Her proposes a new diasporic aesthetic built on groundlessness.

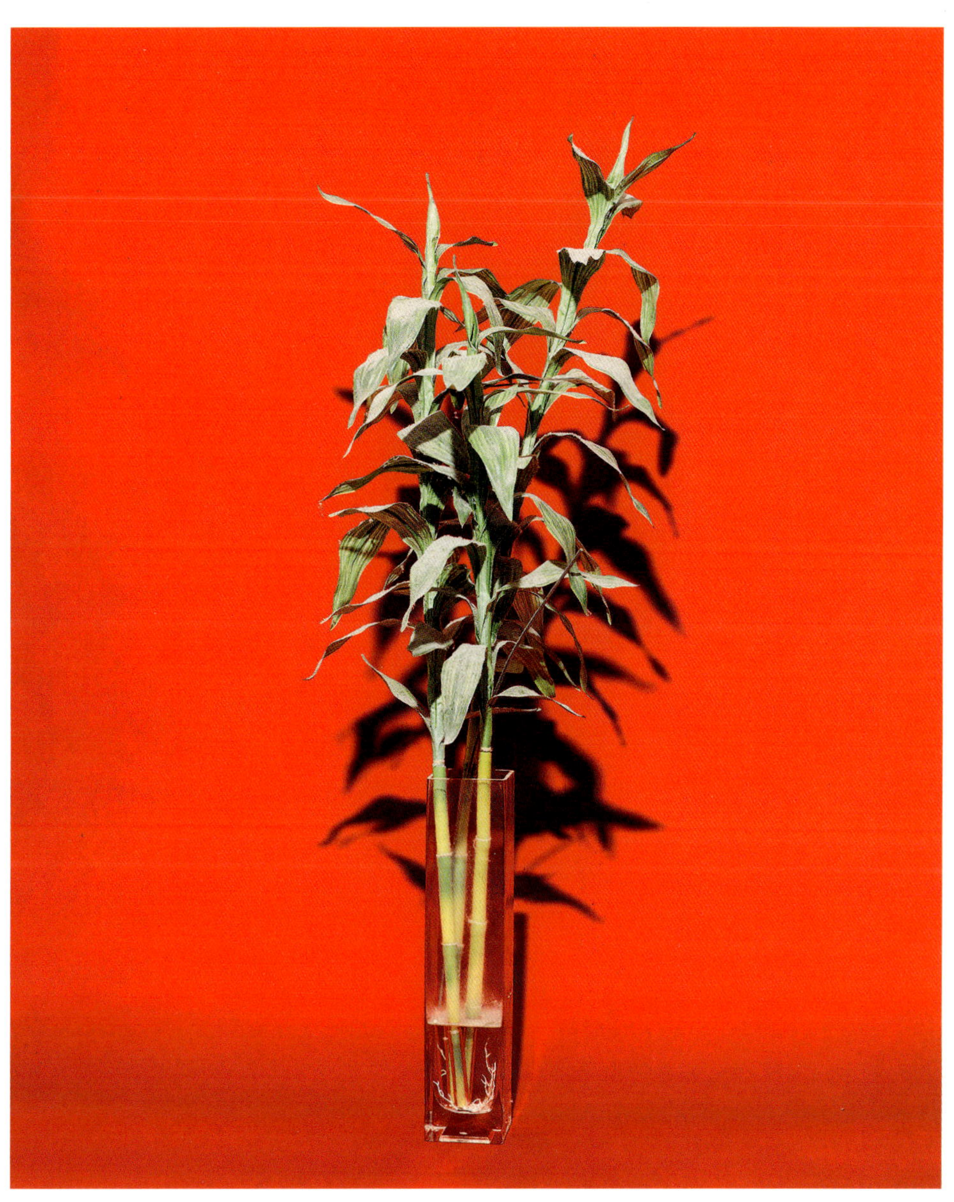

untitled, 2016, from the *My Mother's*
Flowers series, archival pigment print

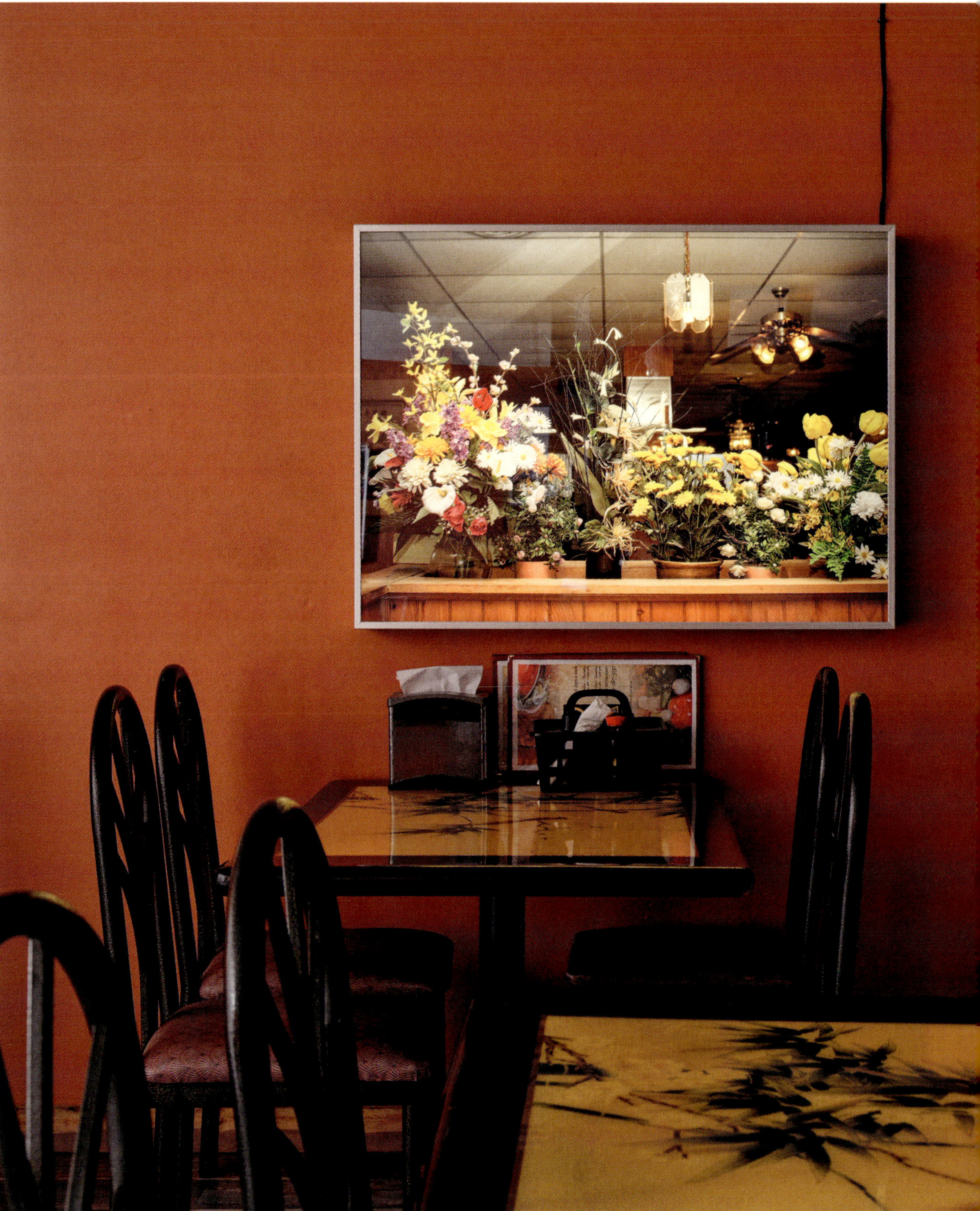

Pao Houa Her: The Imaginative Landscape, installation view at Thai Café, Sheboygan, Wisconsin, 2025

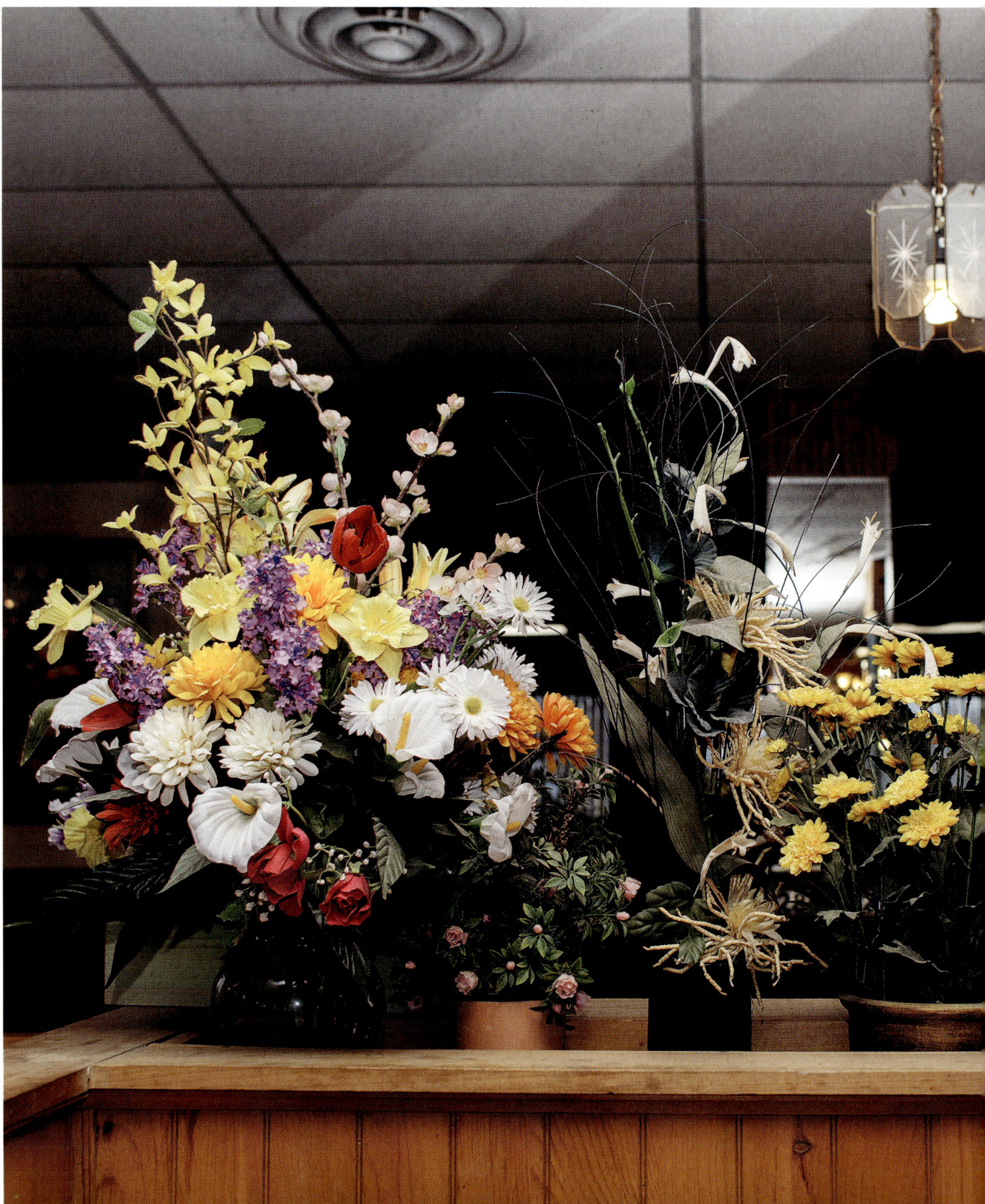

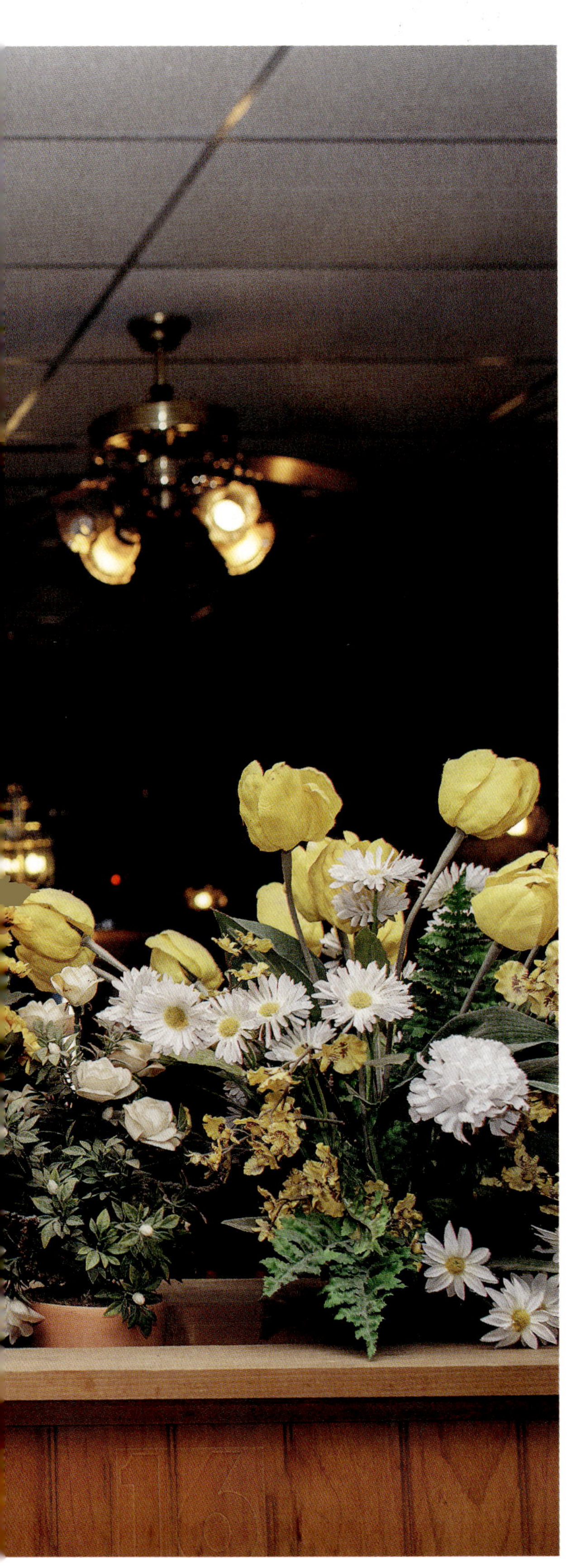

untitled (fake flowers from restaurant), 2019,
from *The Imaginative Landscape* series,
archival pigment print

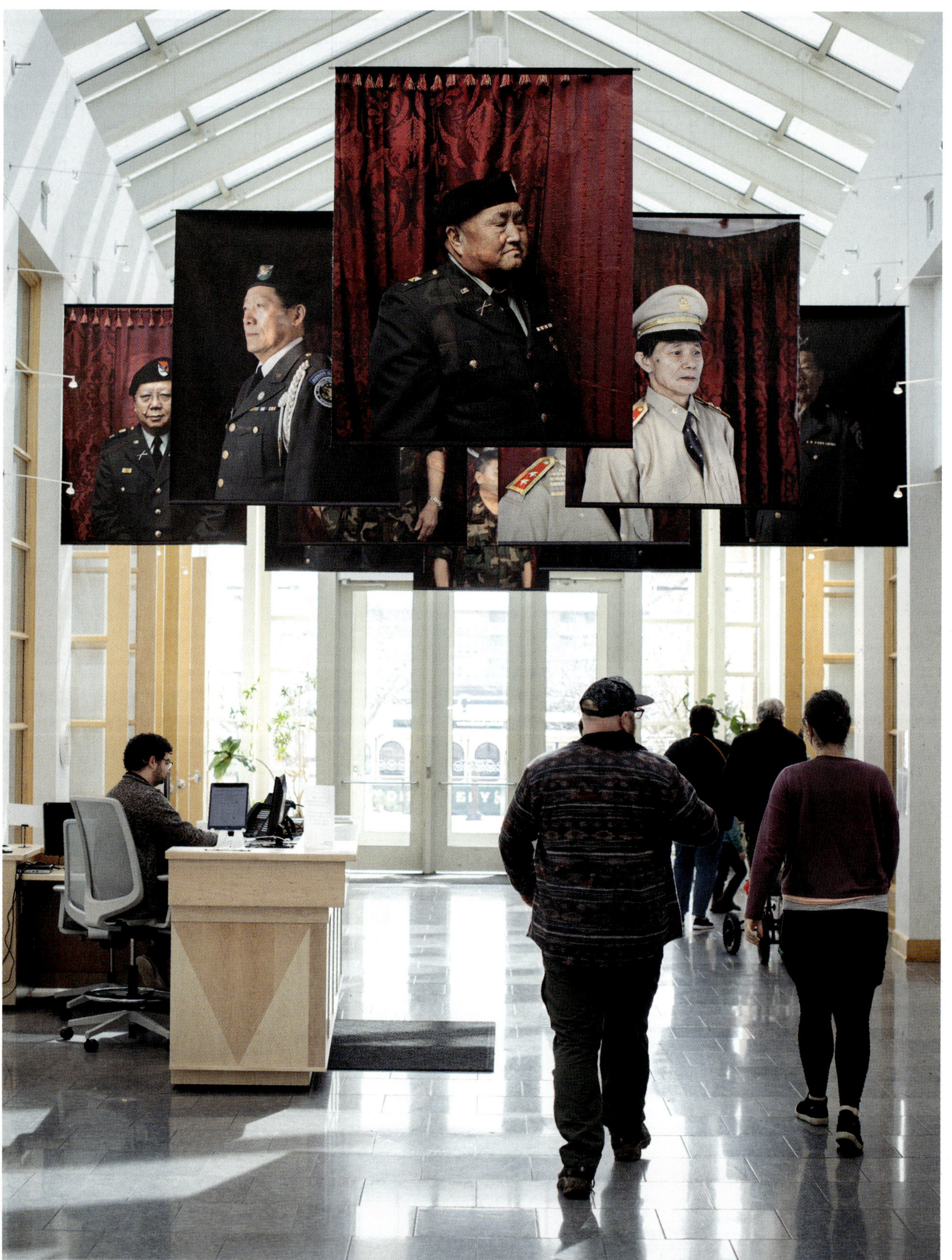

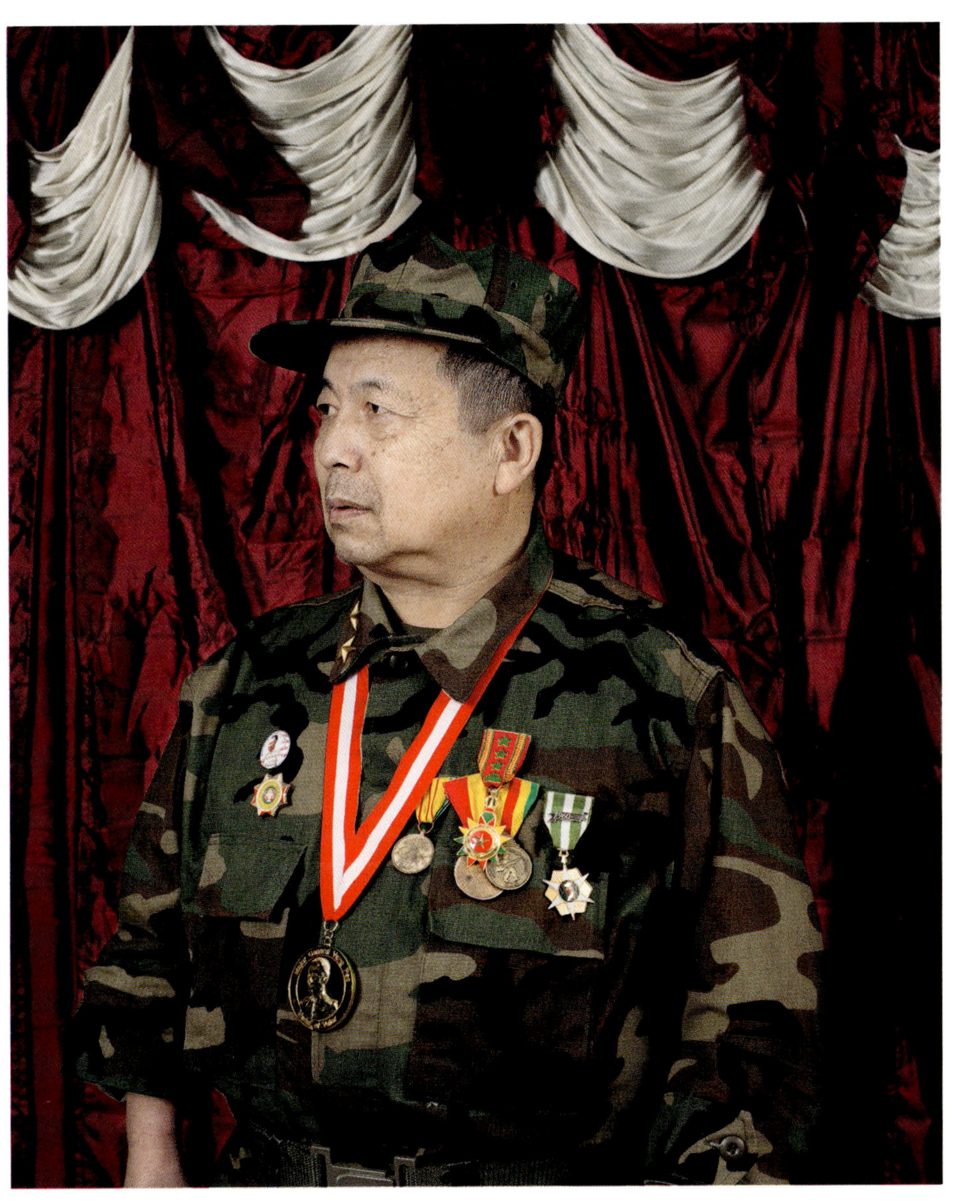

Hmong Veteran, 2014, from the *Attention*
series, archival pigment print

Left:
Pao Houa Her: The Imaginative Landscape,
installation view at the John Michael Kohler
Arts Center, Sheboygan, Wisconsin, 2025

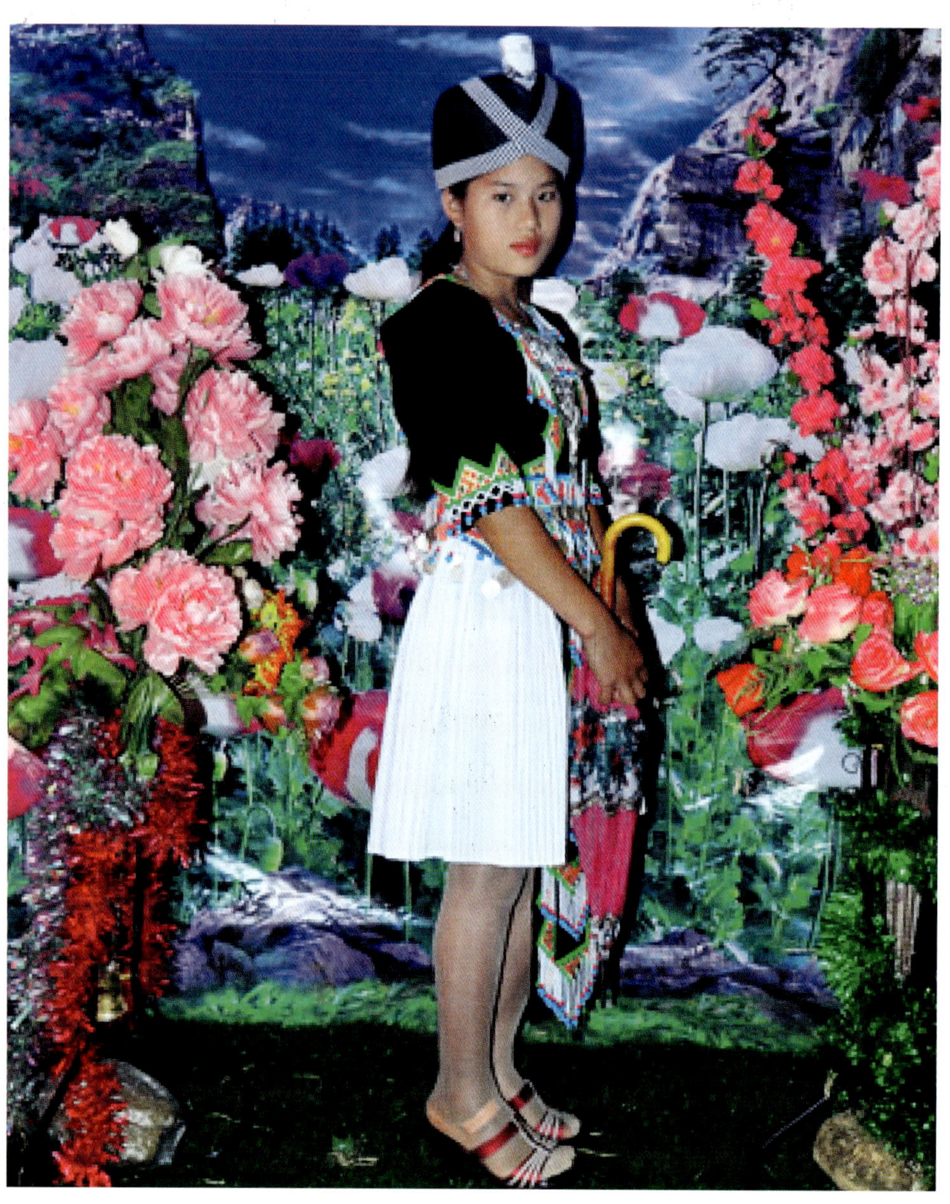

untitled, 2016, from the *My Mother's Flowers* series, archival pigment print

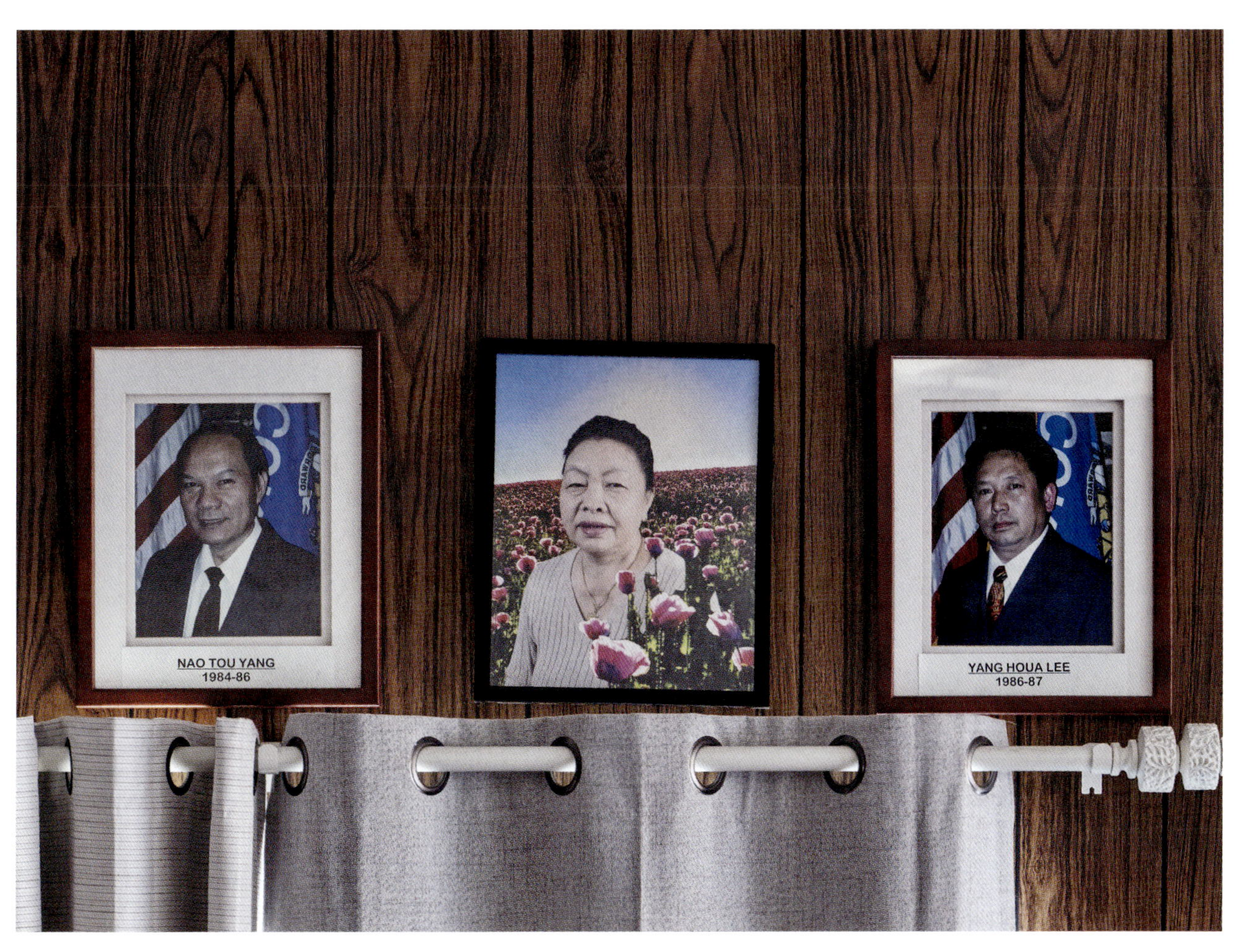

Pao Houa Her: The Imaginative Landscape, installation view at the Hmong Mutual Assistance Association, Sheboygan, Wisconsin, 2025

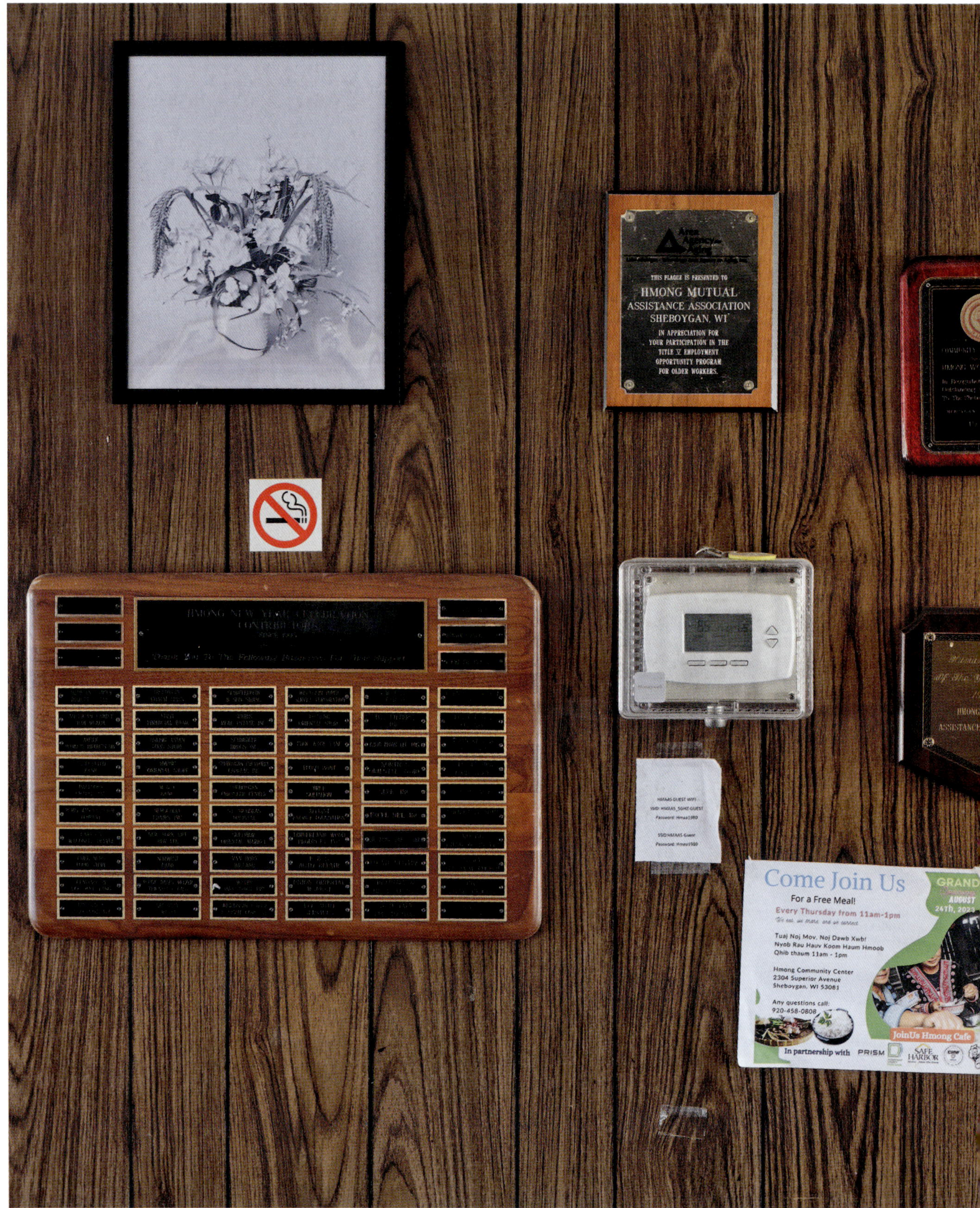
THIS PLAQUE IS PRESENTED TO
HMONG MUTUAL
ASSISTANCE ASSOCIATION
SHEBOYGAN, WI
IN APPRECIATION FOR
YOUR PARTICIPATION IN THE
TITLE V EMPLOYMENT
OPPORTUNITY PROGRAM
FOR OLDER WORKERS.
Come Join Us
GRAND
AUGUST 24th, 2023
For a Free Meal!
Every Thursday from 11am-1pm
Tuaj Noj Mov, Noj Dawb Xwb!
Nyob Rau Hauv Koom Haum Hmoob
Qhib thaum 11am - 1pm
Hmong Community Center
2304 Superior Avenue
Sheboygan, WI 53081
Any questions call:
920-458-0808
JoinUs Hmong Cafe
In partnership with PRISM SAFE HARBOR

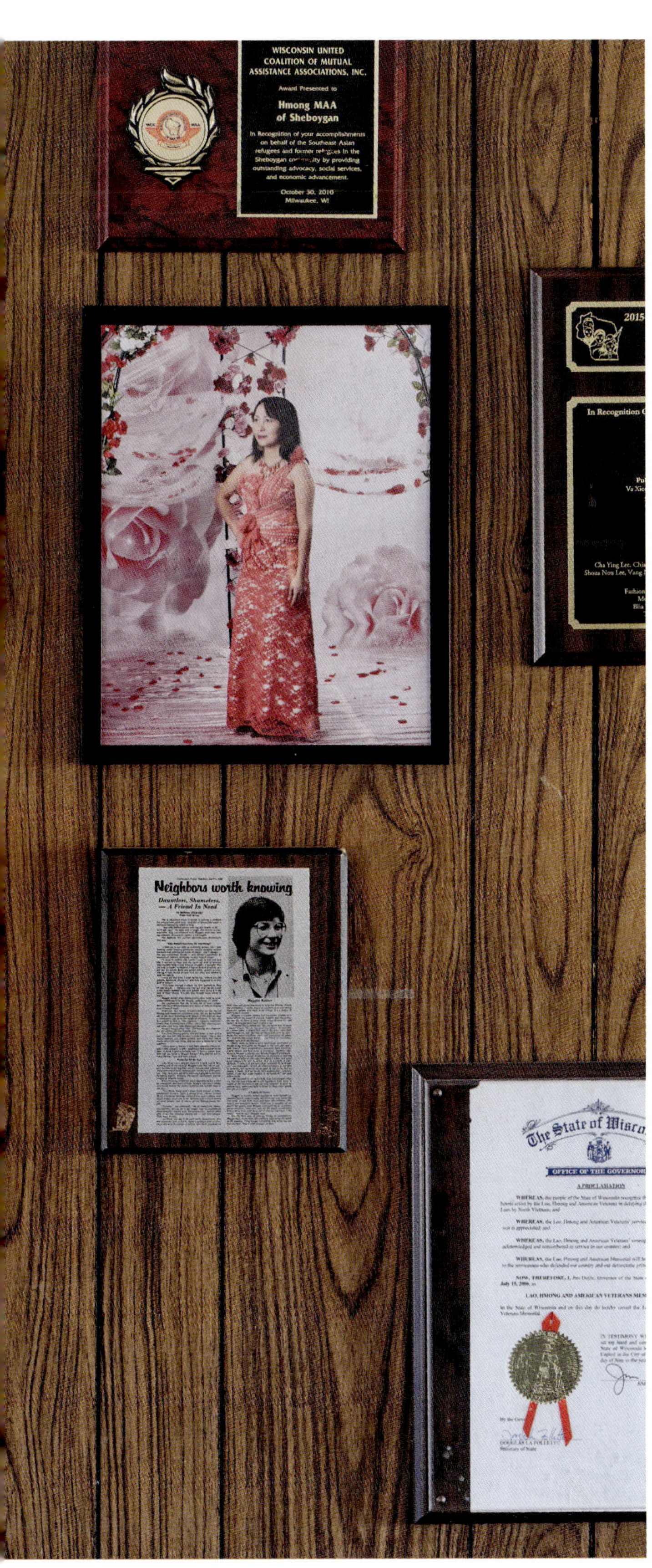

Pao Houa Her: The Imaginative Landscape, installation view at the Hmong Mutual Assistance Association, Sheboygan, Wisconsin, 2025

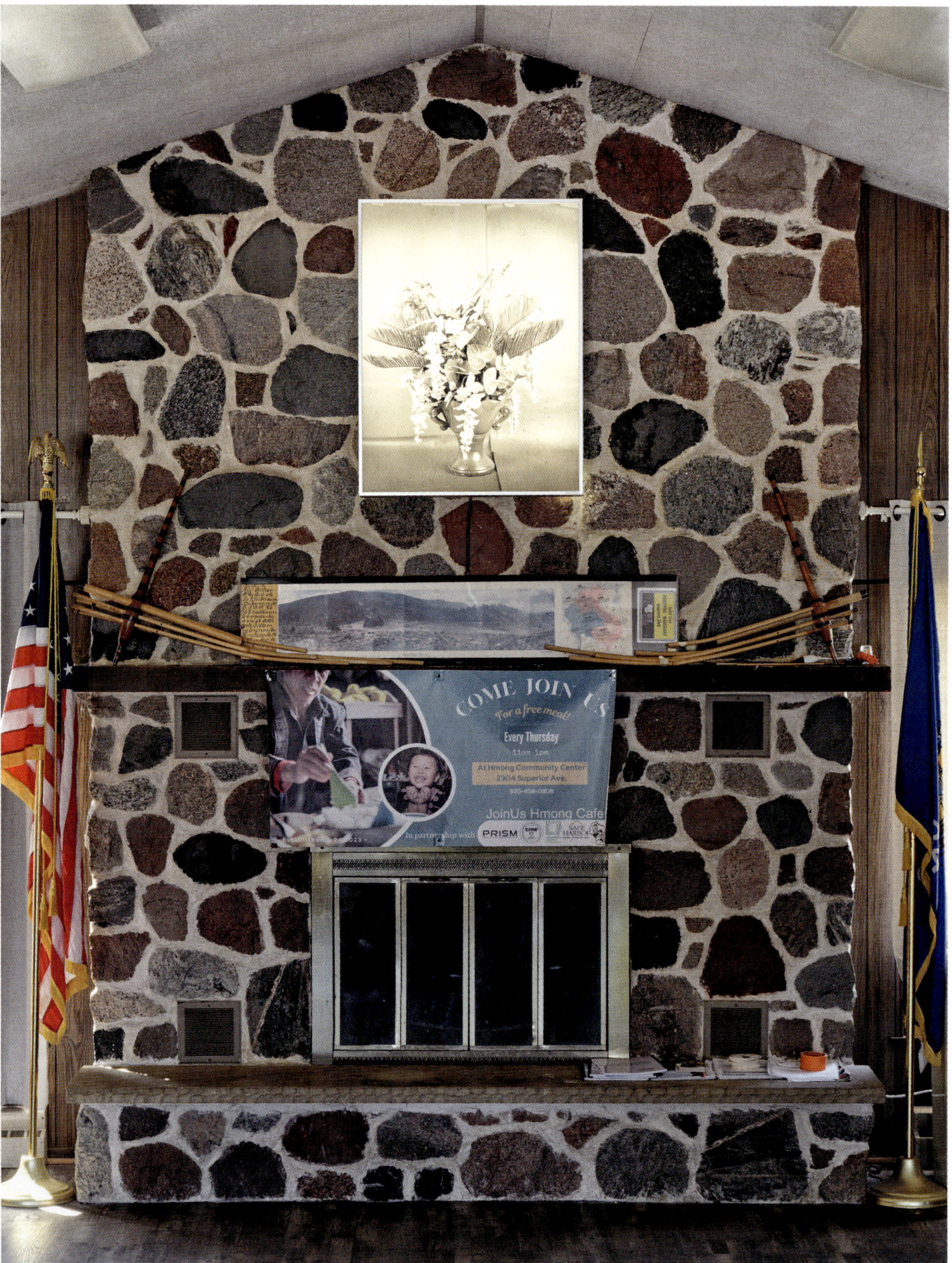
COME JOIN US
For a free meal!
Every Thursday
11am - 1pm
At Hmong Community Center
2304 Superior Ave.
920-458-0808
JoinUs Hmong Cafe
In partnership with
PRISM
SAFE HARBOR

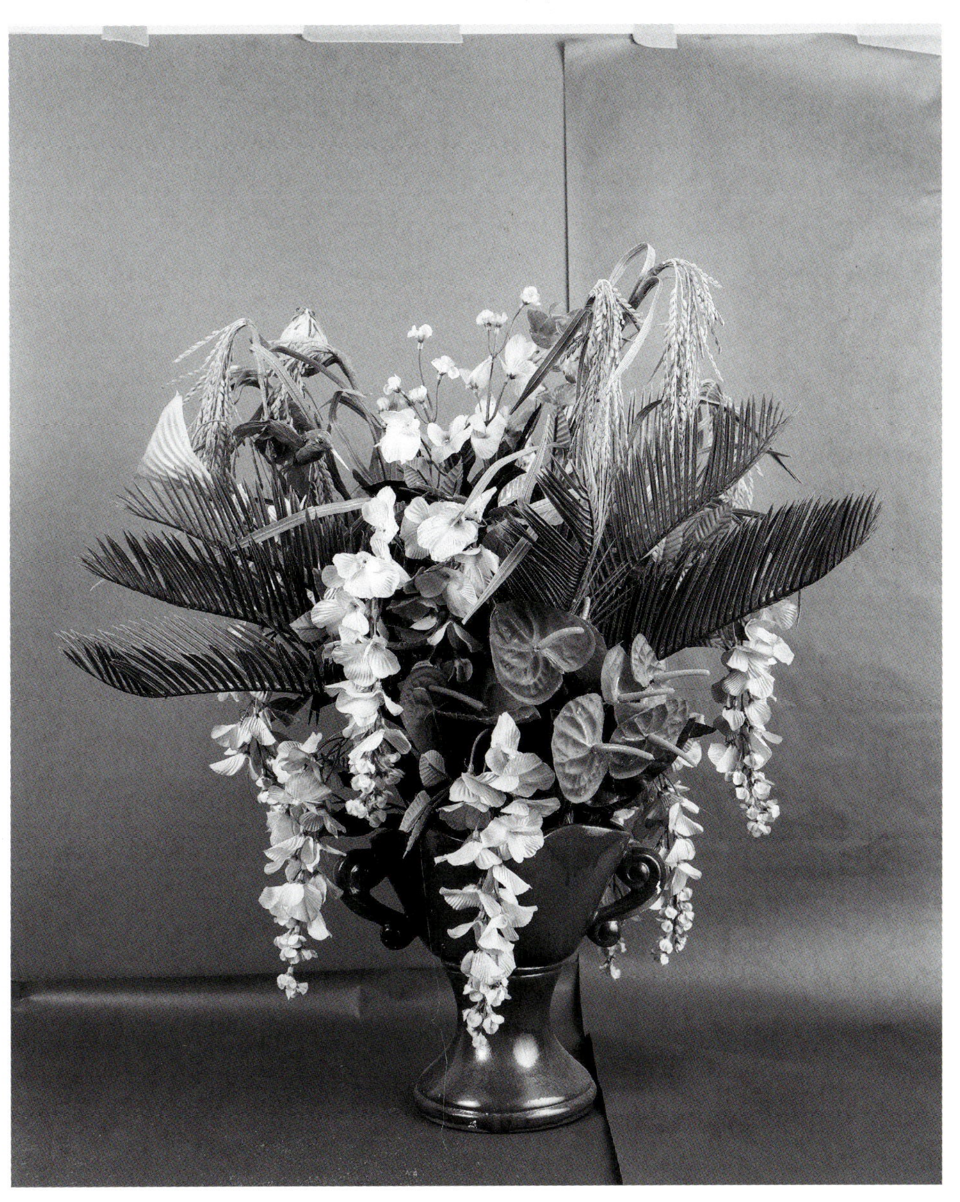

untitled, 2016, from the *My Mother's
Flowers* series, archival pigment print

Left:
Pao Houa Her: The Imaginative Landscape,
installation view at the Hmong Mutual
Assistance Association, Sheboygan,
Wisconsin, 2025

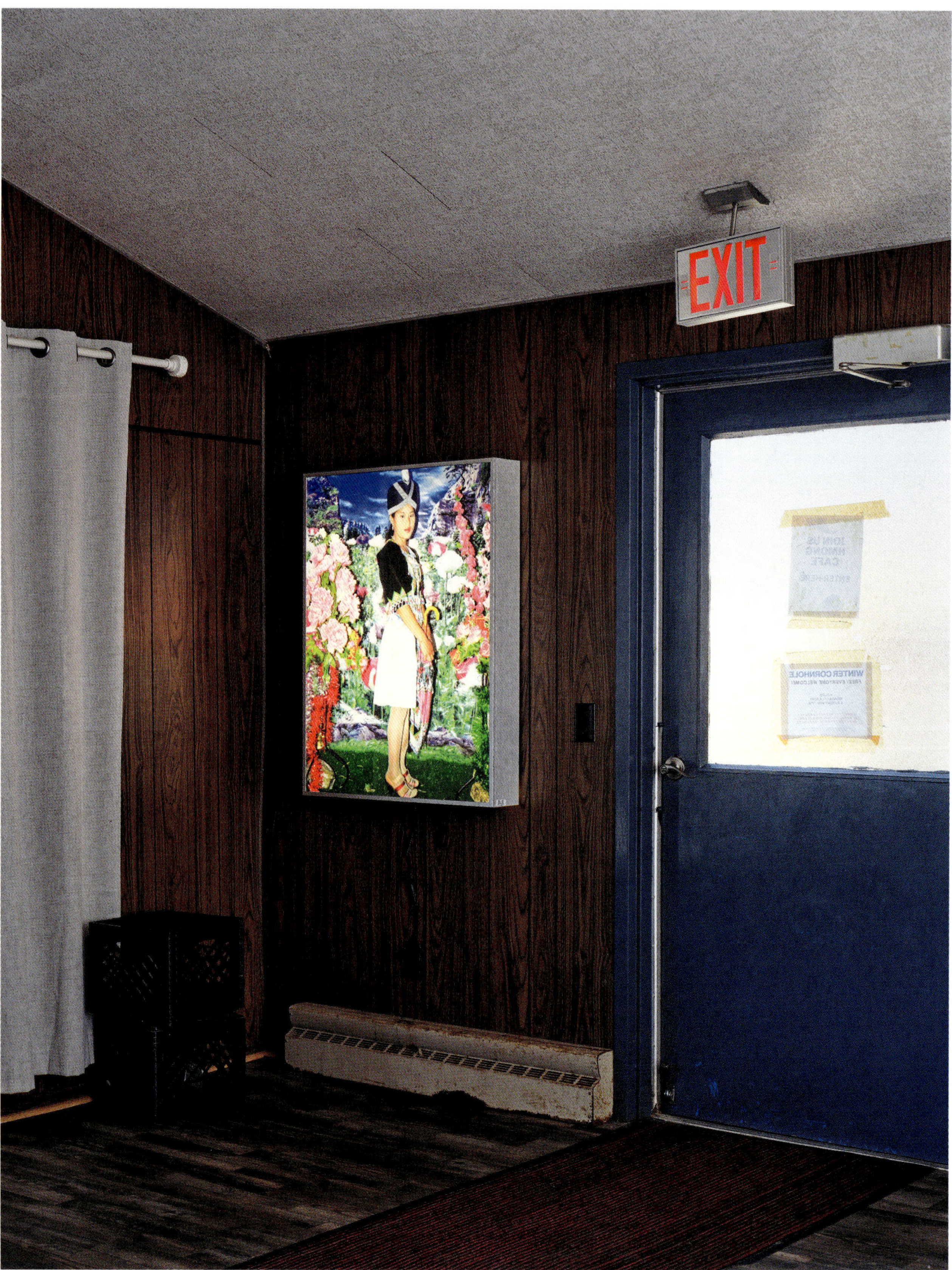

EXIT

Pao Houa Her: The Imaginative Landscape,
installation view at the Hmong Mutual
Assistance Association, Sheboygan,
Wisconsin, 2025

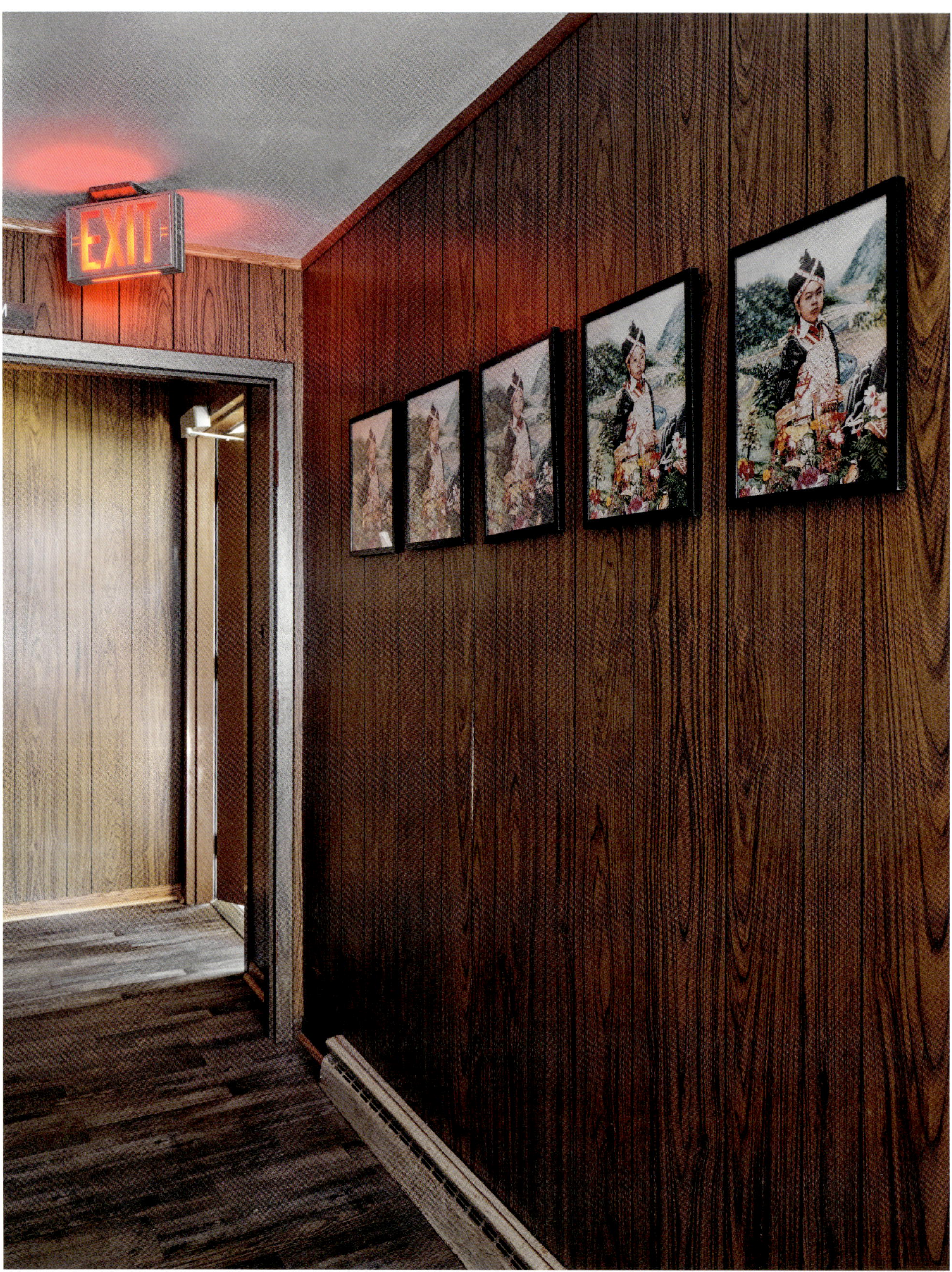

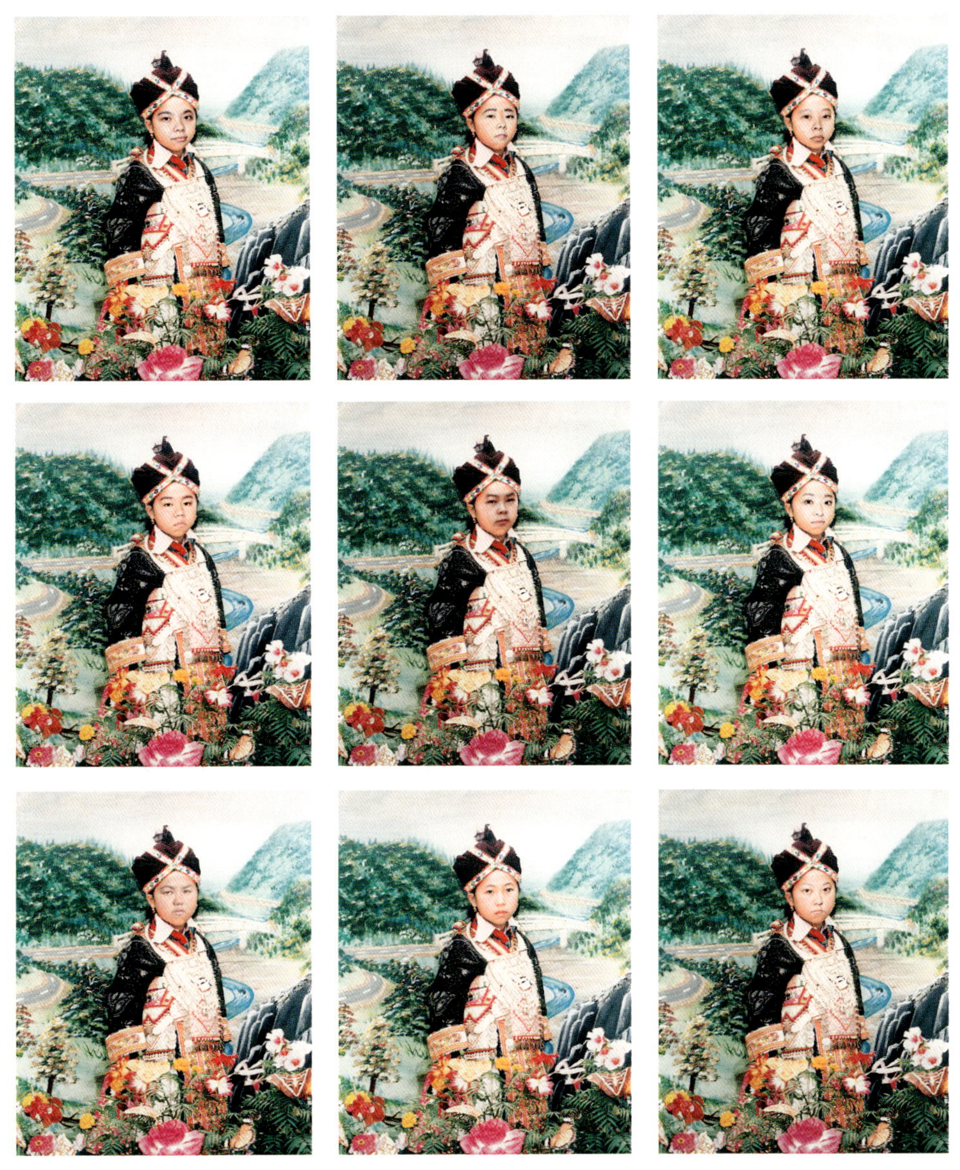

My grandmother's favorite grandchild, 2017,
from the *My grandfather turned into a tiger*
series, nine archival pigment prints

Left:
Pao Houa Her: The Imaginative Landscape,
installation view at the Hmong Mutual
Assistance Association, Sheboygan,
Wisconsin, 2025

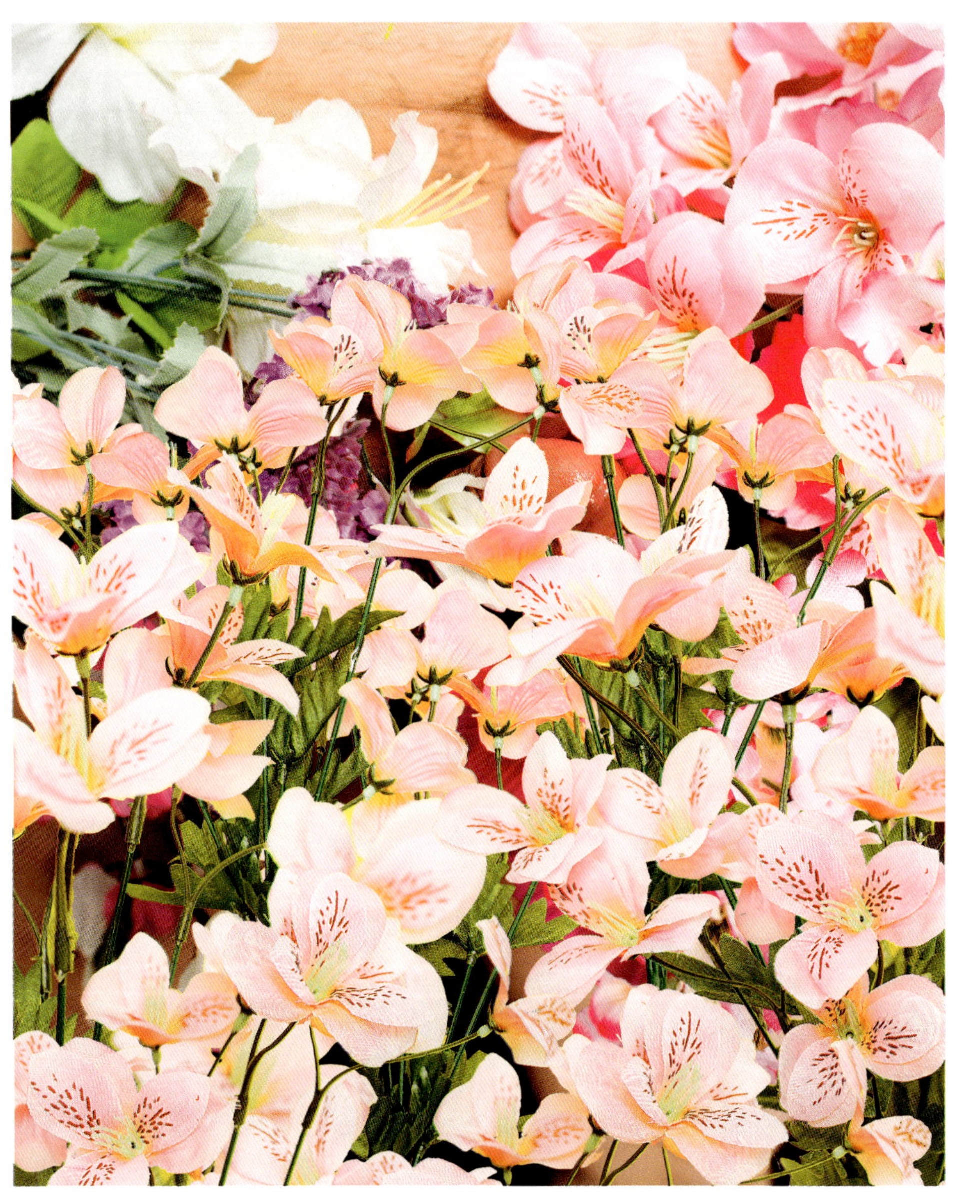

Flower penis, 2017, from the *My grandfather turned into a tiger* series, 3D lenticular print

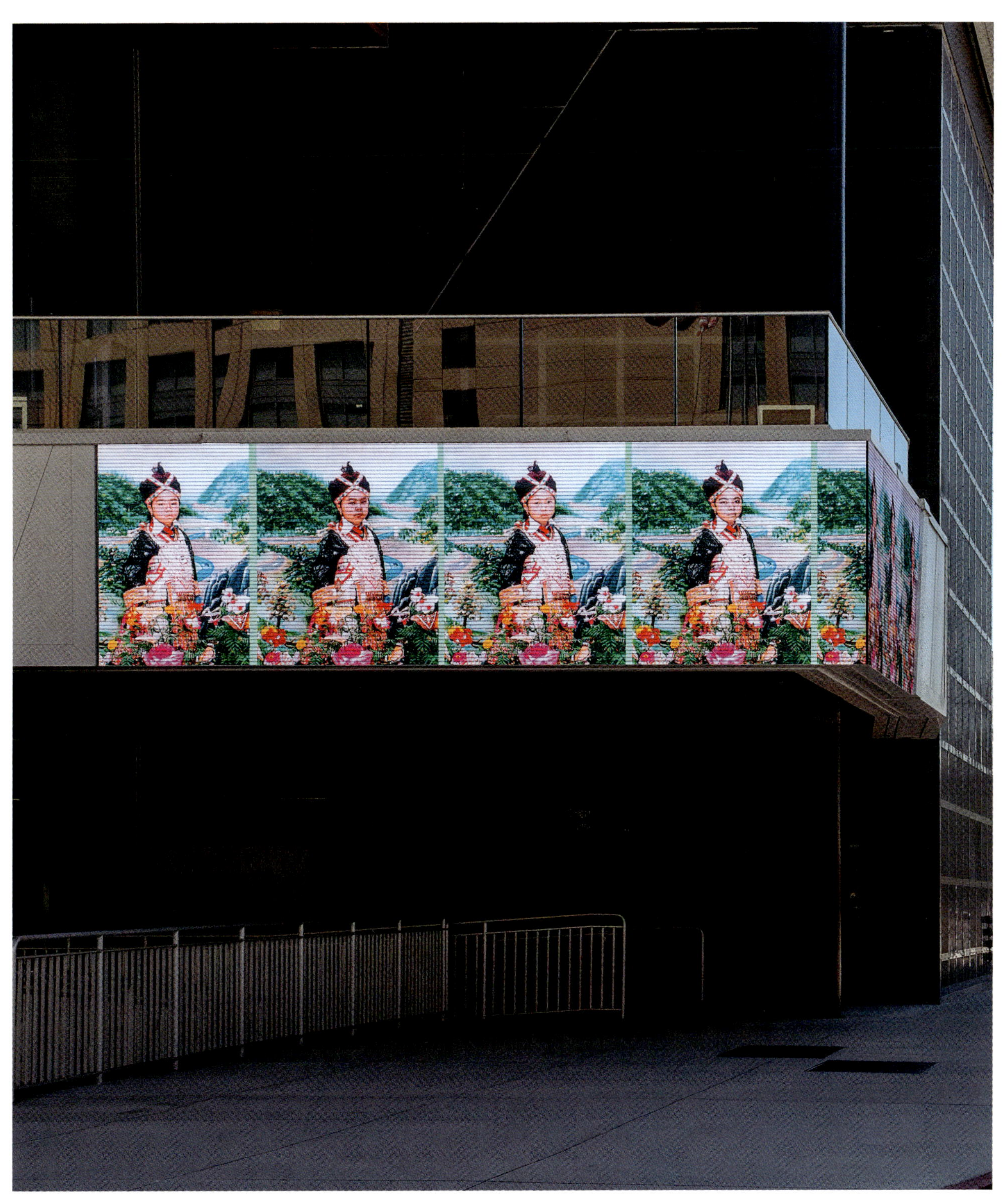

Pao Houa Her: The Imaginative Landscape,
installation view, downtown San José,
California, 2025

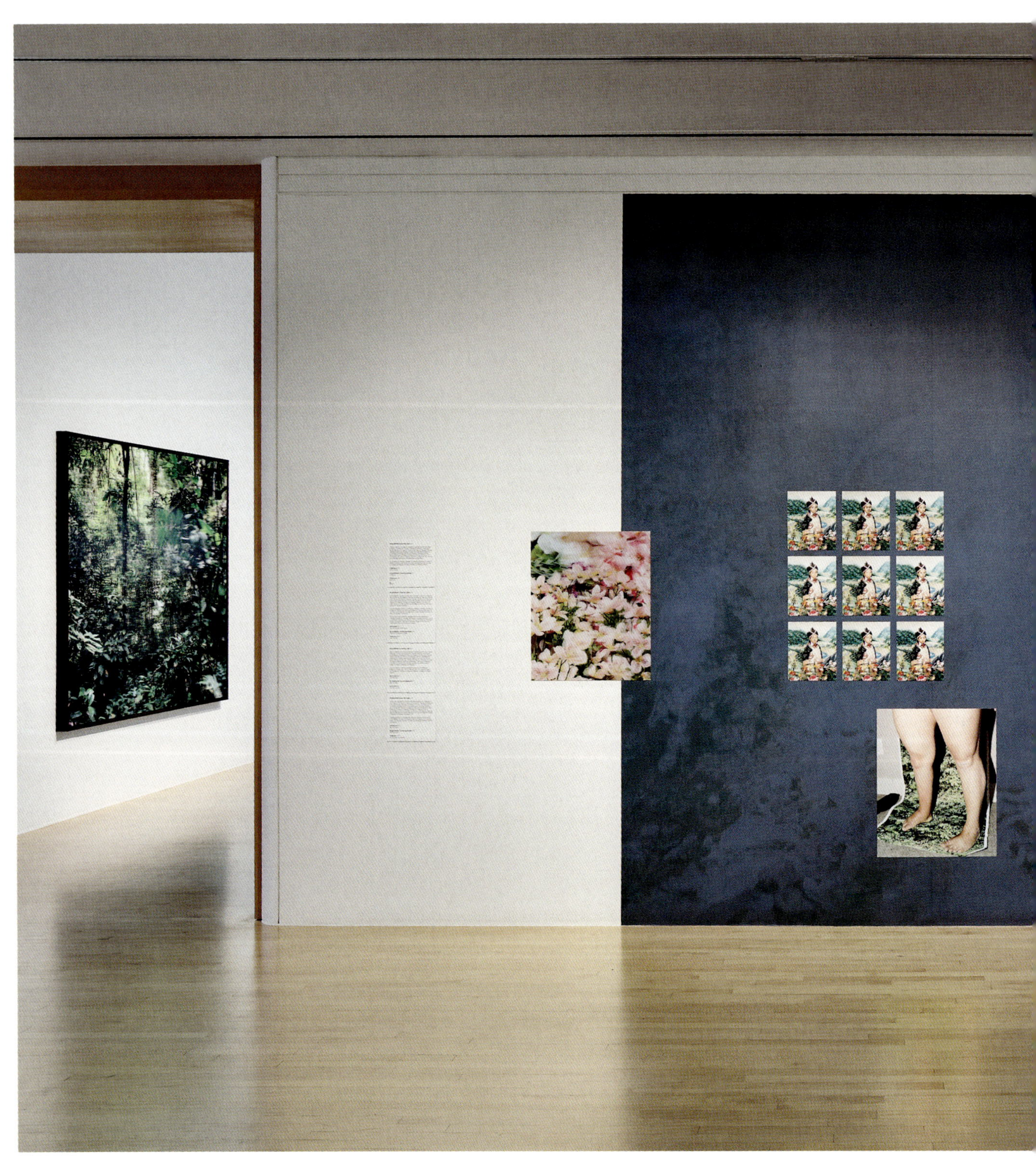

*Pao Houa Her: The Imaginative
Landscape*, installation view
at San José Museum of Art, 2025

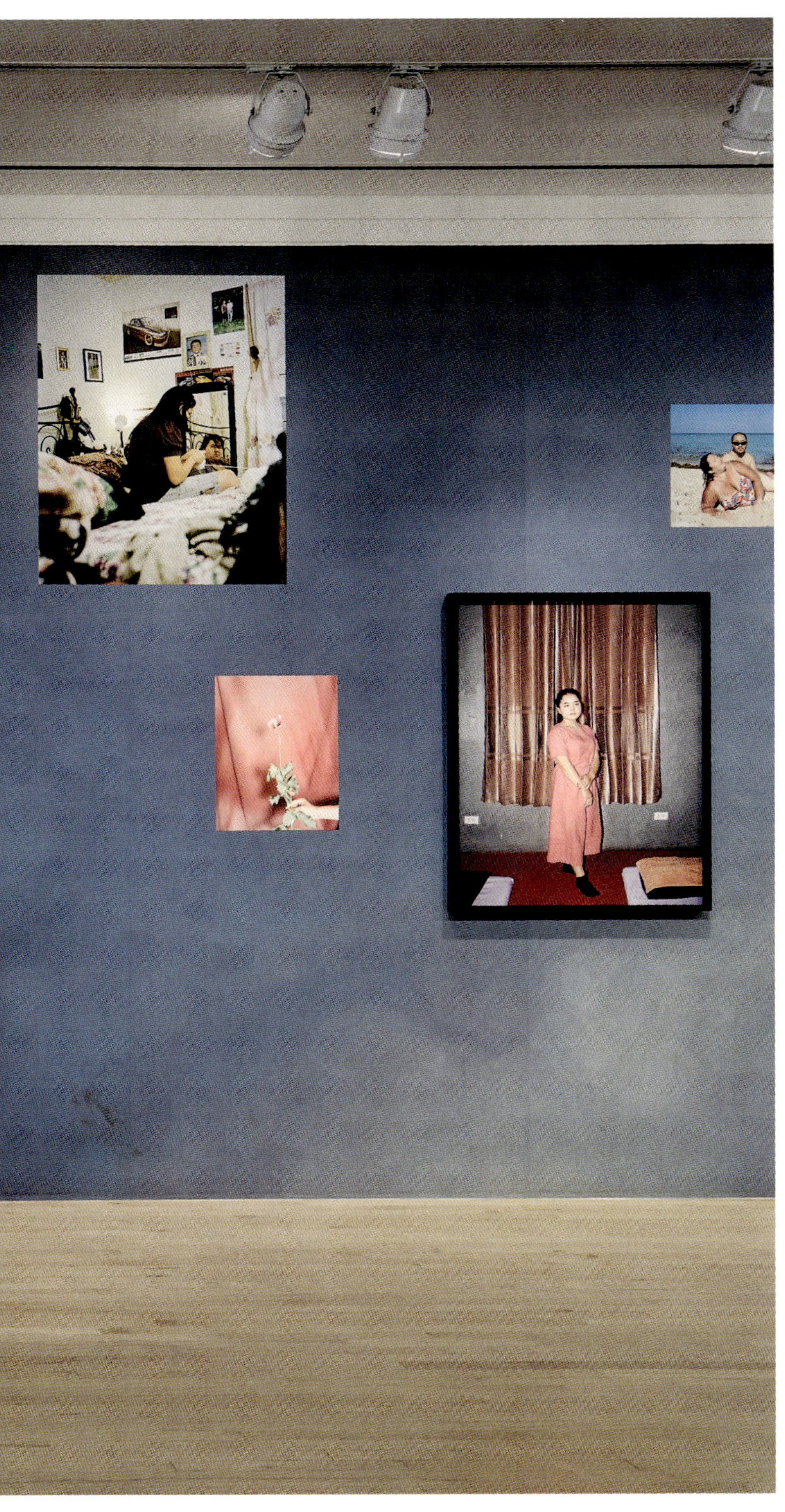

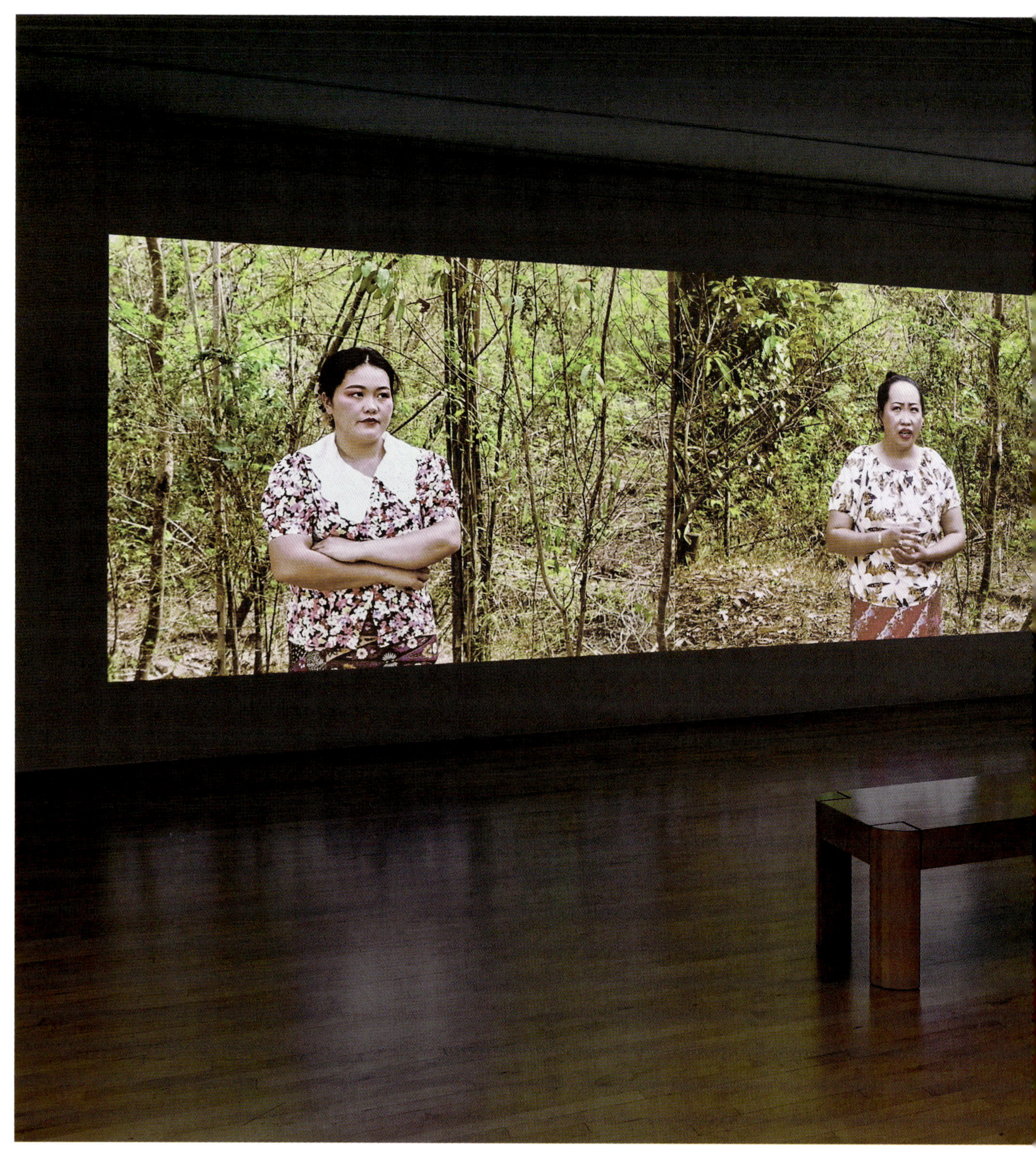

A Conversation Between 4 Hmong Women, 2025, four-channel video, 26 minutes, looped. Pao Houa Her: The Imaginative Landscape, installation view at San José Museum of Art, 2025

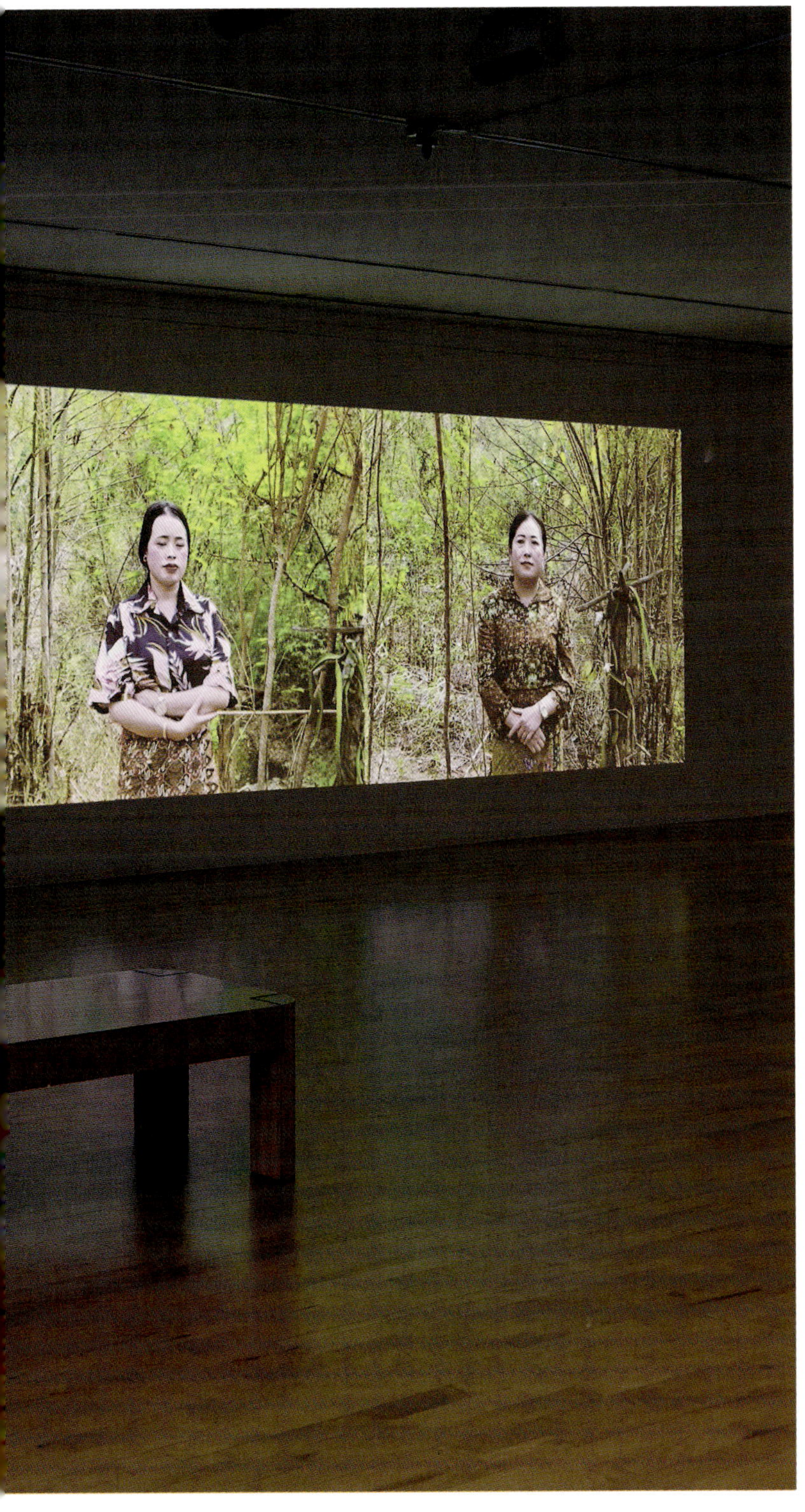

Kwv Txhiaj in the Valley of the Widows, 2023,
single-channel video, 24 minutes, looped.
Pao Houa Her: The Imaginative Landscape,
installation view at the John Michael Kohler
Arts Center, Sheboygan, Wisconsin, 2025

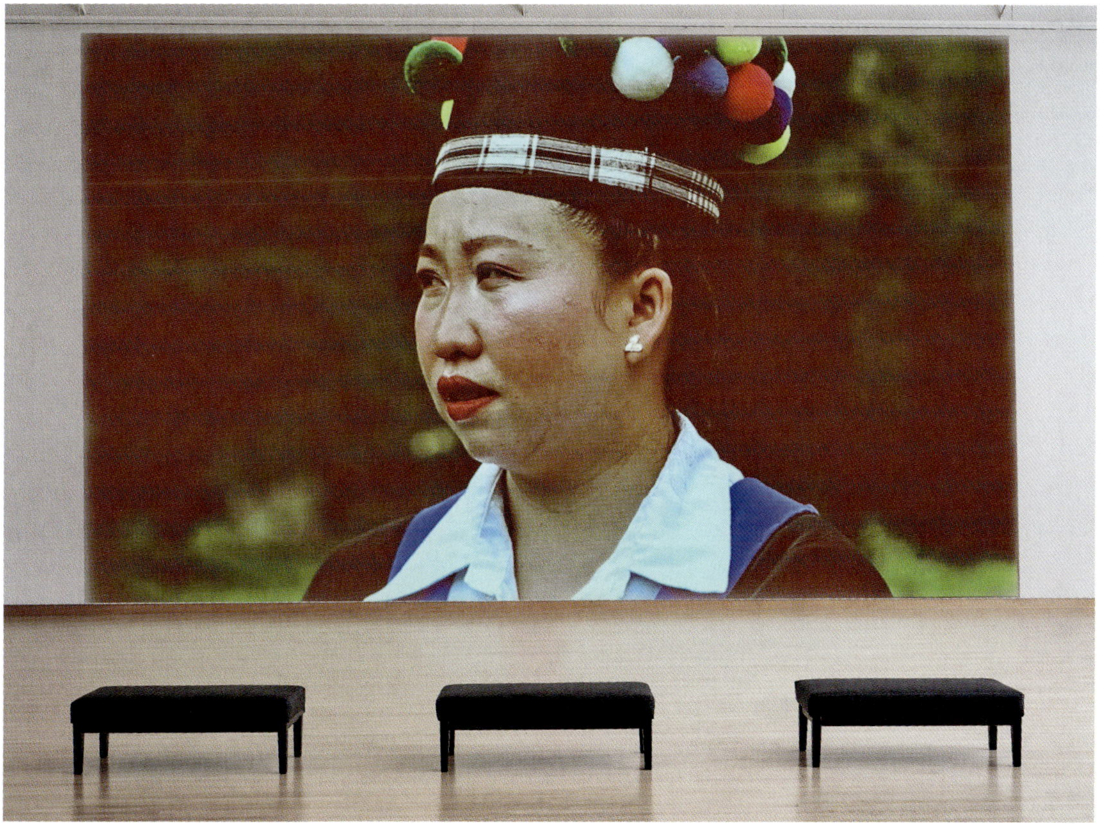

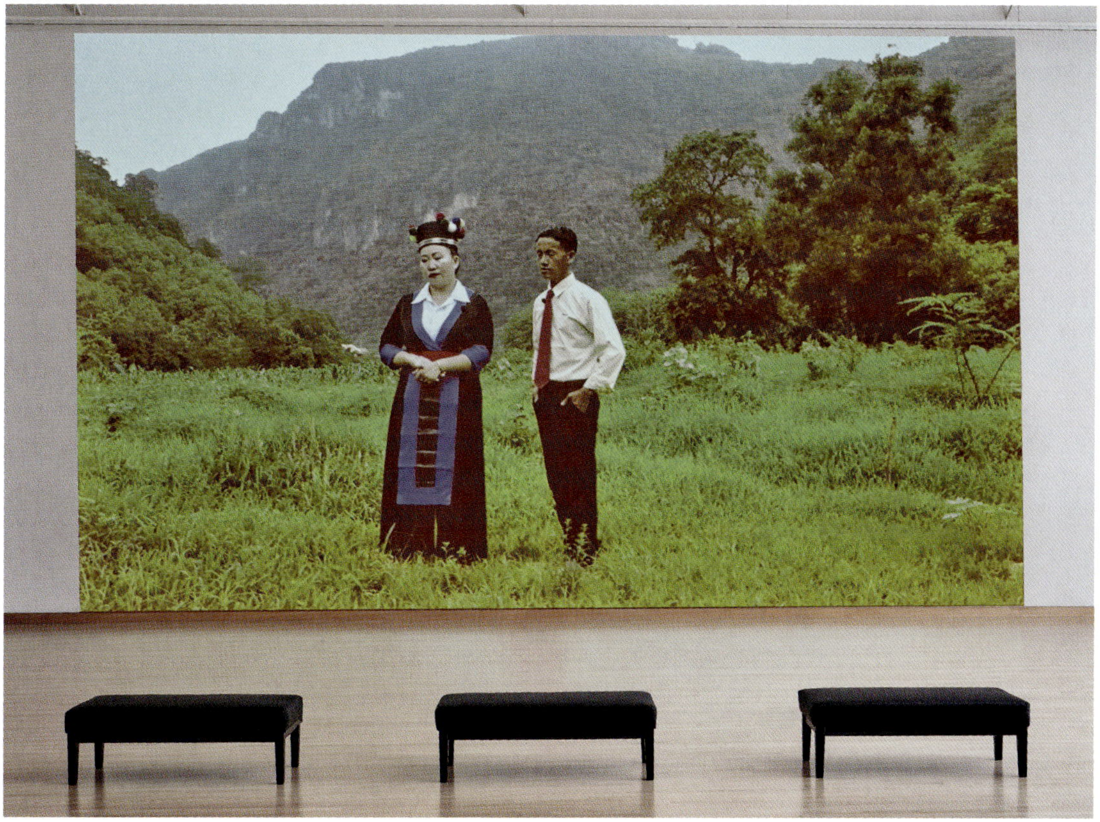

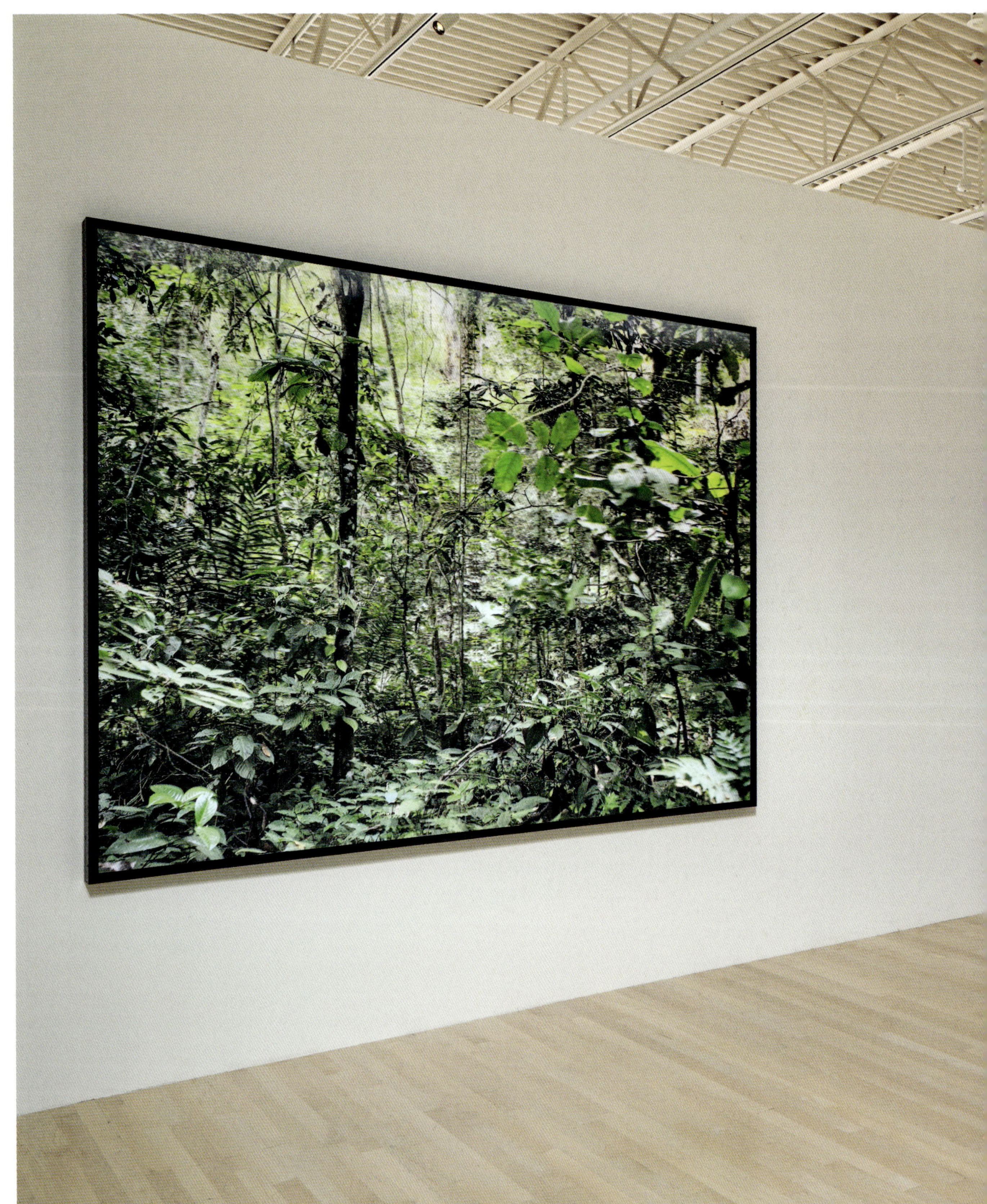

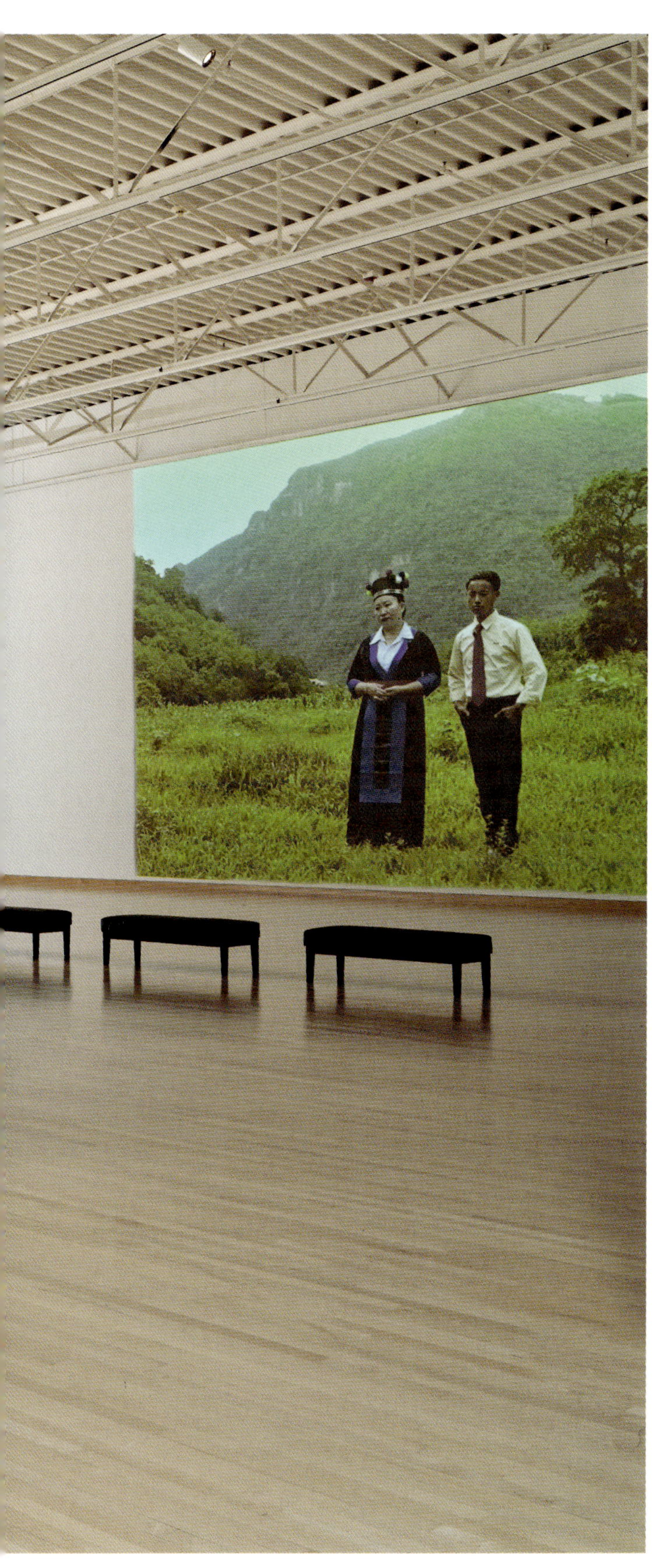

Pao Houa Her: The Imaginative Landscape,
installation view at the John Michael Kohler
Arts Center, Sheboygan, Wisconsin, 2025

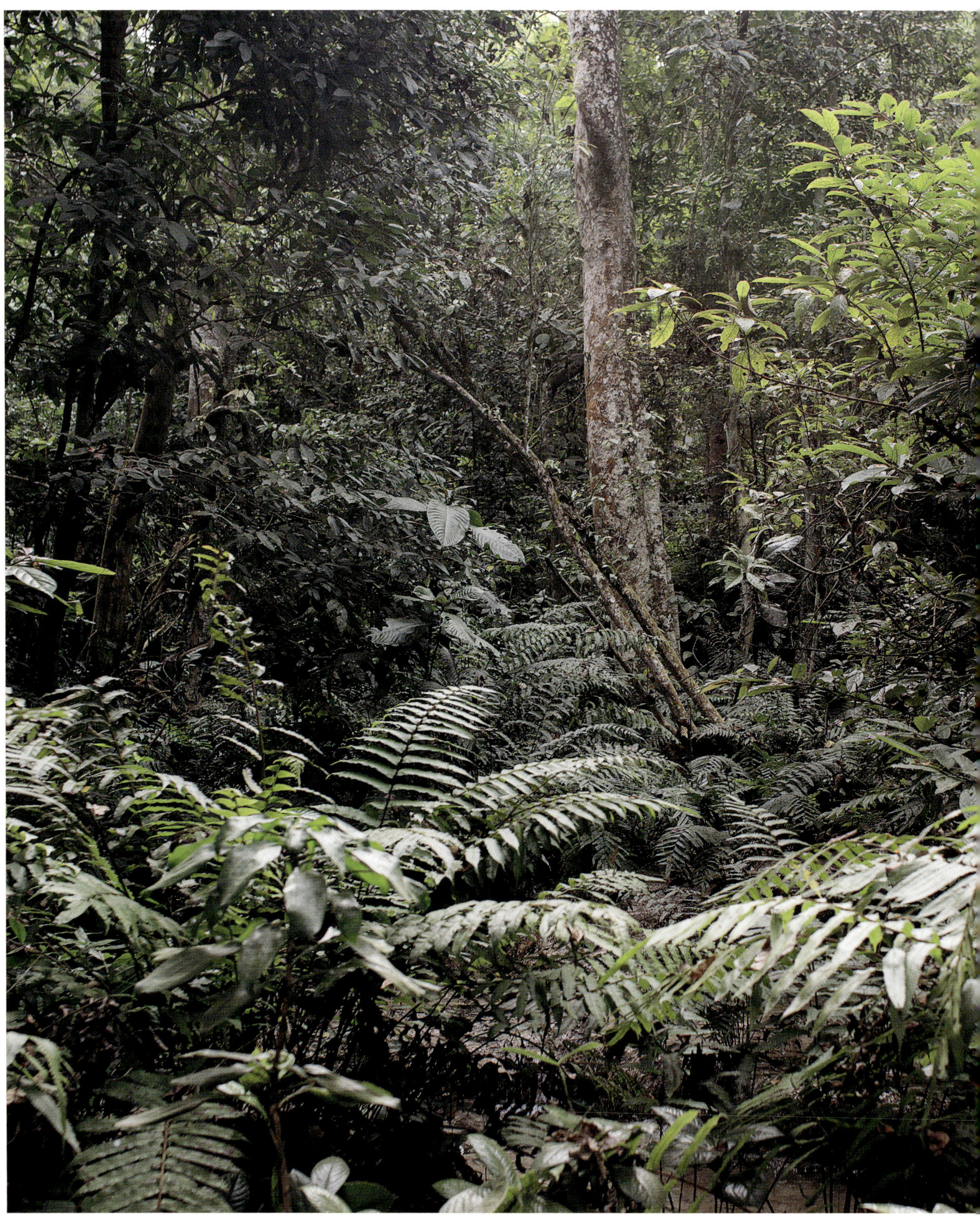

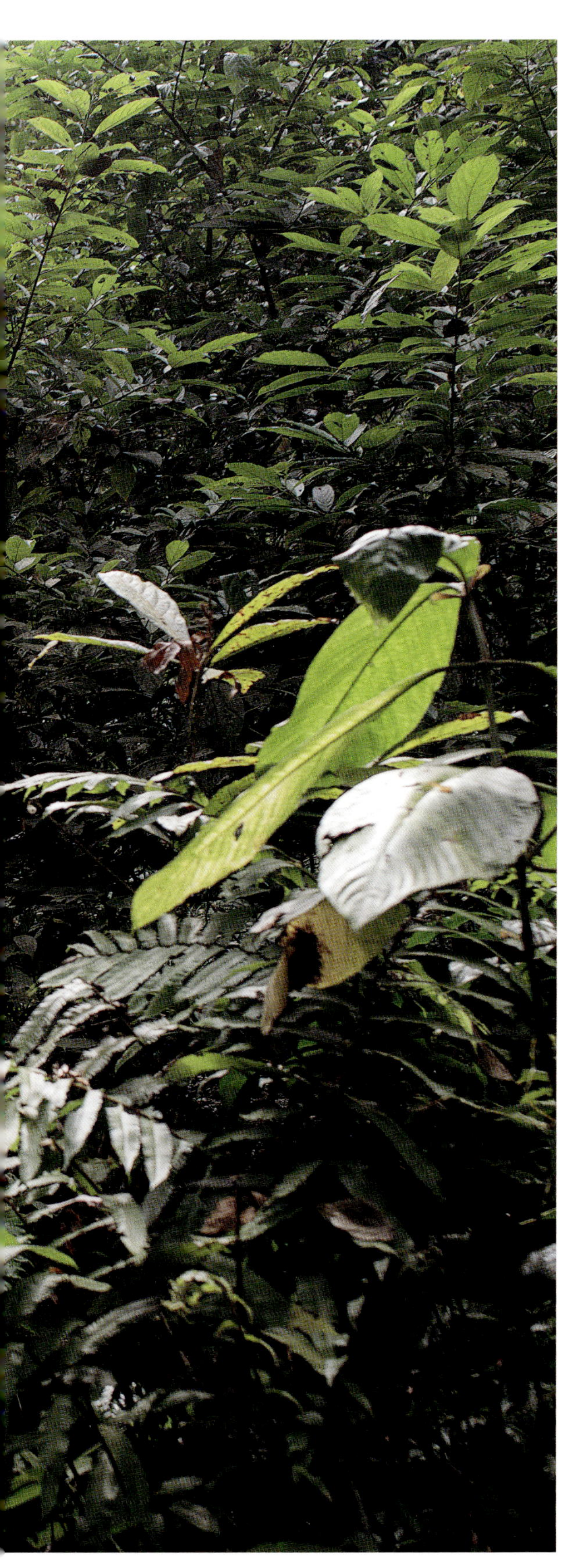

untitled, 2022–24, from the *Pictures of paradise* series, 3D lenticular print

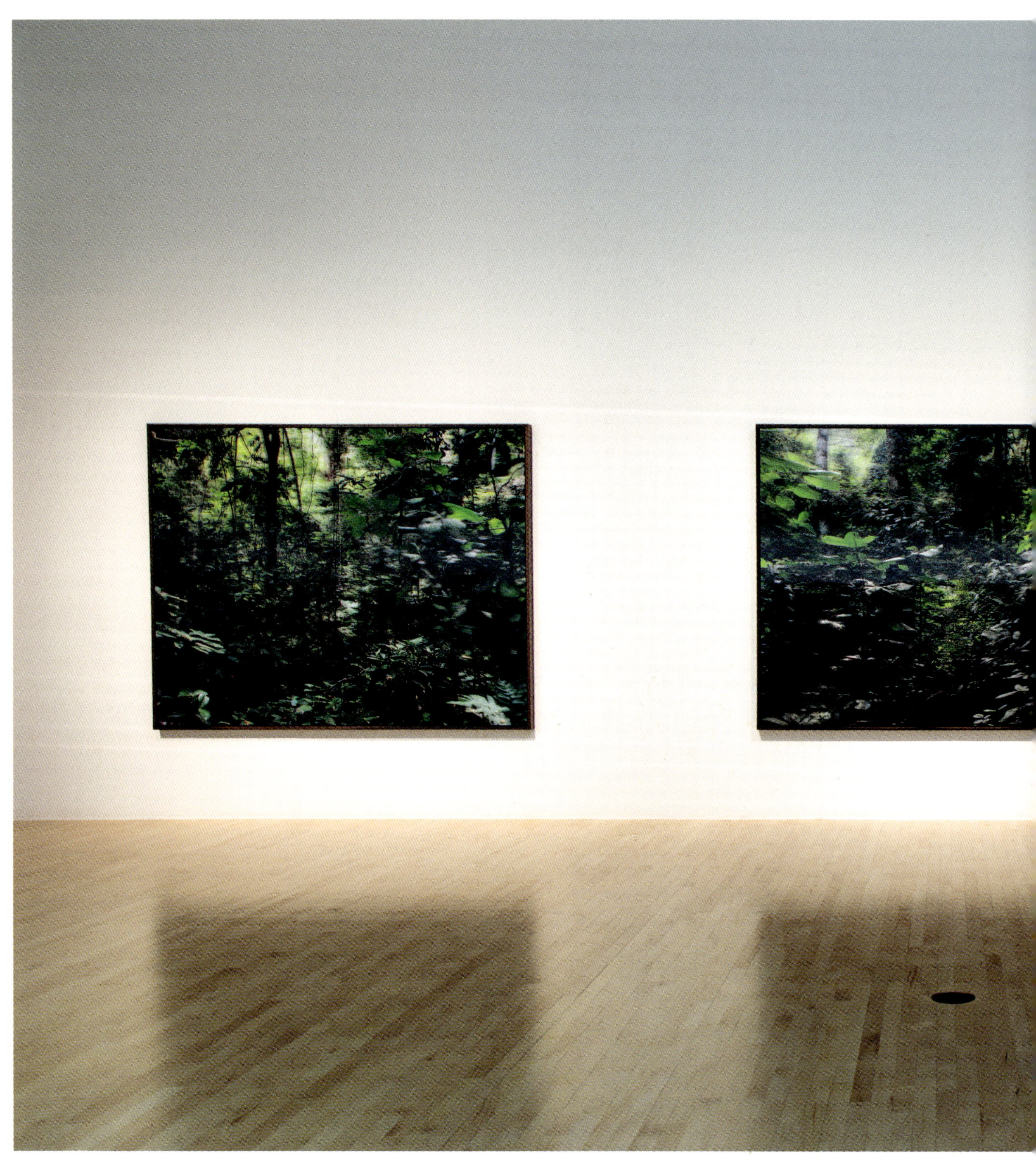

*Pao Houa Her: The Imaginative
Landscape*, installation view
at San José Museum of Art, 2025

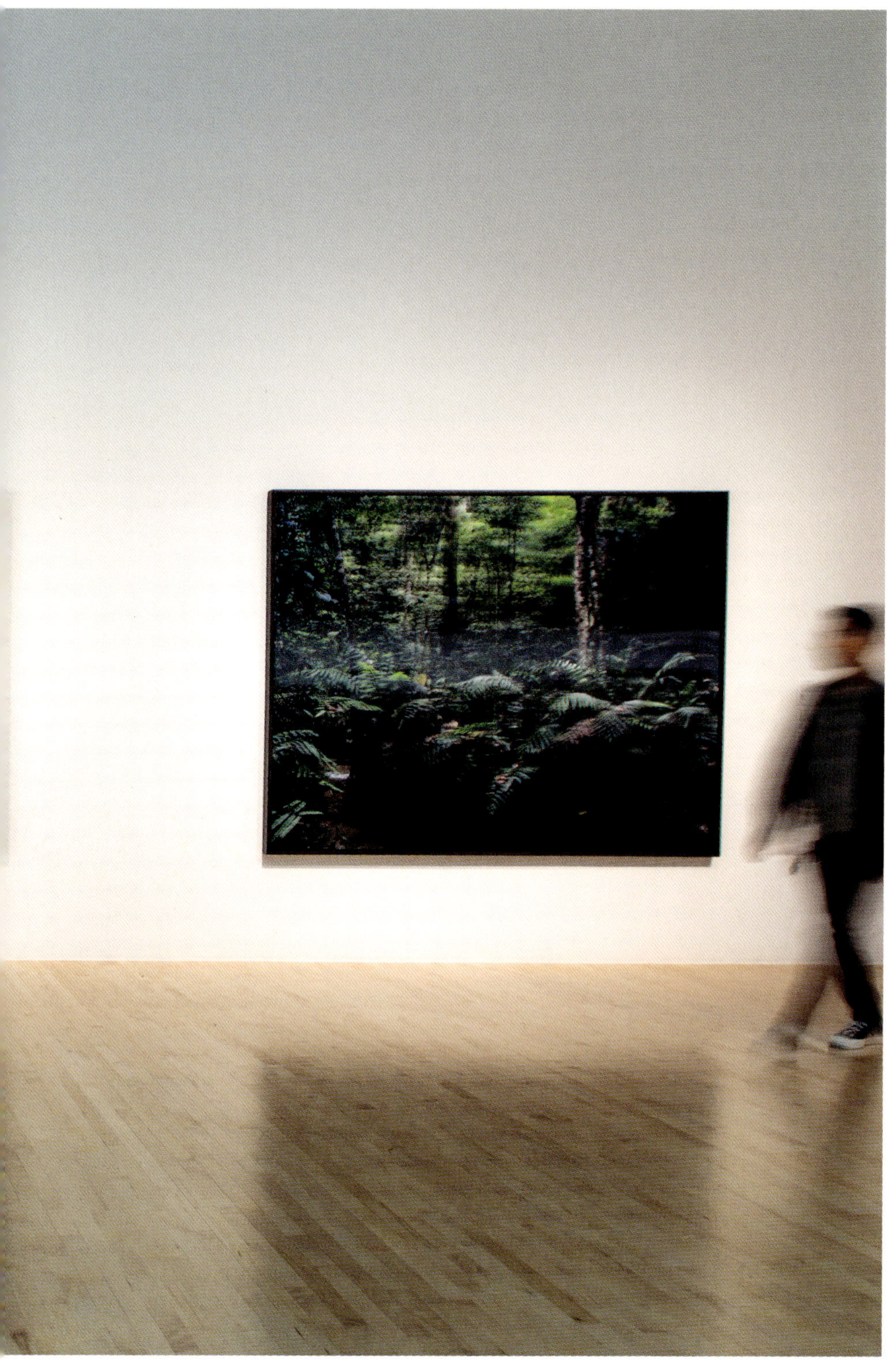

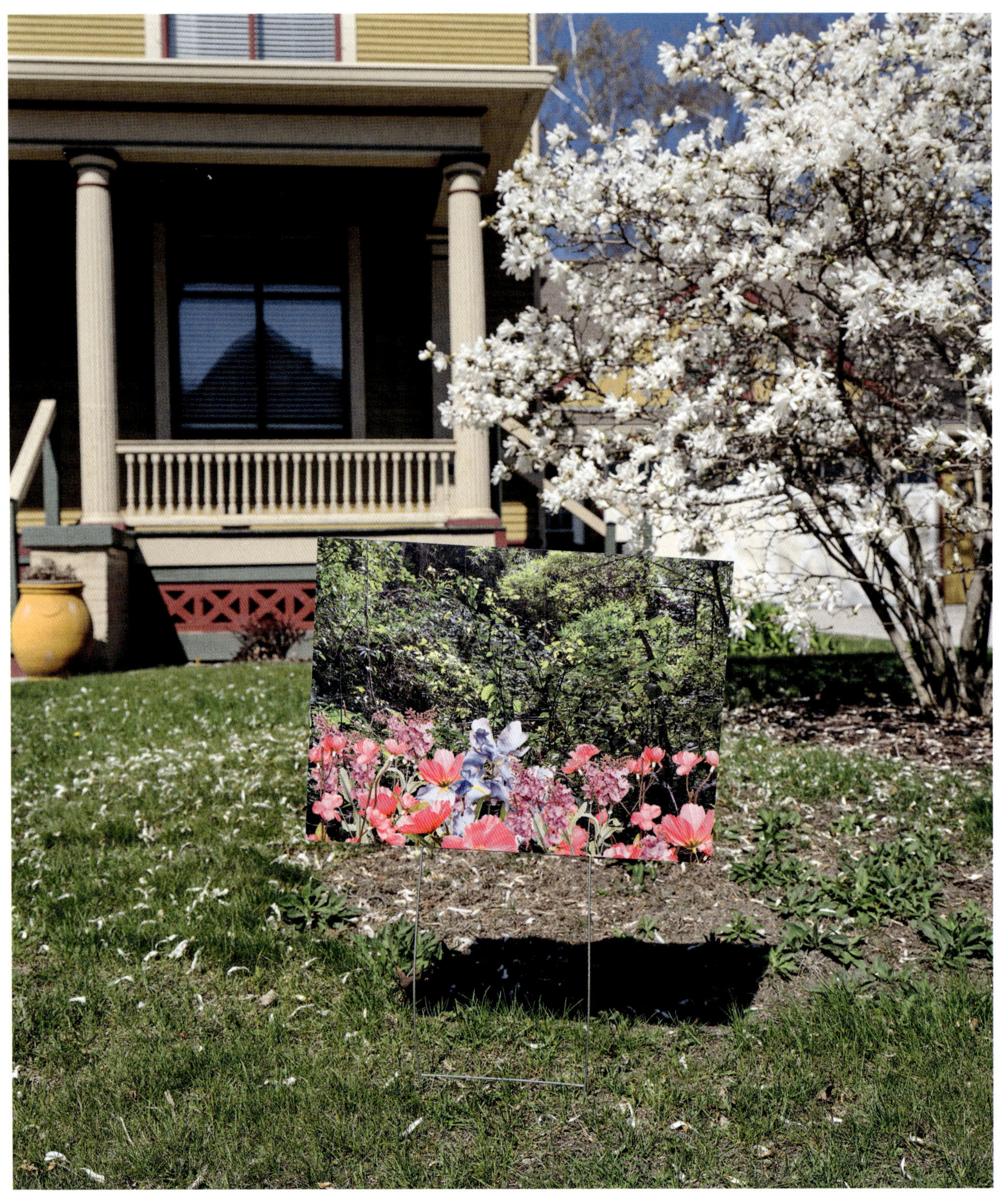

Pao Houa Her: The Imaginative
Landscape, installed yard sign,
Sheboygan, Wisconsin, 2025

IN CONVERSATION

PAO HOUA HER *and* JODI THROCKMORTON

Hours flew by as Pao Houa Her and I sat down in my office at the John Michael Kohler Arts Center (JMKAC) to discuss her exhibition and the long but incredibly rewarding week we had just spent together installing her work at several locations throughout Sheboygan. Each place was transformed by Her's art and vision and, in turn, her art was understood anew through the particularities of each place. Her's approach to site-specificity pushes the boundaries of audience engagement, making her art an active part of daily life rather than a static object to be observed.

We had a lot to discuss. There was the moment with Judge Natasha Torry in her courtroom, where Her's work—a series that brings forward Hmong distrust of the US legal system—is installed on faux-wood paneled walls hung with traditional portraits of past judges. The juxtaposition of her images with the established visual symbols of authority is striking and prompts new conversations about representation and inclusion in judicial spaces. Torry shared an early reaction to the images in the courtroom with Her: a Hmong man had paused before Her's work and remarked on how comforted he felt seeing his community represented in that space. It was a moment of quiet validation—an affirmation that Her's work was not just being seen but was actively resonating with those it sought to reach.

At the Thai Café, owners Choua and Kou Lee dimmed the lights so that Her's glowing lightboxes illuminated the dance floor, tables, and plastic menus in a joyful glow. The restaurant, a hub for both Hmong and non-Hmong patrons, took on an almost ethereal quality as Her's images blended into the ambiance. It was easy to imagine the dance floor full, guests on stage singing karaoke, and the work itself becoming part of the memories created in that space. Here, Her's art was not confined to a frame on a white wall—it was dynamic, immersive, and deeply connected to the life of the community.

And finally, the day we visited the weekly free lunch offered at the Hmong Mutual Assistance Association was

"

memorable. Her stood before elders of the Sheboygan Hmong community, sharing the meaning behind the images that, as she put it, were "disrupting" their space. At first, there was nervousness. Some members of the audience seemed unsure of what to make of these contemporary images intruding upon their familiar gathering space. But then, laughter broke the tension, questions were asked, and some elders even requested that Her take their photo. Her's work sparked a dialogue, and it also held space for a lively game of bingo. It was an example of how her work exists to invite conversation and coexistence with the rhythms of everyday life.

Her work isn't confined to traditional gallery spaces—it lives in the world, engaging directly with the people it represents. For example, at Hmongtown Marketplace, in St. Paul, Minnesota, she installed light boxes in collaboration with Midway Contemporary Art in the middle of a bustling food court, integrating her work into the rhythm of daily life. These lightboxes coexist with the space, waiting for someone to take a moment to notice them, to be moved by them, to recognize something of themselves in them.

Held weeks before the exhibition opened in Sheboygan, my conversation with Her explores the significance of her work in public and community-centered locations and fine art spaces alike. The discussion highlights how her work engages with themes of identity, memory, and belonging, and addresses the complexities of Hmong American experiences and the tension between visibility and exclusion.

We reflect on the challenges and rewards of placing art in unconventional venues, where access is dictated by different rules than in a traditional museum framework. These settings invite different forms of audience engagement, sometimes making visitors uneasy, yet also fostering deeper connections. The exhibition's structure, spanning multiple locations in Wisconsin and California, mirrors the dispersed nature of Hmong communities and acknowledges their resilience in forging new homelands. Through this work, Her not only broadens the scope of contemporary art but also redefines who gets to experience it and on whose terms, leaving a lasting impact on both the art world and the communities she represents.

What follows is a glimpse into our exchange, distilled from a dialogue shaped by history, identity, and the profound act of representation.

My sincere thanks go to Pao Houa Her. This project challenged us both; we wondered how it would be received by both community members and people well-versed in contemporary art. Her is at her best when she is listening to people's responses to her work and thinking through how it could be encountered in their spaces. It is Her's resilience, openness, honesty, and adaptability that made this exhibition possible. I am incredibly grateful to her for allowing us to care for her images in Sheboygan.

—

JODI THROCKMORTON In thinking about how this project evolved into something spanning not just Sheboygan but also the San José Museum of Art—how did that come about?

PAO HOUA HER I remember that you and Lauren [Dickens] visited me at my studio, and we were talking about where my work exists in the world. I was specifically talking about a lightbox that was shown both at the Walker Art Center and at Hmongtown Marketplace[1] [*untitled* (*fake flowers from restaurant*) 2019, from *The Imaginative Landscape* series] and how that same image felt very different in those two spaces. That conversation sparked the idea of thinking about how my work could exist in the community—about accessibility.

JT We installed that same image yesterday at the Thai Café. Can you talk more about what it means for your work to exist in different locations, like the Walker Art Center, Hmongtown Marketplace, or the Thai Café in Sheboygan?

PHH I think a lot about what it means to be an artist in the context of being a Hmong American daughter. My parents always operated in survival mode—that was their way of living. And they instilled that mindset in me and my siblings. To survive in America, we had to focus on staying above the poverty line—education, working constantly.

Growing up, I was torn between what it meant to be American and what it meant to be a Hmong daughter. My parents didn't have the tools to help me navigate those identities, so I rebelled. I did things they didn't want me to do. That ultimately led me to become an artist. It's the only way I know how to express myself, ask the questions I want to ask, and do the research I need to do. That has always been at the core of my identity as an artist.

It's both liberating and terrifying to share this work with my community. It's scary because I feel like many in my community don't have the tools I've had to interpret my work. But it's liberating because it's important for Hmong people to see themselves represented in ways beyond becoming a doctor, lawyer, or office worker.

When I was talking to Natasha [Judge Natasha Torry] yesterday, she mentioned a Hmong man at the courthouse [Sheboygan County Circuit Court] who appreciated the Hmong portraits. Moments like that feel monumental. They reaffirm why I do this work.

JT   Ideally, we'd love for everyone to come to the Arts Center, but the reality is that's not always possible. What does it mean to you that this person—who likely never would have stepped foot in the Arts Center—had a moment with your work, even though we don't know why he was at the courthouse?

PHH   For me, it's important that he saw my work in a space that might otherwise feel foreign to him. It's crucial for people to see images that look like them—to feel a sense of belonging.

I think about when I first discovered photography. In my Introduction to Photography class at community college, we learned about Diane Arbus[2] and all the photography canons. But then I saw the work of Wing Young Huie,[3] and I recognized people—my grandmother, my uncle, people from my community. That was the moment I realized why I needed to make the work I do.

JT   I want to go back to something you said earlier about the *After the Fall* series in the courthouse and what that series means, especially in that context.

PHH   When you suggested putting *After the Fall* in the courthouse, I was really excited because that body of work talks about the legal system. *After the Fall* is about a Hmong man who went to senior centers and advertised investment opportunities, claiming he was working with the US government and the UN to create a new country for Hmong people. Many elders gave him money because they believed in this dream. But the FBI got involved in 2015 and investigated him.

2   Diane Arbus (1923–1971), a New York City-based photographer, best known for her distinctive black-and-white portraits.

3   Wing Young Huie (b. 1955, Duluth), a photographer based primarily in Minneapolis.

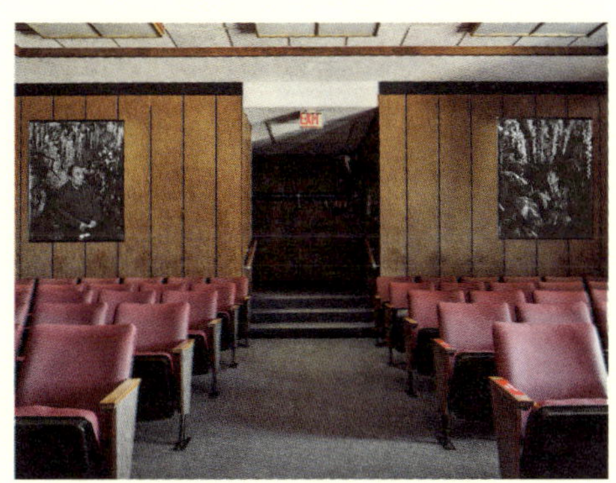

I found the story fascinating because it mirrored the longing many Hmong people have to return to Laos and create a homeland. That dream is very much rooted in the elders' experiences, and I wanted to make work that reflected their feelings of longing for home.

In my work, I used portraits of people in a senior daycare center and combined them with images of the Como Park Zoo and Conservatory [in St. Paul, Minnesota]. I wanted to create a metaphor for how the community exists in an artificial, man-made space. The conservatory's plants, though from other parts of the world, exist and thrive there, much like my community exists in an environment that isn't our original home. The images in *After the Fall* can swindle viewers, making them believe they're seeing something real when it's not. The play between the real and the artificial is key. It's about making people see beyond the surface and question the layers beneath.

JT   What does being a Hmong daughter and an artist mean to you?

PHH   I think a lot about patriarchy in my community. There are deep-rooted traditions that still exist today. Hmong daughters are viewed differently than sons. But I've been lucky—my parents didn't impose too many of those gendered expectations on me. I've had to push against the idea that, as a wife, my role is to serve and take care of my husband's family. My husband has always supported my career, which made my parents more accepting. But my mom has warned me that my career might lead to divorce or rejection from the family. Despite those fears, I feel fortunate. I've been able to do the work I do, and that's something I don't take for granted.

I think that there are a lot of difficulties though. When I was making my *Attention* series, it was really hard to talk to Hmong men and to say, "I'm making work about Hmong soldiers and I was wondering if I could come and take a photo of you?" My dad had to call them and ask them on my behalf. It's so interesting when you think about that series in relationship to patriarchy. This body of work is really beautifully honoring the service [of Hmong veterans].

JT   But it still required you to find a way to cross this chasm of patriarchy and to have your father reach out to these men?

 Having supportive parents to do that for you, even if they didn't fully understand why you wanted to photograph Hmong veterans, was really great.

And also, thinking about the Hmong men in the community—when I showed this work in 2015 at the Minneapolis Institute of Art, it was around the time when President Obama signed the Stolen Valor Act of 2013.[4] I remember Hmong men in the community being concerned about the photographs I had made. They worried that the veterans in my work could be prosecuted under the Stolen Valor Act. Having people in the Hmong community—especially men—ask me, "Do you know what you're doing? Do you know the can of worms you're potentially unleashing?" was really wild. Even now, after all these years, I'm still processing it. These are veterans who fought for the Americans, who agreed to fight for the Americans, who are now here in the United States, and whose desire is simply to be recognized by the US government. They're trying to reinsert themselves into a history that they were very much a part of but have been all but forgotten.

I'm also interested in the power of the uniform itself. I think about it like Superman and Clark Kent—when Clark takes off the uniform, he's just a regular person, but when he puts it on, he becomes something else. For these men, the uniform acts as a superhero suit. Without it, they're just any other Hmong elder. But when they put it on, they feel important. The Hmong community gives them a kind of recognition they wouldn't get otherwise.

JT   Can you talk about the moment you discovered they were creating their own uniforms and teaching themselves to play "Taps" and fold the flag?

PHH I always knew Hmong veterans existed, but I had never really done any research on it. I remember coming home during my second year in grad school. My dad asked if I wanted to attend an uncle's funeral, and I said yes. I brought my camera.

I knew my uncle had fought in the war, but I didn't know to what extent. As we were waiting for the casket to be carried in, I saw three men dressed in white walk in, playing trumpets. The sound wasn't polished, but it was familiar. I couldn't quite place it. Then the casket entered, draped with an American flag, flanked by three older Hmong men in uniform. They

4   President George W. Bush signed the Stolen Valor Act of 2005, making it illegal to falsely claim military honors. In 2012, the Supreme Court ruled it unconstitutional. In response, President Barack Obama signed a revised Stolen Valor Act in 2013, making such false claims illegal only when intended for material gain.

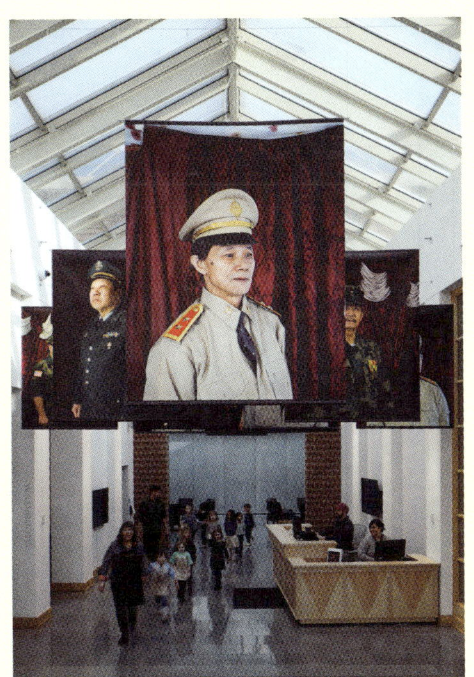

Pao Houa Her: The Imaginative Landscape, installation view at the John Michael Kohler Arts Center, Sheboygan, Wisconsin, 2025

rolled the casket down, turned it, and folded the flag into a triangle. But instead of giving it to my aunt, they handed it to their son. Watching this, I felt like I was witnessing something surreal. I couldn't wrap my head around it.

Later, I saw my best friend's father at the procession. I had met him a few times at her house, so I approached him and asked, "What branch of the military were you in?" He responded, "We were part of the Special Guerrilla Unit." I asked, "Oh, what branch is that?" And he told me, "Oh, that's not part of any US military branch." Then he pulled out a piece of paper detailing his time in the war and his training. I asked if he carried that paper with him everywhere, and he said yes—especially at moments like this.

That's when I started asking about his uniform. "Where is this from?" I asked. He looked at me and said, "Daughter, the US Army doesn't support us. We actually belong to the Lao-Hmong Association Special Guerrilla Unit. We have chapters spread across the United States, including one in Minnesota."

He explained how they have to buy their own uniforms, often sourcing them from secondhand military supply stores or eBay. Some of the medals they wore had been personally made and distributed by General Vang Pao. This completely unraveled my assumptions. Previously, I thought the Hmong elders I had seen in uniform were wearing original military-issued garments. Learning the truth made me even more curious about the organization, how these men were navigating the political system, and how they were lobbying for recognition.

JT   And then there's the heartbreaking aspect of the Stolen Valor Act.

PHH Absolutely. Talking to Hmong men and women currently serving in the US military, I found that while many empathized with these veterans, they also leaned on the argument that there's a legal order in the military, and these elders were overstepping their bounds.

That was so difficult to process. These men risked their lives for the United States, yet they were being accused of violating military law simply by wearing a uniform that represented their service.

JT   What strikes me most is that these men want recognition so badly that they go out of their way to search for uniforms and medals on eBay. And yet, this is seen as an "illegitimate" way to honor their service—because they didn't go through a system that never recognized them in the first place.

PHH   These men were not considered US soldiers but "allies" of the United States. If they had been enlisted, the US government would have been responsible for supporting them. But instead, the US has a history of recruiting allies to fight for them—only to abandon them once the war is over. That's exactly what happened to these Hmong veterans. Now, even in 2015, 2020, 2025, these veterans are still fighting for recognition.

JT   Yes, and even now, a bill has been put forward in Wisconsin [at the state, not federal, level], but as Vue Yang [a Sheboygan Hmong veteran] pointed out, many of these men have died. They're never going to receive financial or official recognition for what they did.

PHH   And yet, it's still so important to have work that acknowledges their story. Whether or not people understand its significance immediately, it needs to be there.[5]

JT   One of the things I initially thought was a problem—that not all these spaces would be open at the same time—you saw as a benefit. You talked about *creating* barriers or allowing them to exist. Maybe a person that is not Hmong has to step into the Hmong Mutual Assistance Association and feel a little uncomfortable. That's part of it.

PHH   In Sheboygan, people will encounter the work in their everyday spaces. In San José, most of the access is through the museum doors. That shifts the dynamic entirely. It'll be really interesting to see how people engage with the work differently in these two locations, especially since many of the same works will exist in both places.

Or maybe Hmong folks step into Paradigm to experience that space. Or they visit the Kohler Arts Center to see what a museum show looks like. These different points of access allow communities to interact and integrate in new ways.

5   The *Attention* series was at one point proposed for Sheboygan City Hall; plans were set aside amid the complexities of municipal process, and installed in the Arts Center.

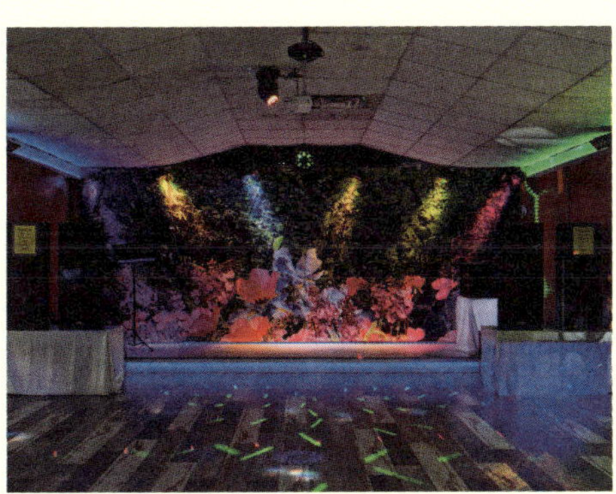

Pao Houa Her: The Imaginative Landscape, installation view at the Thai Café, Sheboygan, Wisconsin, 2025

JT When we first went to the courthouse, I remember meeting Natasha and going through security, thinking, *I'm going to make people go through security to see this artwork.* That felt complicated. But then I realized—this is part of the experience. Art audiences, who might not usually navigate these spaces, will now have to go through the same process as everyone else to see the work.

PHH Yeah, and that's okay. It's okay to be a little uncomfortable. It puts everyone on the same level. There's no privileged access. If you want to see the work at the Hmong Mutual Assistance Association, you have to go when they're open. Maybe that means attending a community lunch. If you're coming from New York expecting to see the show on *your* timeline, well—you have to be here on *the pace of the town.*

JT Yes! The *pace of the town.* That's a perfect way to put it. And that idea really sets the tone for the lunch that we experienced at the Hmong Mutual Assistance Association. It felt like a moment when we both got to witness the work in action.

PHH Getting to eat with everyone was really special. One thing I always find fascinating, and not just fascinating but also fun and scary at the same time, is when Hmong people encounter my work. There's always this self-doubt that comes up right away, but then it settles down a bit.

I was focused on themes that I thought they could relate to. For instance, I talked about my work with veterans and about the pieces in the space. The two bodies of work on display were *My Mother's Flowers* and *My grandmother's favorite grandchild.*

JT Can you share more about *My Mother's Flowers*?

PHH *My Mother's Flowers* consists of floral images—still lifes of flowers that my mother collected and later retired to the basement. When I talked about these images, I noticed a lot of the elder Hmong women nodding in agreement. They told me, "Yes, we have things like that. We love filling our houses with flowers, especially fake flowers."

Then, I shifted to discussing this very specific website that I was obsessively combing through in the early 2010s.

Between 2010 and 2015, I would check it at least once a day, if not once a week. The website, tojsiab.com, connected Hmong American men with Hmong Laotian girls.

It was pre-Facebook, pre-Hmong dating on social media. Hmong men would browse the site, where Hmong Laotian women would upload photos. Many of these women took their pictures to internet cafes, where the staff would Photoshop them before uploading. The site ranked them based on views—there was a "Top 50" every day, then a weekly and monthly ranking.

JT   So, you were interested in how people photographed themselves and how technology played a role in that?

PHH   Exactly. I was fascinated by how they posed, how their images were altered, and how men engaged with them. Some images had faces cut out and pasted onto different bodies. Others had skin whitening or nose elongation—Western beauty standards imposed through Photoshop.

I religiously screen-grabbed these images, collecting them for years. I first learned about the site through an uncle who met a woman there. He was sending her money, believing she was completing paperwork to come to the US. He spent nearly his entire life savings—$85,000—only to be catfished.

JT   Wow. That must have been heartbreaking.

PHH   It was. But it's not an uncommon story in the Hmong community. I shared this story yesterday at the lunch, and the room reacted in fascinating ways. The men said, "No, we don't like girls from that website." But the women responded, "Oh yes, those are exactly the girls these men like." It sparked a really interesting debate.

JT   That's such a powerful conversation. It reminds me of how you connect themes of beauty and artifice in your work. Like, even the way your mother collected artificial flowers— there's something there, right?

PHH   Yes, absolutely. My mother loved the idea of the American Dream, and for her, that meant having flowers everywhere. We were too poor for fresh flowers, so she bought artificial ones from thrift stores and dollar stores, rearranged them, and displayed them for years. When she tired of them, she retired them to the basement but never threw them away.

Similarly, in my archive of images from tojsiab.com, I noticed a pattern: women often photographed themselves next to flowers. There's a long history of the female body as a vessel for youth and fertility, and I wondered—were these women consciously or subconsciously playing into that imagery?

JT One work that really stands out in the exhibition is your video *Kwv txhiaj in the Valley of Widows* (2023). If you're open to talking about it … it's a centerpiece of the exhibition in the main gallery. It's incredibly moving and has really strong cultural ties. Can you talk about the making of it?

PHH I became really interested in *kwv txhiaj*.[6] I've lived with these *kwv txhiaj* videos all my life. My parents are avid listeners, and they watched videos of *kwv txhiaj* regularly. I have an uncle whose job was to go to Laos, make *kwv txhiaj*, bring it back, and sell it. The video cassettes and videotapes were always present in our homes, no matter where we lived.

As a child, teenager, and even as a young adult, I knew they existed, but I never really paid attention to them. It wasn't until recently—around 2020 or 2021—that I started engaging with them. One New Year's at the senior center where my mother worked, a woman approached me and said, "I want to sing you a *kwv txhiaj*." So she did—this beautiful song about her experiences during the Hmong New Year, her role as the singer, and the preparation involved.

Then I traveled to Laos in 2023. Before I left, I had been working with a videographer, Ka Xiong, who collaborates with me on my *kwv txhiaj* videos. I told him I was coming to Luang Prabang on a specific date and asked him to find a Hmong man and woman to sing *kwv txhiaj* next to each other. He agreed, and when he asked what they should sing about, I told him: grief and loss.

I think he took my request literally because he knew I had lost my husband in 2021. When he went to find the singers, he told them I wanted them to sing about my husband's passing. By the time I arrived in Luang Prabang, he had already explained my story to them. When they picked me up, they asked, "Tell us about your husband." I thought they were just curious, so I shared our story—how we had been together since childhood, built a life together, and how he passed away unexpectedly from a brain hemorrhage.

JT   And they decided to sing about that specifically?

PHH   Yes. I didn't have the heart to tell them not to. A part of me wanted them to sing about grief and loss, but I didn't expect them to tailor it to my personal story. And yet, they did. The result was this incredibly beautiful song about a man's death and how he waits for the woman he left behind. She sings about her loss, how they didn't have children, and ultimately, it became a story about my husband and me.

    What's fascinating is that later, I learned about a place in Luang Prabang called the Valley of Widows, where they filmed the video. There's a local legend about a Hmong man who fell in love with a woman from the mountains. The village wanted him back, so they tried to kill her but ended up killing him instead. She avenged his death and then perished. The mountain landscape is said to form her body. It was surreal to discover this story after making the video.

JT   How did you feel about the video after that?

PHH   I sat with it for a long time. I sent it to my gallerists and said, "I made this, but I don't know what to do with it." The two singers in the video are revered in the Hmong community. They improvised the song on the spot, and it was stunning. I wasn't sure if or how it would fit into my practice.

    In some ways, this piece is the most personal work I've ever made. I can't even watch the video because every time I do, I start crying. And it's not just about understanding the lyrics—I don't even know how to sing *kwv txhiaj* or fully grasp its structure—but the song moves me deeply.

JT   And this will be the first time you're showing it publicly?

PHH   Yes, the first time in its entirety.

JT   Are you worried about how that will feel—seeing and hearing it in the gallery?

PHH   Absolutely. My mom has asked about it, but I haven't shared it with her yet. It's incredibly personal. I think I'm open to talking about many things, but I've never shared this much about my husband before. It's new for me.

JT   The lenticulars [from the series *Pictures of paradise*] feel like a perfect bridge to this work.

PHH   Yes. In late 2022 and early 2023, my parents decided to take my siblings and me to Laos. It was the first time they had returned in over twenty years. My dad took us on a tour of the places where he and my mother hid in the jungle while fleeing. He and my uncle shared stories about survival—how they had to clear land, find food, and build shelter while being pursued.

JT   Even amid danger, life continued.

PHH   Yes, people lived, loved, and gave birth in those jungles. I think about the jungle as both a place of life and a place of secrets. It's thick, overgrown, and unwilling to reveal its past. That's why the work needed to be lenticular—because the jungle is surreal. It exists, it's tangible, but the reality of what happened there feels unreal. The depth, the layers—it all had to be conveyed in that format.

JT   The lenticular images truly capture that sense of depth— you feel like you have to push through them.

PHH   Exactly. I wanted the viewer to interact with them in a way that reflects that impenetrability. Much like history, the jungle covers things up. You can't just see everything clearly; you have to navigate through layers.

JT   I really like that the images are large enough that they change the way the viewer moves. You have a bodily experience, a physical relationship to them. That was a shock to me because you can't just stand straight in front of them and consume the photo like we do with others—you have to move and look.

PHH   That's really important and very much part of the viewer's experience. I often talk about the dance that needs to happen when you're looking at images. And in this case, it's quite literal—you have to move in order to see them.

JT   I was reading about you being photographed in a refugee camp as one of your earliest memories. Have you heard the Ocean Vuong interview with Krista Tippett on *On Being*?

PHH   No, what did he say?

JT   He talks about the cover photo of *Night Sky with Exit Wounds*—it looks like a happy picture of a little boy with two loving women. But in reality, they were in a refugee camp. They paid for that photo with three cups of rice. That made me think about what I read about you.

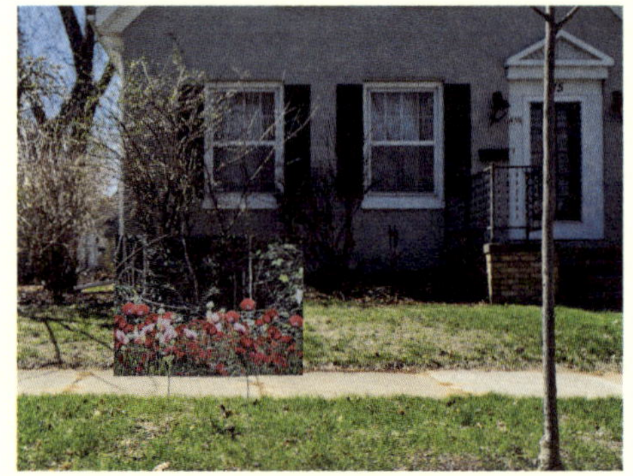

Pao Houa Her: The Imaginative Landscape, installed yard sign, Sheboygan, Wisconsin, 2025

PHH   That's fascinating. I had a conversation with Lauren [Dickens] recently about refugee camp photographers. I suspect they knew that people were going to be separated and saw an opportunity to create images that would become the only tangible connection for many families. My grandmother, for example, commissioned a photograph of my cousin because she knew they would be separated forever. That photo was the only one she allowed on her wall for the rest of her life. It moved with her from house to house.

JT   Wow. And now that photo lives in your house?

PHH   Yes, and it will likely be in every house I live in after this. But it's insignificant to my parents and uncles.

JT   That's so interesting. But for you, it holds so much weight.

PHH   Absolutely. That single photograph is what drives my research into portraiture and Hmong studio photography. It encapsulates everything that genre embodies.

JT   One of the things we've talked about is what scares us about this project. Can you reflect on that? What's scaring you, and how do you balance artistic risk with community expectations and your own expectations?

PHH   When I think about this work, I often think about who it is for, why it exists, and whether people will understand it. Those questions are always on my mind. Over the years, I've grown more confident in saying that my work is for Hmong people. Maybe not all of them right now, but in the future, I hope they will engage with it, talk about it meaningfully, and critique it in ways that are productive for them.

But the thing that gives me anxiety is how the community will receive the work. Even though it's for the Hmong community, I worry about what they will say about it. Isn't that wild? The hope is that they talk about it, that it opens up space for larger conversations. But that's also the thing that scares me the most.

JT   Did yesterday's lunch [at the Hmong Mutual Assistance Association] make you feel better, or do you still feel the same way?

PHH   Still the same. I don't know if this is an artist thing, but anytime you make something and send it into the world, the big question is always, "How will people perceive it?" And it does matter to me. I welcome—and think it's important to have—criticism and critiques of my work, but that's also what scares me.

As an artist of color, I try really hard to be sensitive to issues within my community. I want to be aware of the sensitivities present, but I'm also interested in talking about them and bringing them to the forefront. Often, my community does a good job of putting on a public face and not addressing internal issues. I'm interested in those internal issues. For instance, yesterday we talked about a dating website and how there's an ongoing problem in our community with older Hmong men going overseas to marry younger Hmong women. Some people might ask, "Why are you bringing this issue to the forefront for outsiders to see? We should be able to fix our problems within our community." I understand that perspective, but I also think it's important to talk about these issues openly.

JT   Yes, and how will the community talk about the work? That's something we don't have control over.

PHH   The Hmong Mutual Assistance Association piece is the one that makes me wonder, are they going to call us and say we have to take it down?

JT   That's been on my mind, too.

PHH   I've been calling that installation a "disruption" rather than just an installation. That's important to acknowledge.

In my community, we celebrate and remember the past, but sometimes, that past needs to be critiqued, too. Disrupting the presidential wall is a way of critiquing—by inserting women into that space.

JT   I think another challenge is that people have to experience this exhibition on its own terms. This isn't a traditional art center or museum experience.

PHH   Right. If you want to see the courthouse installation, you have to go Monday through Friday, nine to five, pass through security, and follow their rules. You can't just walk in whenever you want, like at a museum.

JT   Or to experience your work at the Hmong Mutual Assistance Association, you really need to go to the Thursday lunch from eleven to one and be there. I think the art world says they're ready for this kind of engagement, but will they be? Will they come expecting to see every single piece and be frustrated when they can't? Part of the experience is being rebuffed, being made to think about access.

PHH   Yes. Historically, art has always been experienced on the terms of the institution. But with this project, we are experiencing art on the terms of different institutions—the courthouse, the Hmong Mutual Assistance Association, etcetera. That's really interesting to me.

JT   And some of those places have unexpected access rules. For example, even if the courtroom is in session, people are still welcome to walk in and see the work.

PHH   That experience alone—the uneasiness, being a little uncomfortable—is important. I think about all the times I've felt uneasy going to a museum, not having enough money for admission, or feeling like I wasn't dressed the right way. Now, visitors will have to navigate different spaces on the terms of those institutions.

To go to the Hmong Mutual Assistance Association, you either have to call and make an appointment or come on a Thursday and be part of the community lunch. And you're fed when you're there!

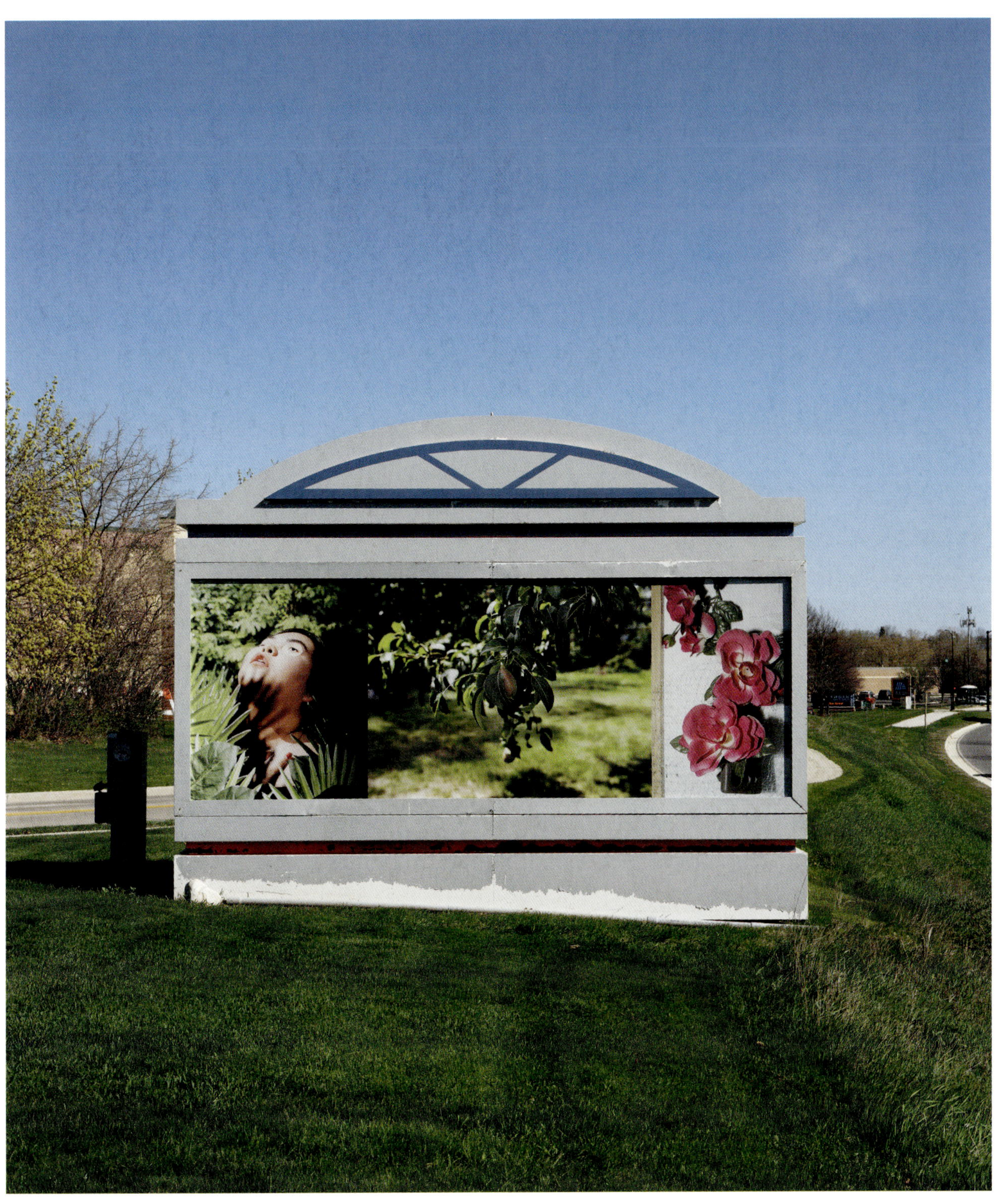

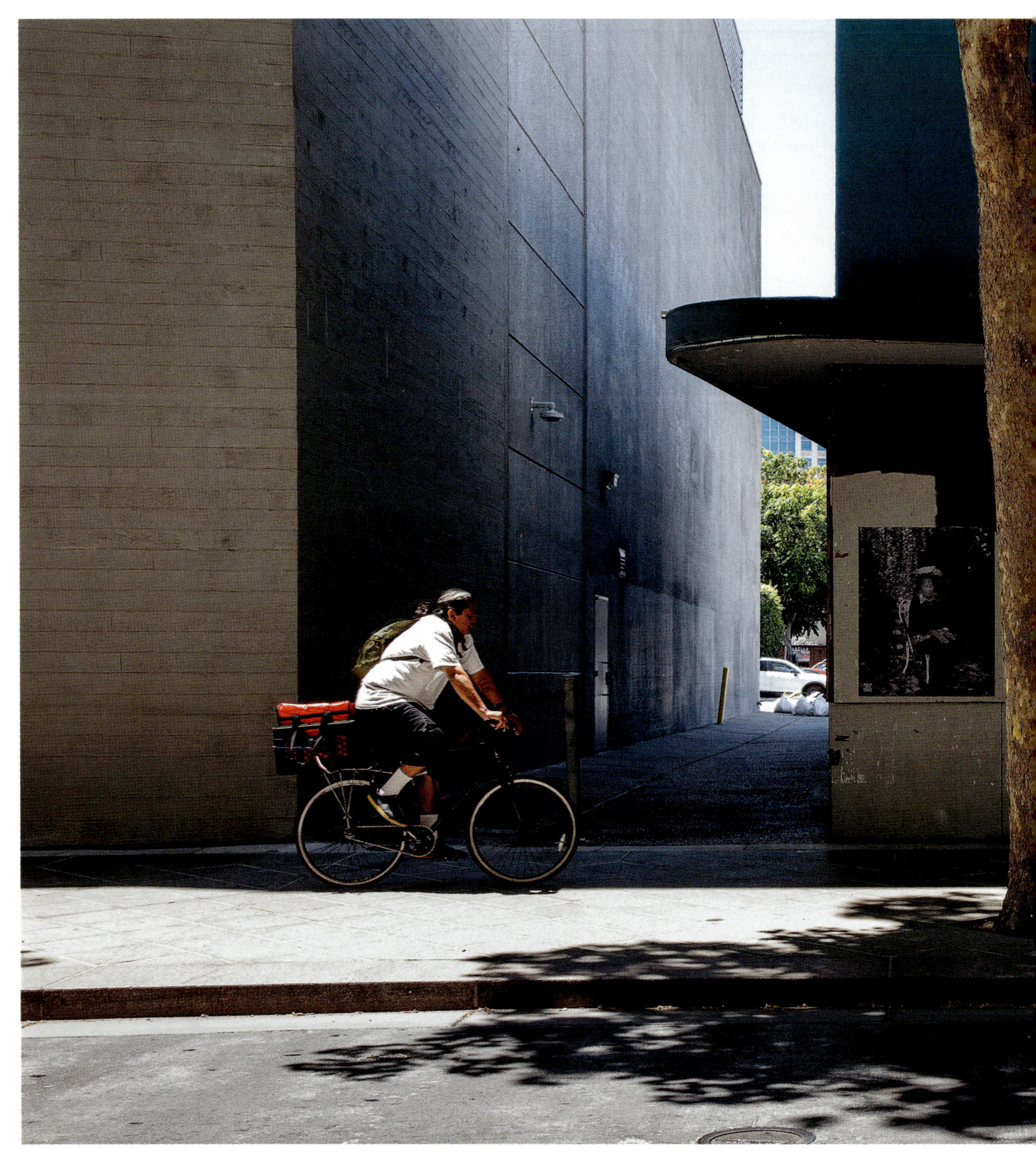

Pao Houa Her: The Imaginative Landscape,
installation view, downtown San José,
California, 2025

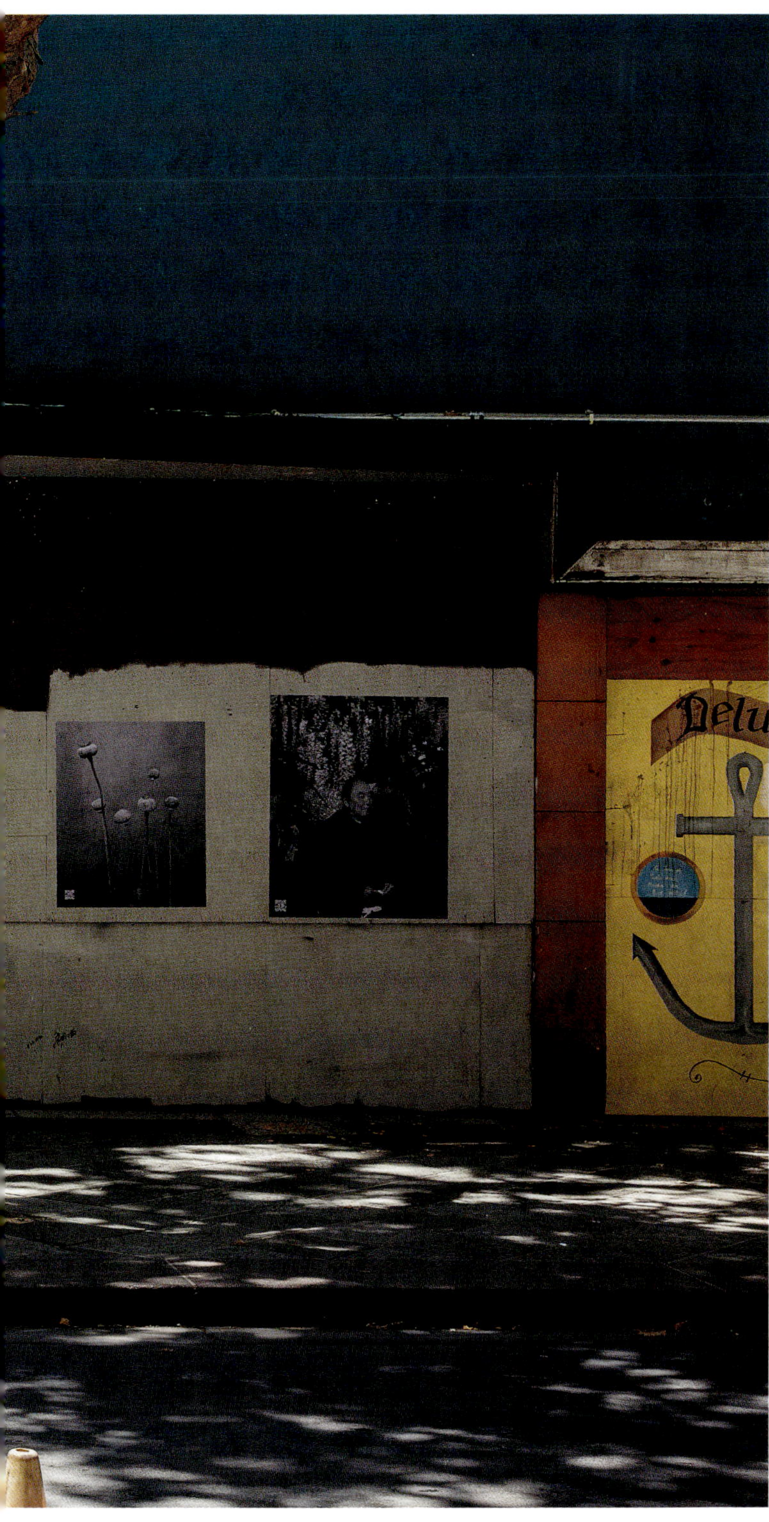

Delu

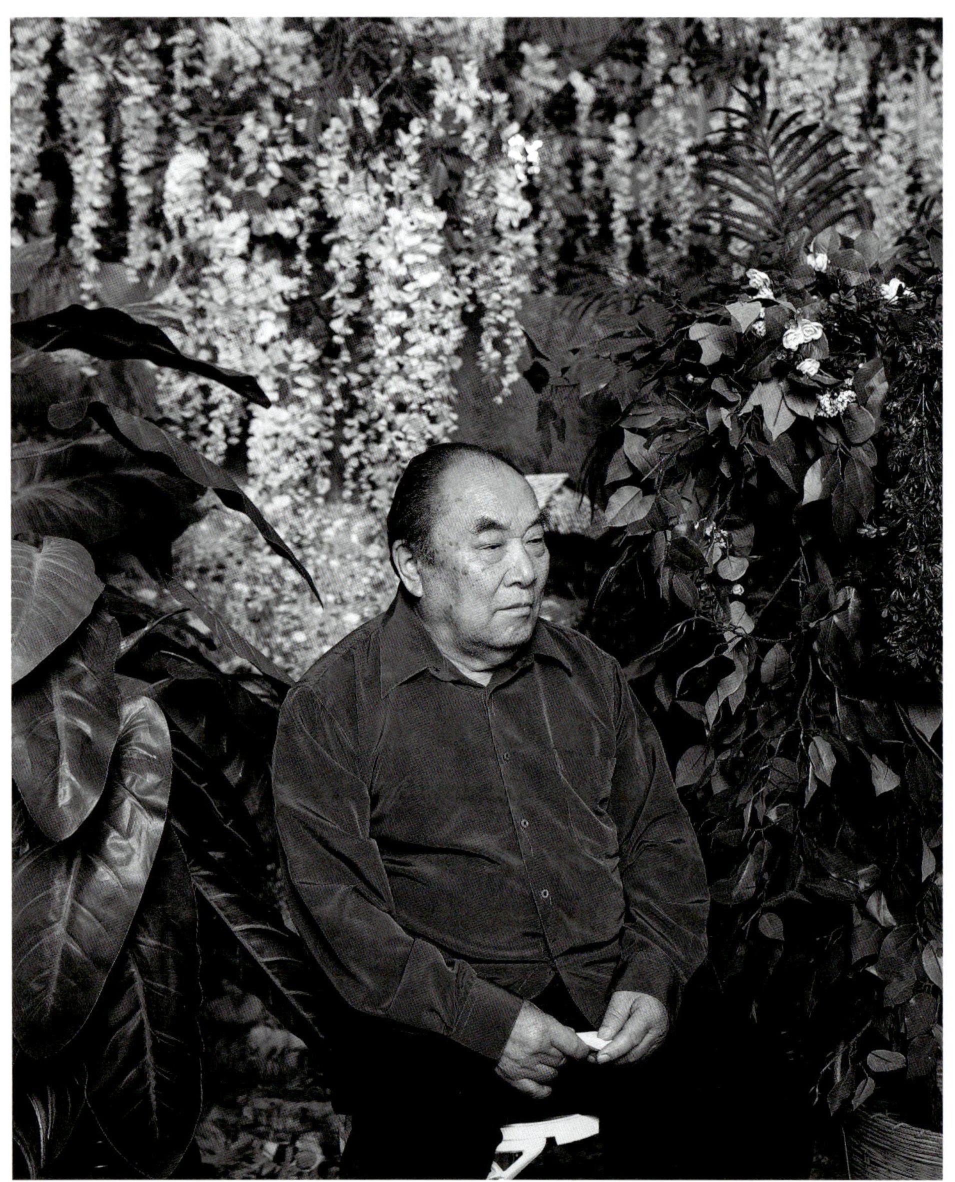

untitled (man sitting), 2020, from
The Imaginative Landscape series,
archival pigment print

Right:
Pao Houa Her: The Imaginative
Landscape, installation view at the
Sheboygan County Circuit Court,
Wisconsin, 2025

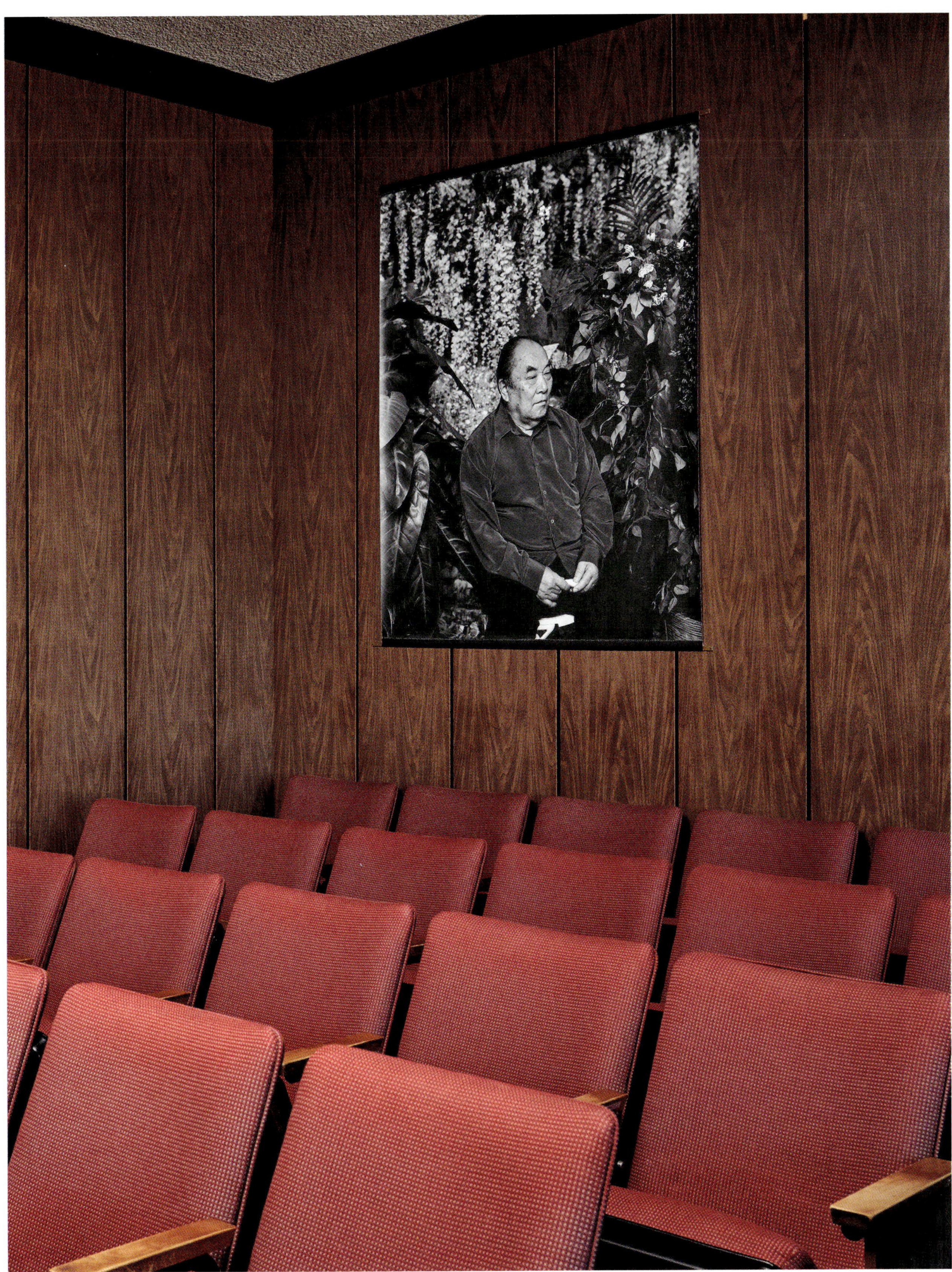

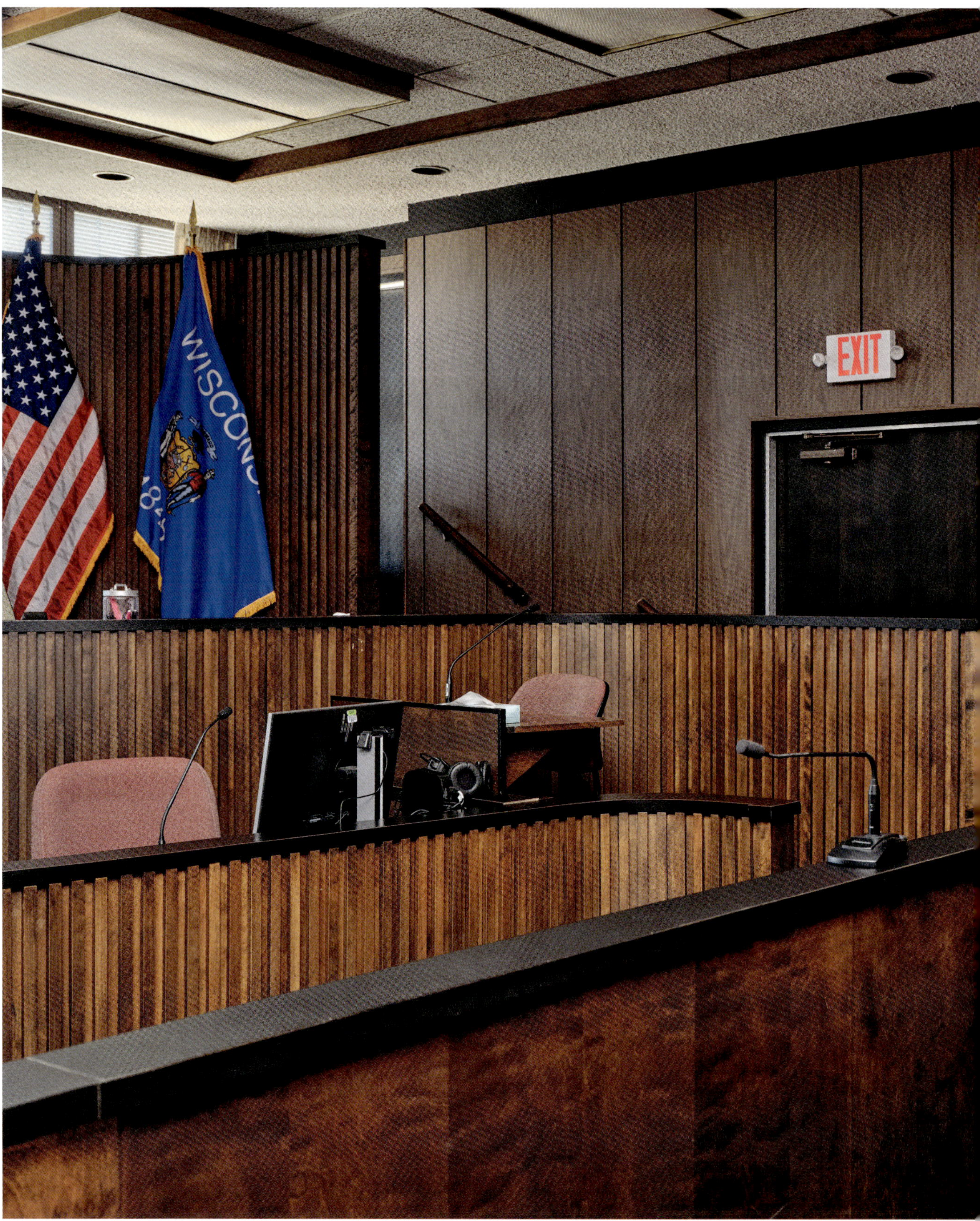
WISCONSIN
1848
EXIT

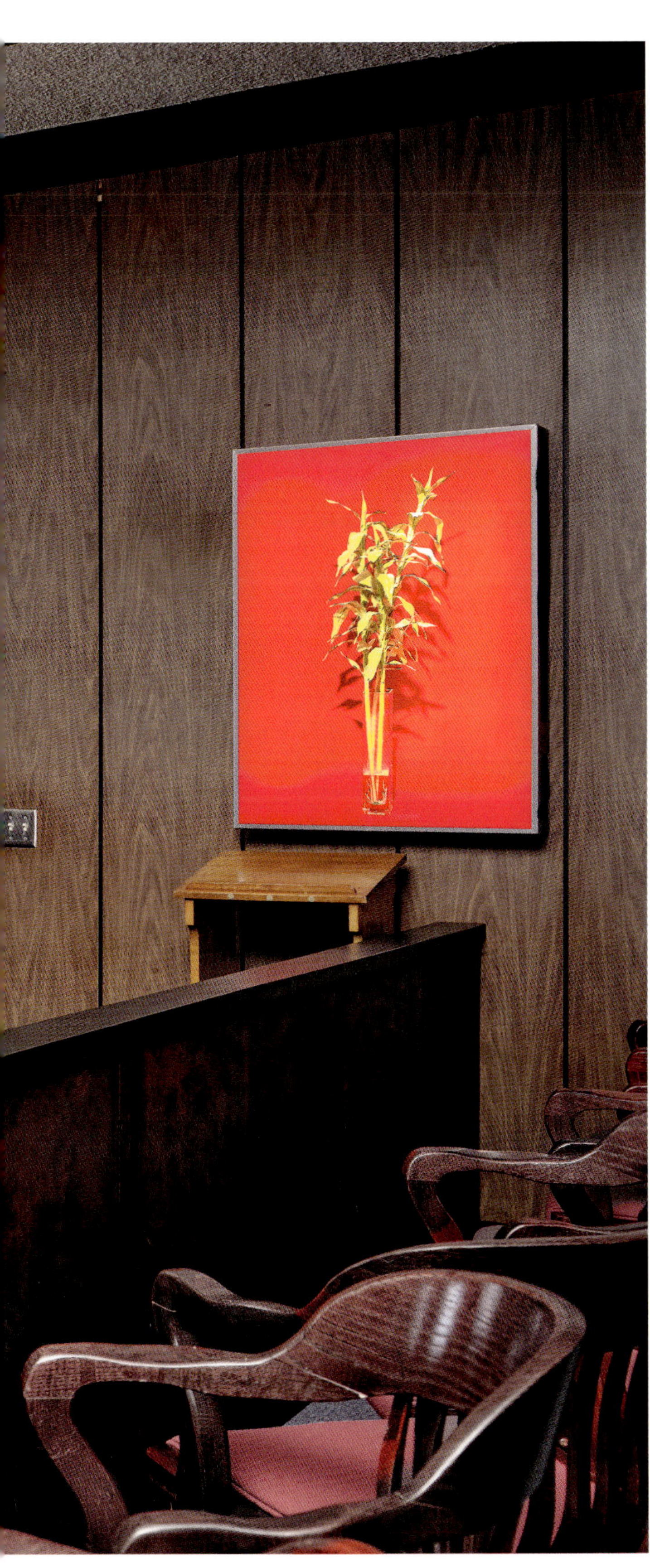

Pao Houa Her: The Imaginative Landscape, installation view at the Sheboygan County Circuit Court, Wisconsin, 2025

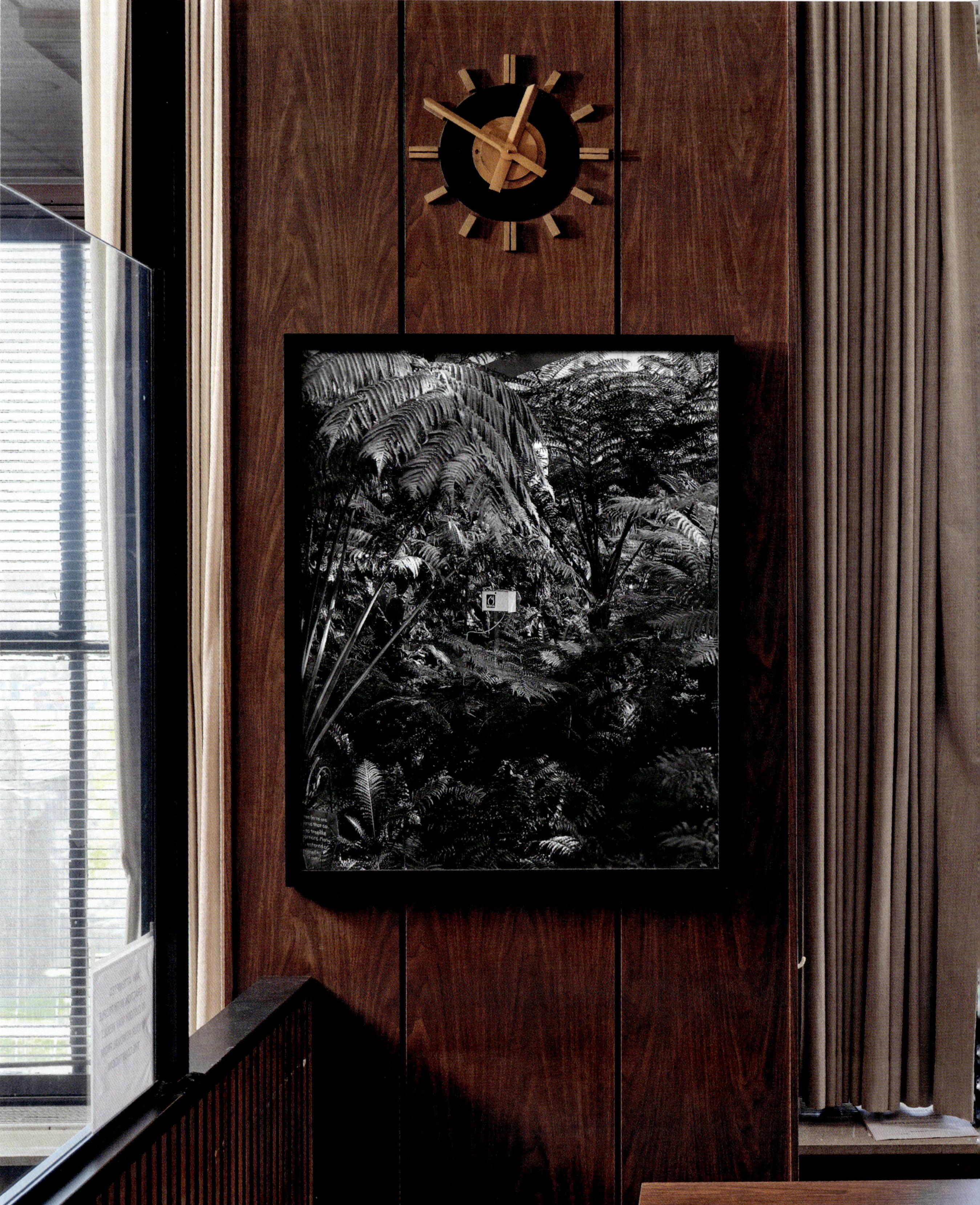

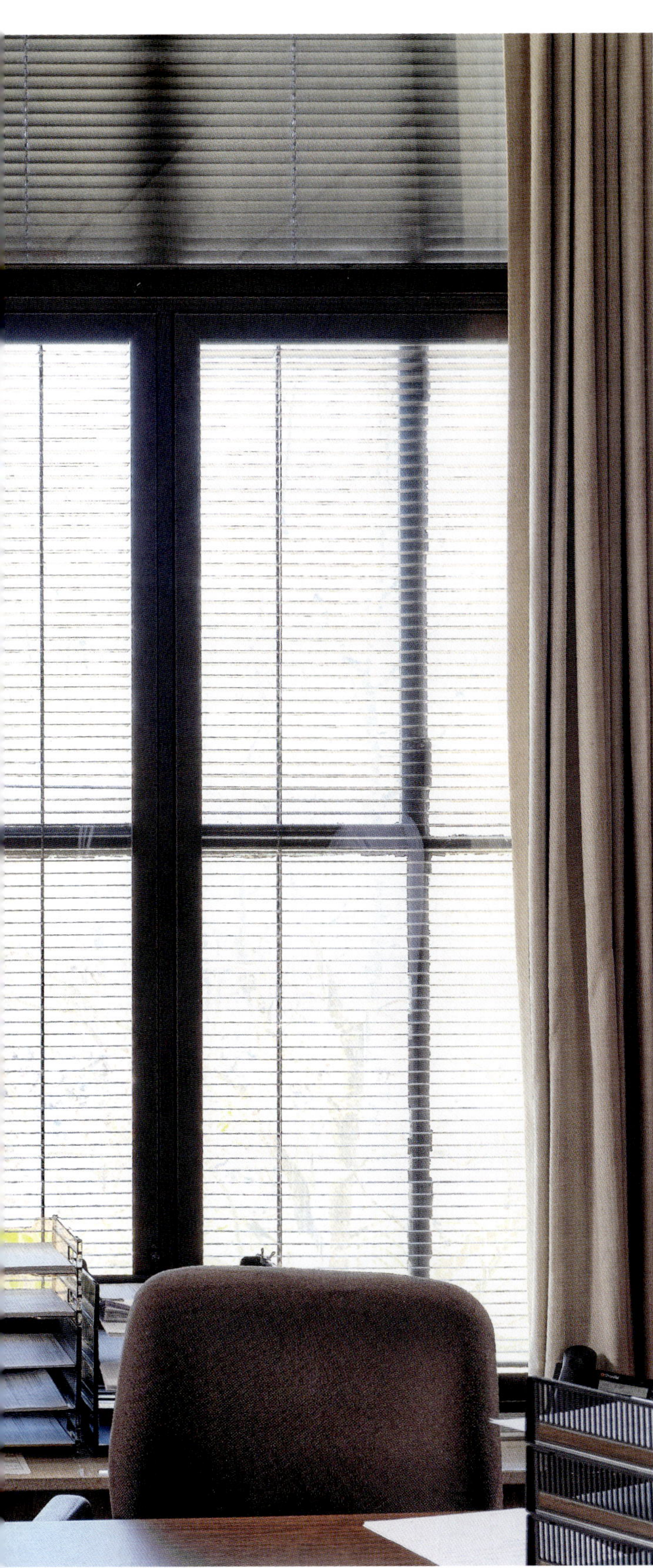

Pao Houa Her: The Imaginative Landscape, installation view at the Sheboygan County Circuit Court, Wisconsin, 2025

untitled (Tais Ka), 2020, from
The Imaginative Landscape series,
archival pigment print

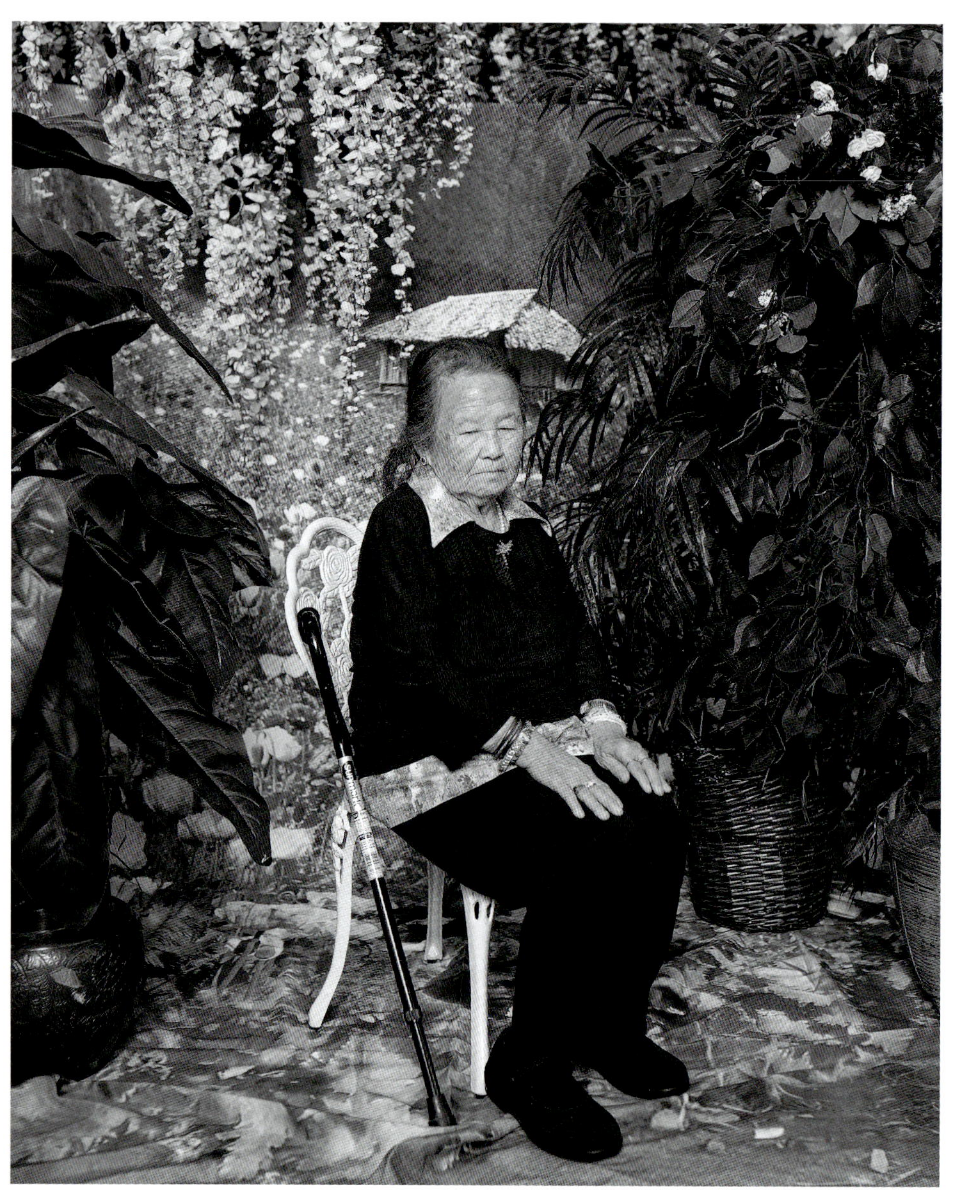

82

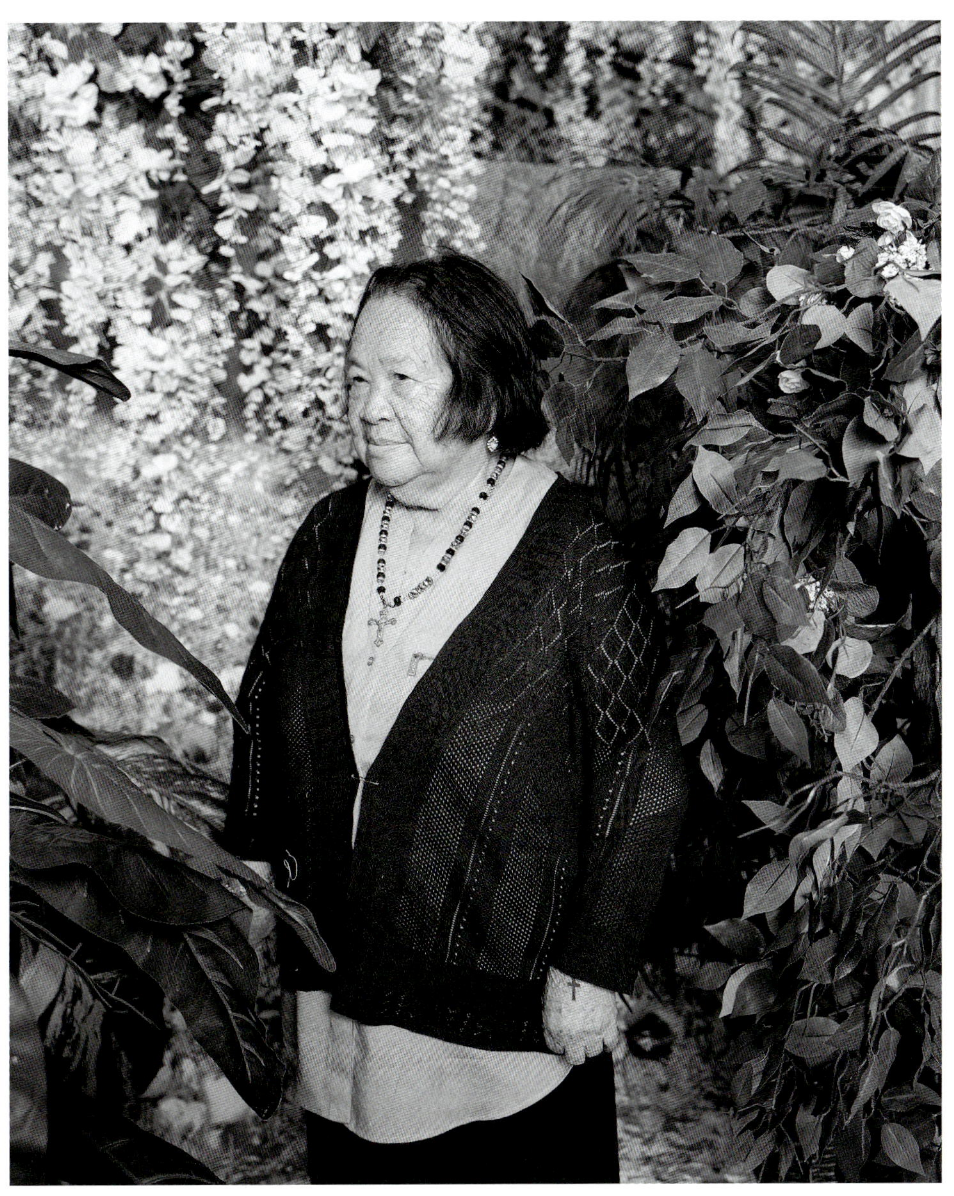

untitled (Tais Shoua), 2020, from
The Imaginative Landscape series,
archival pigment print

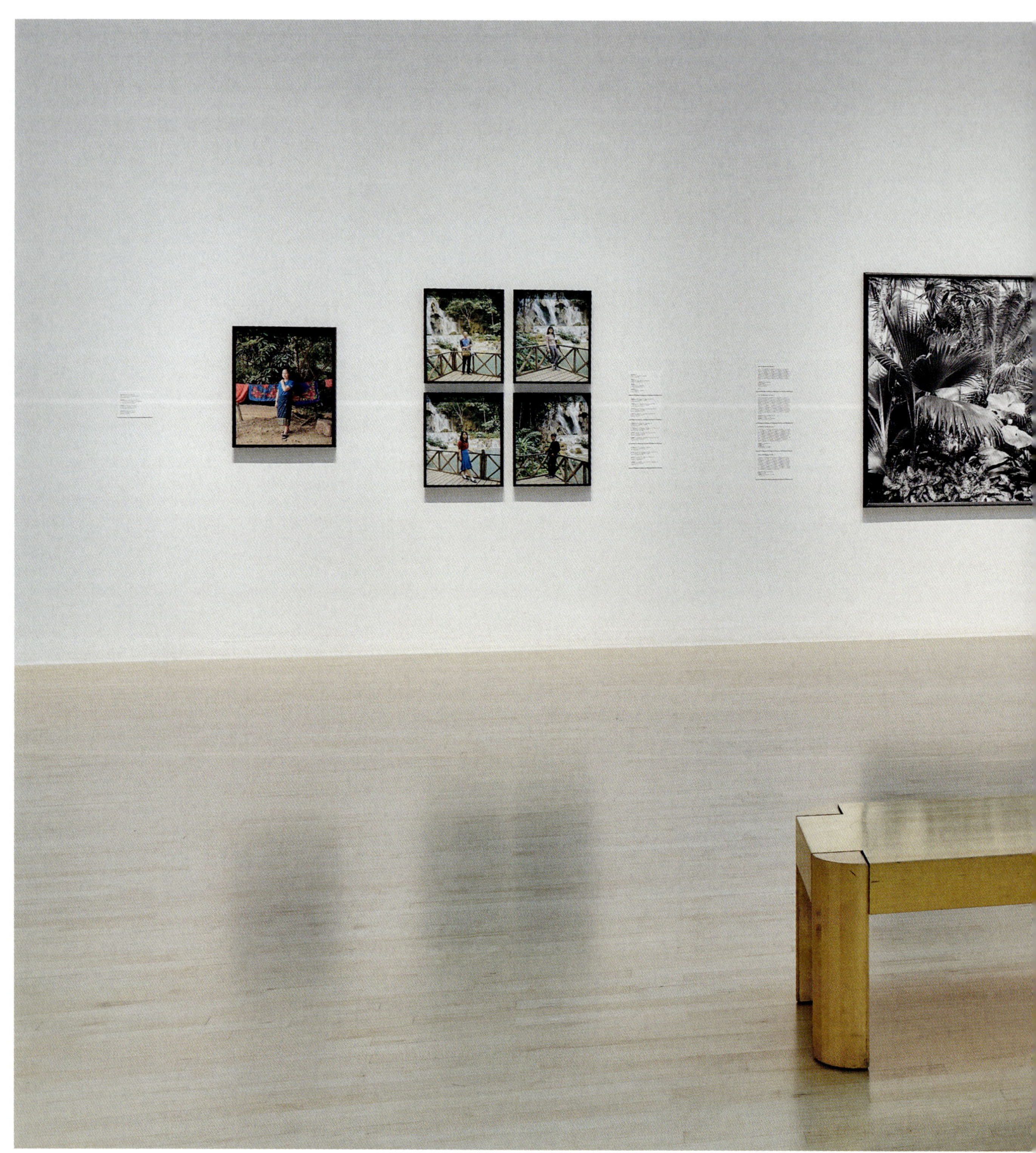

Pao Houa Her: The Imaginative Landscape, installation view
at San José Museum of Art, 2025

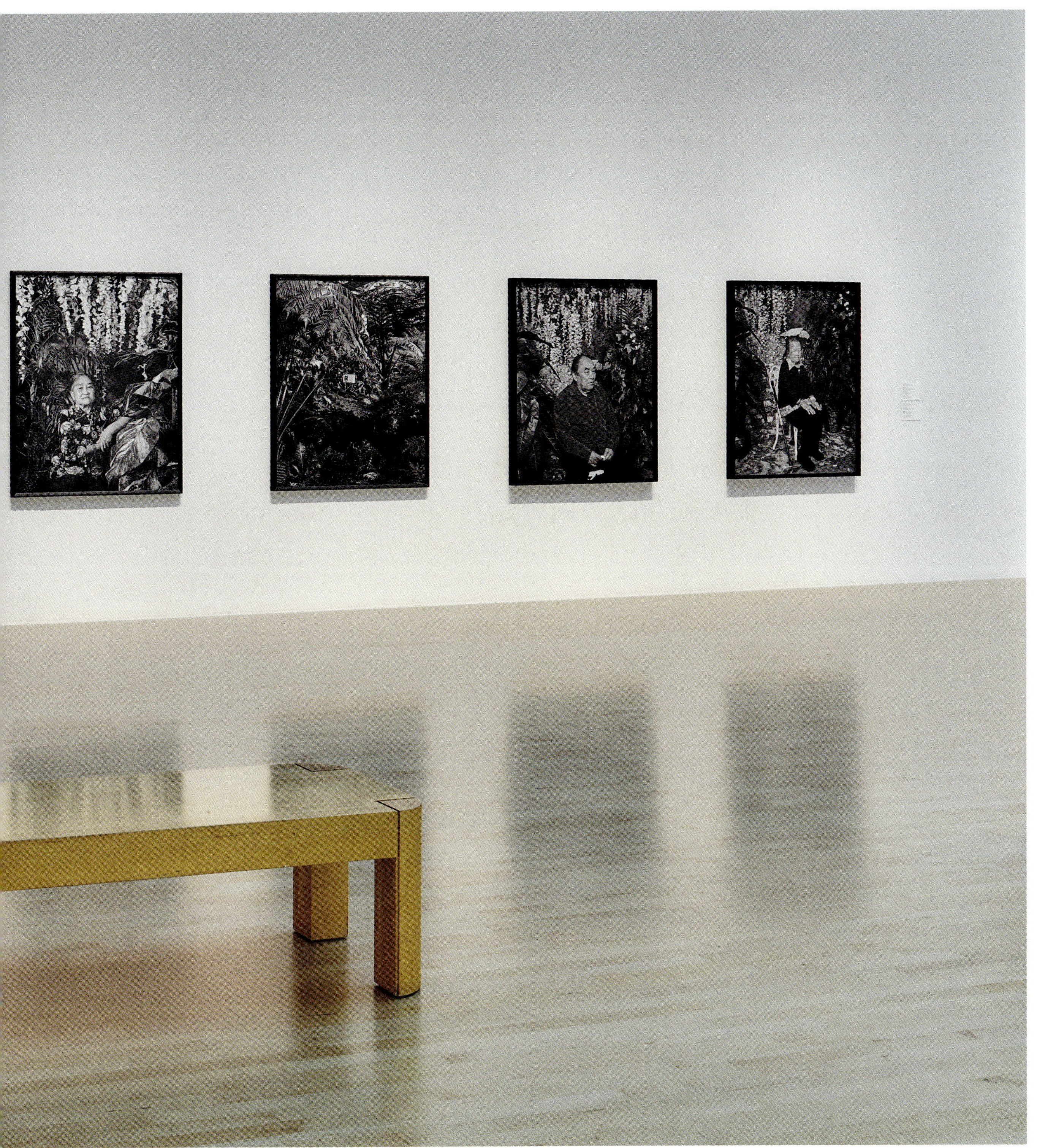

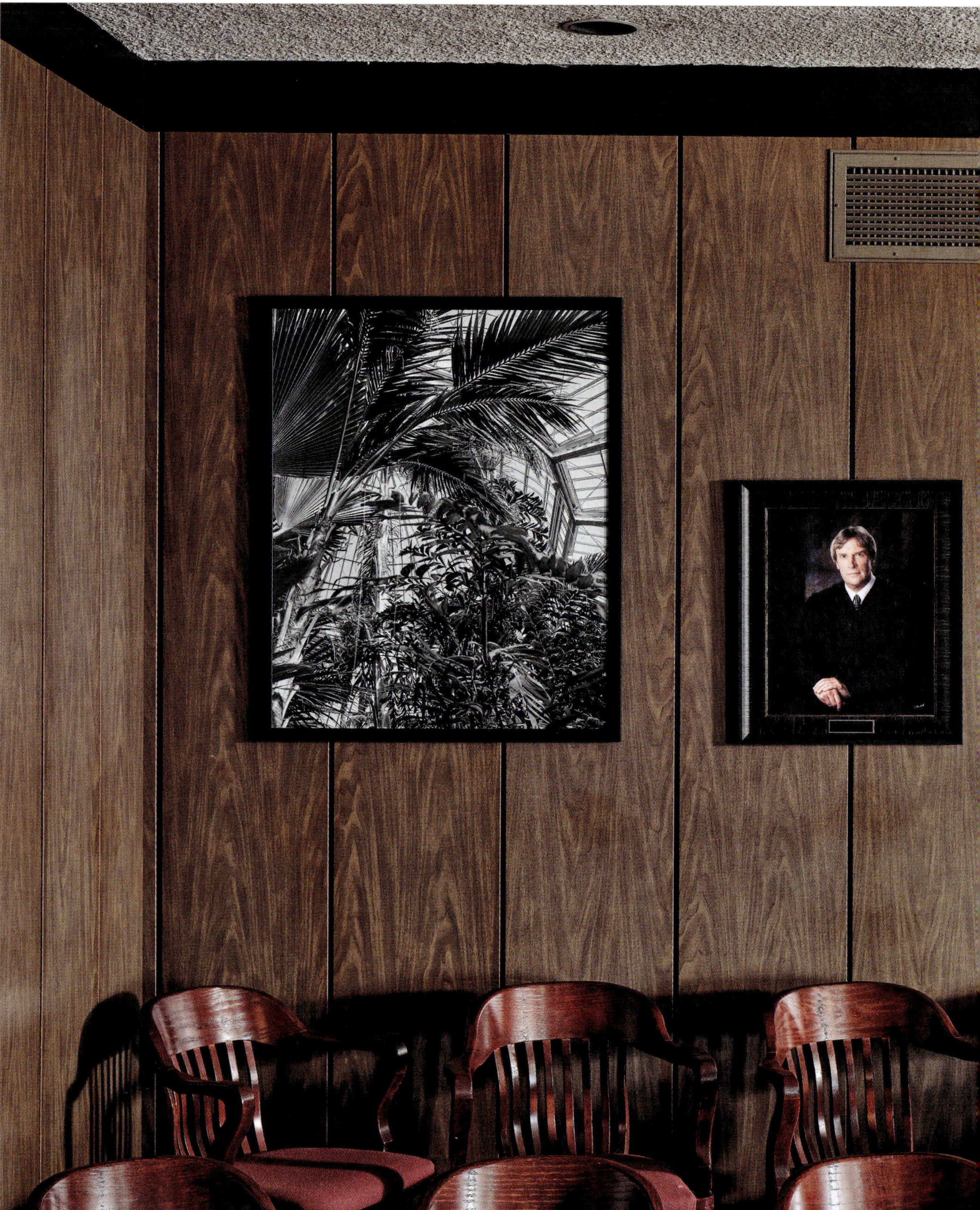

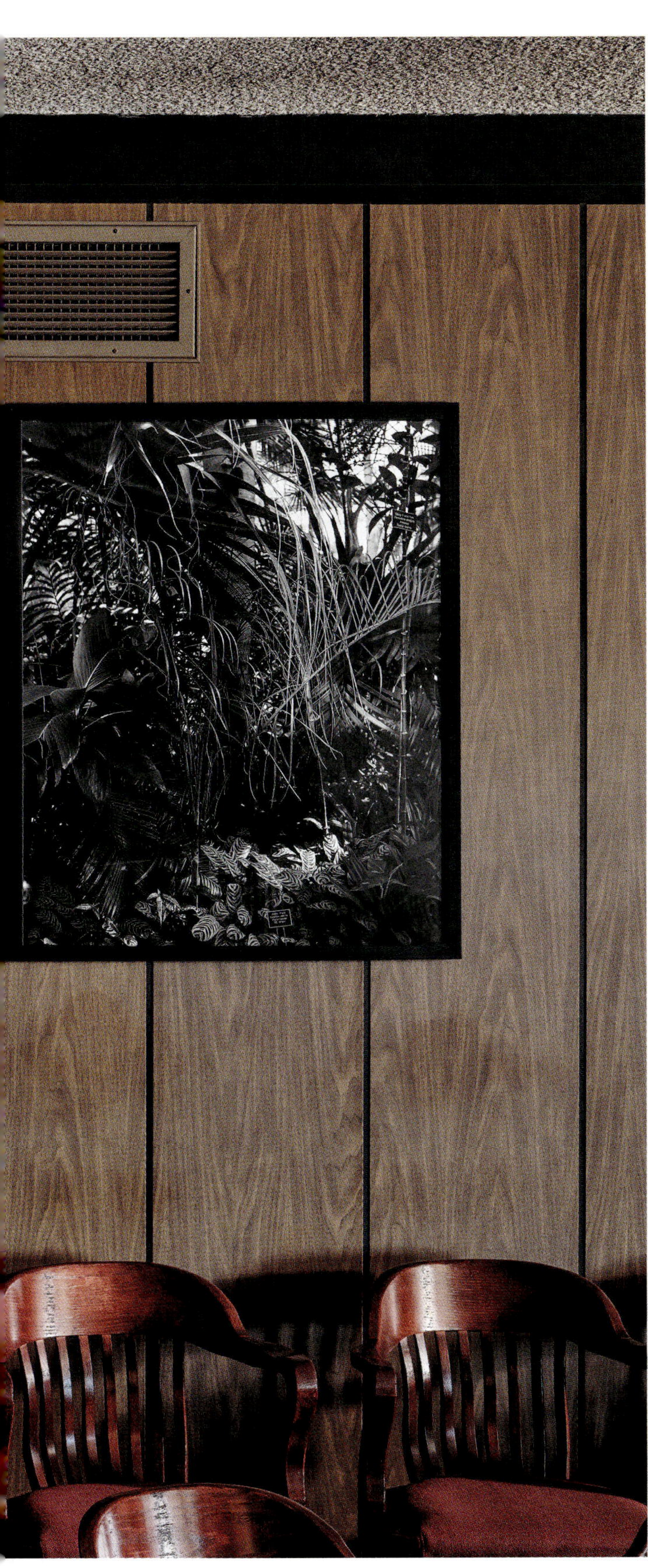

*Pao Houa Her: The Imaginative
Landscape*, installation view at the
Sheboygan County Circuit Court,
Wisconsin, 2025

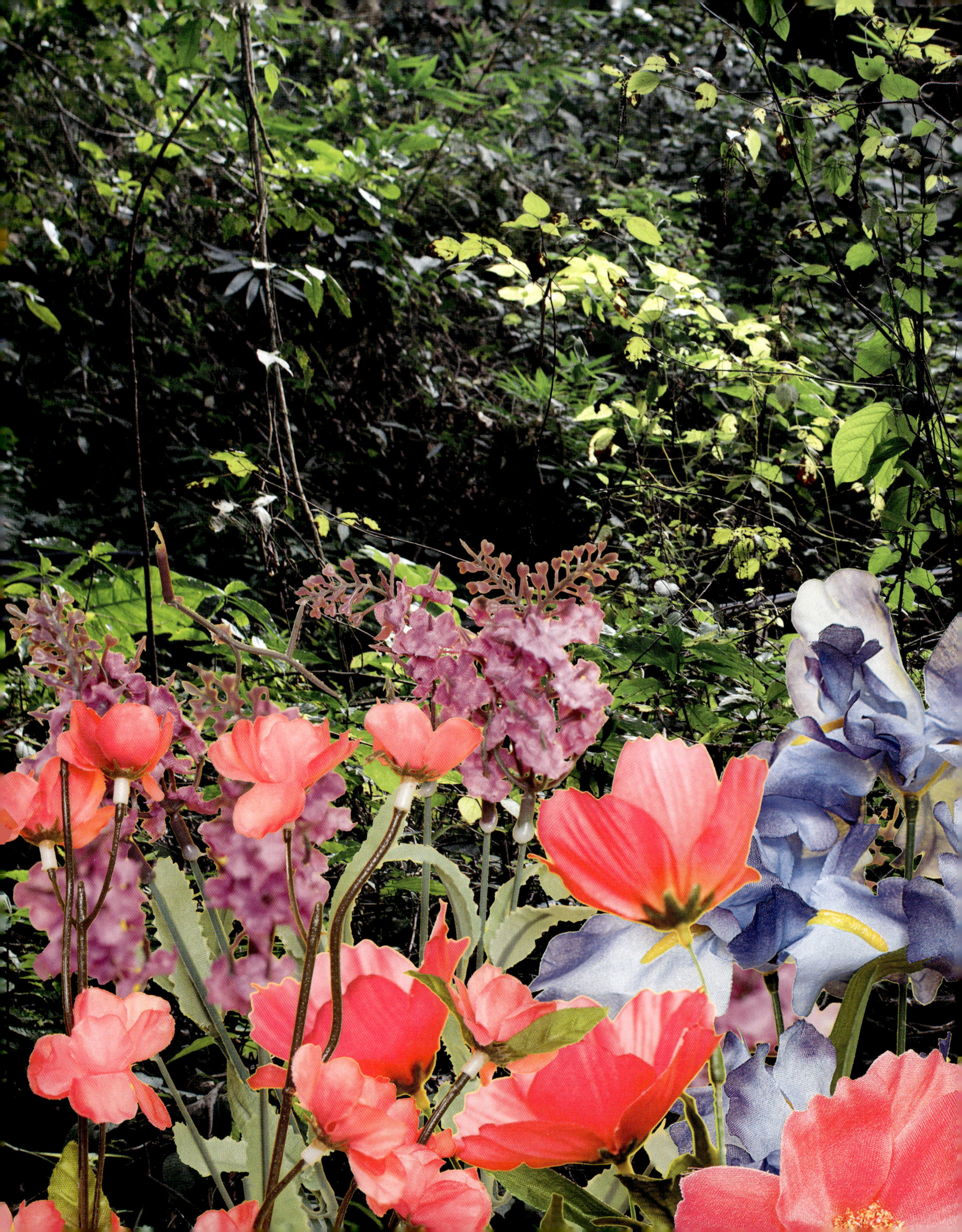

SEEDS
OF HISTORY

PAO HOUA HER

Whenever my *niam tais* (maternal grandmother) spent the weekend with us, I would quietly ask to sleep beside her. Her skin was soft and gentle, and I found comfort in lying close as she shared stories of her childhood in Laos. I listened intently, eager to hear about her walks to the garden, about suitors she once knew, and whether she had ever seen lions or tigers. She often talked about those walks through fields of poppies, where her family cultivated dreams hidden beneath the quiet earth.

In the Hmong community, elders often reflect on those days of prosperity, as a time when the land held more than just crops, but a sense of hope. When I ask why they long to go back to Laos, they speak of those moments, not the land itself, but the feeling of abundance and peace that once seemed within reach.

Through the evolution of studio portraiture in the Hmong diaspora, the image of poppies persists in the background, a quiet reminder of that past. *Seeds of History* seeks to evoke this chapter—recreating a time when fields of poppies stretched across the landscape, a visual meditation on memory, longing, and resilience.

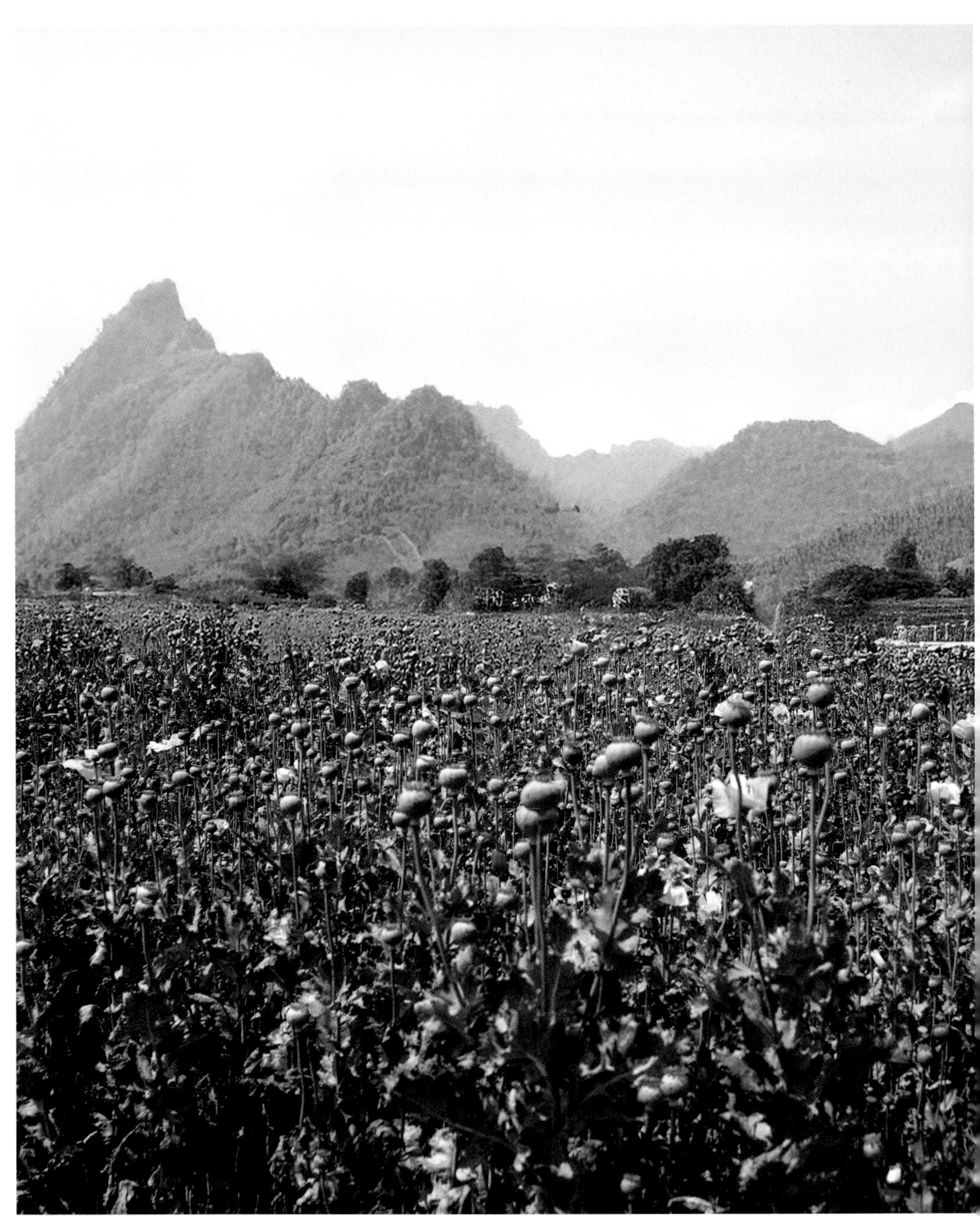

untitled (collaged poppy field and Laos), 2025

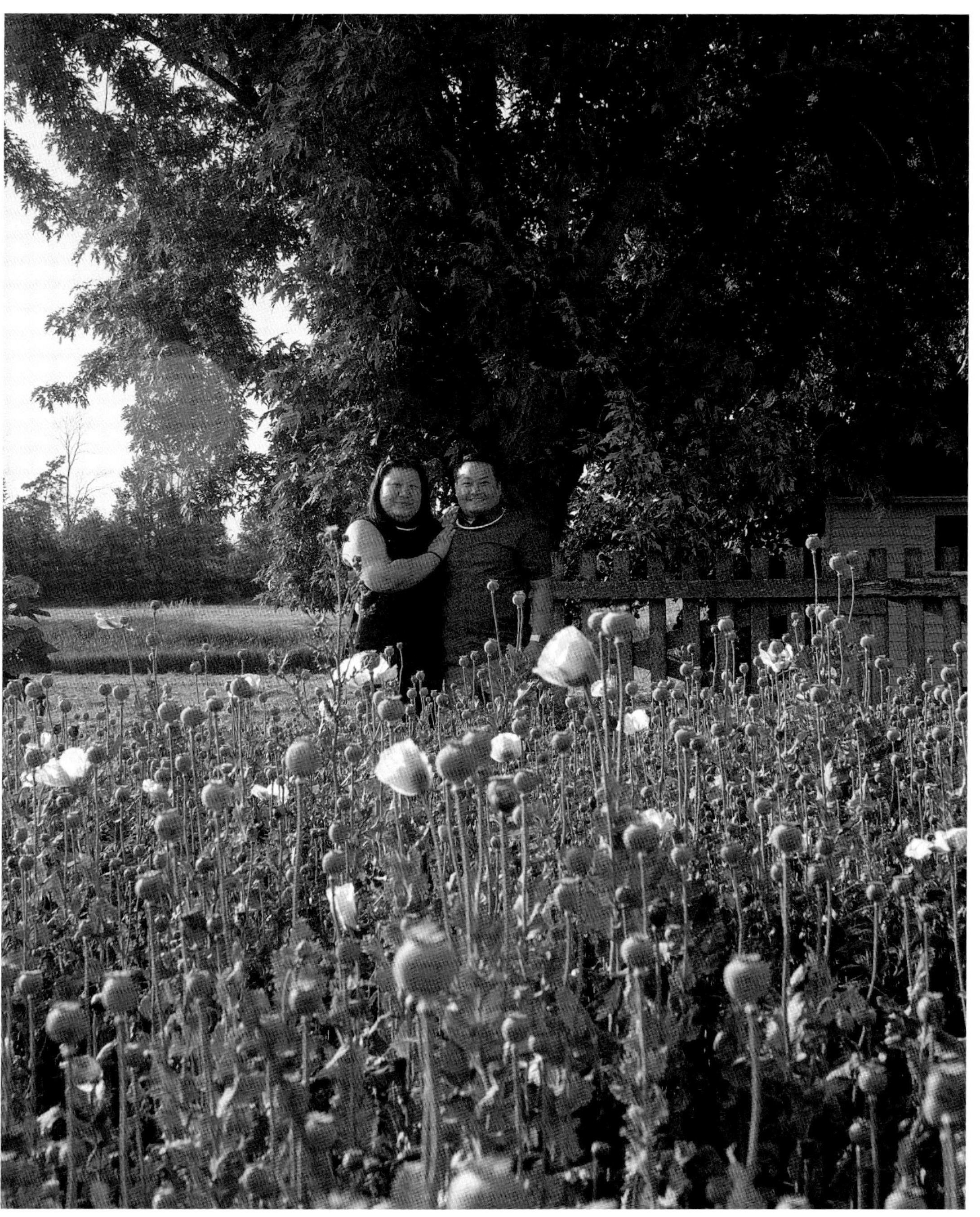

untitled (Shelia Yang and Ge Vang), 2025

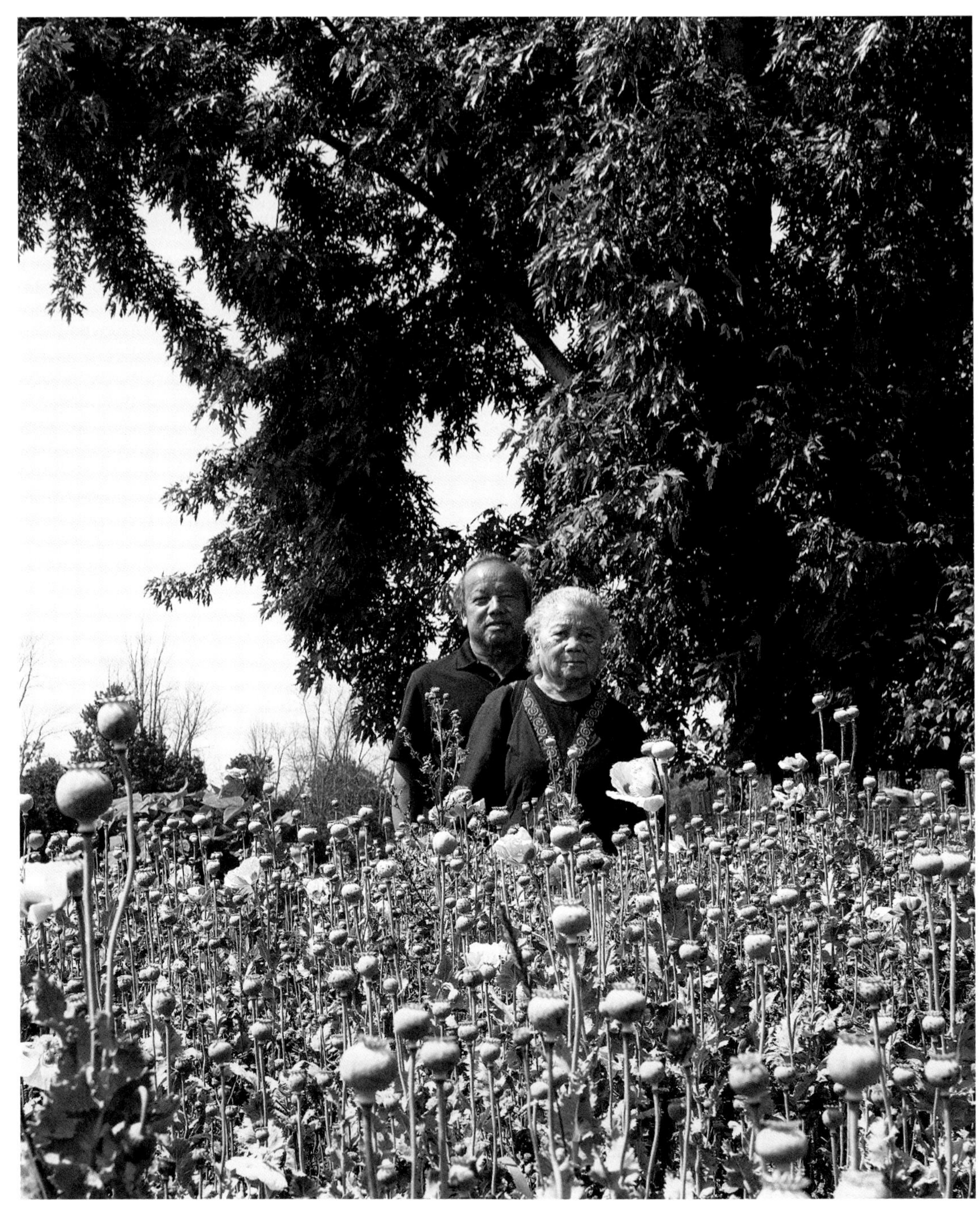

untitled (Xao Yang Lee and Tou Moua Lee), 2025

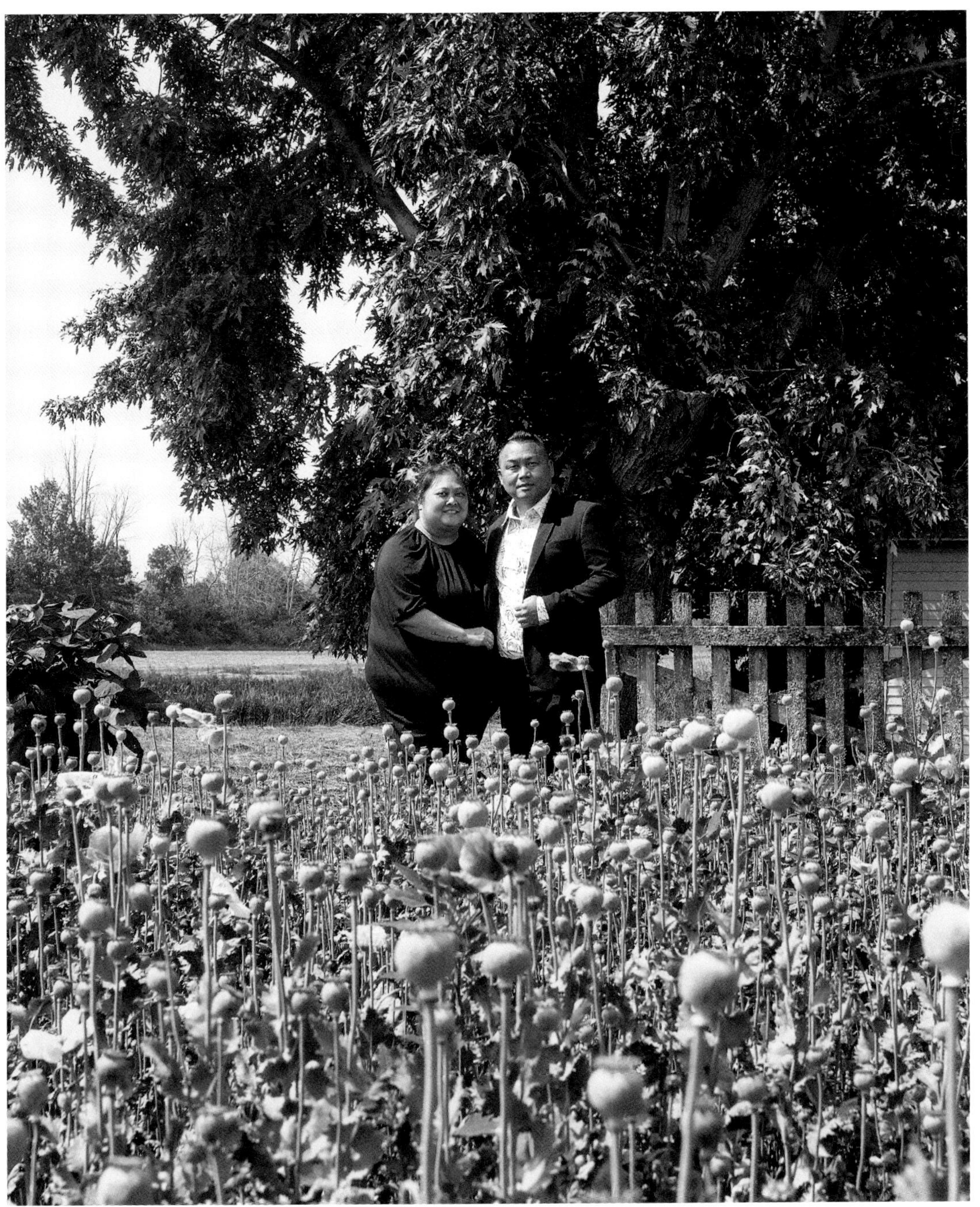

untitled (Choua Lee and Kou Lee), 2025

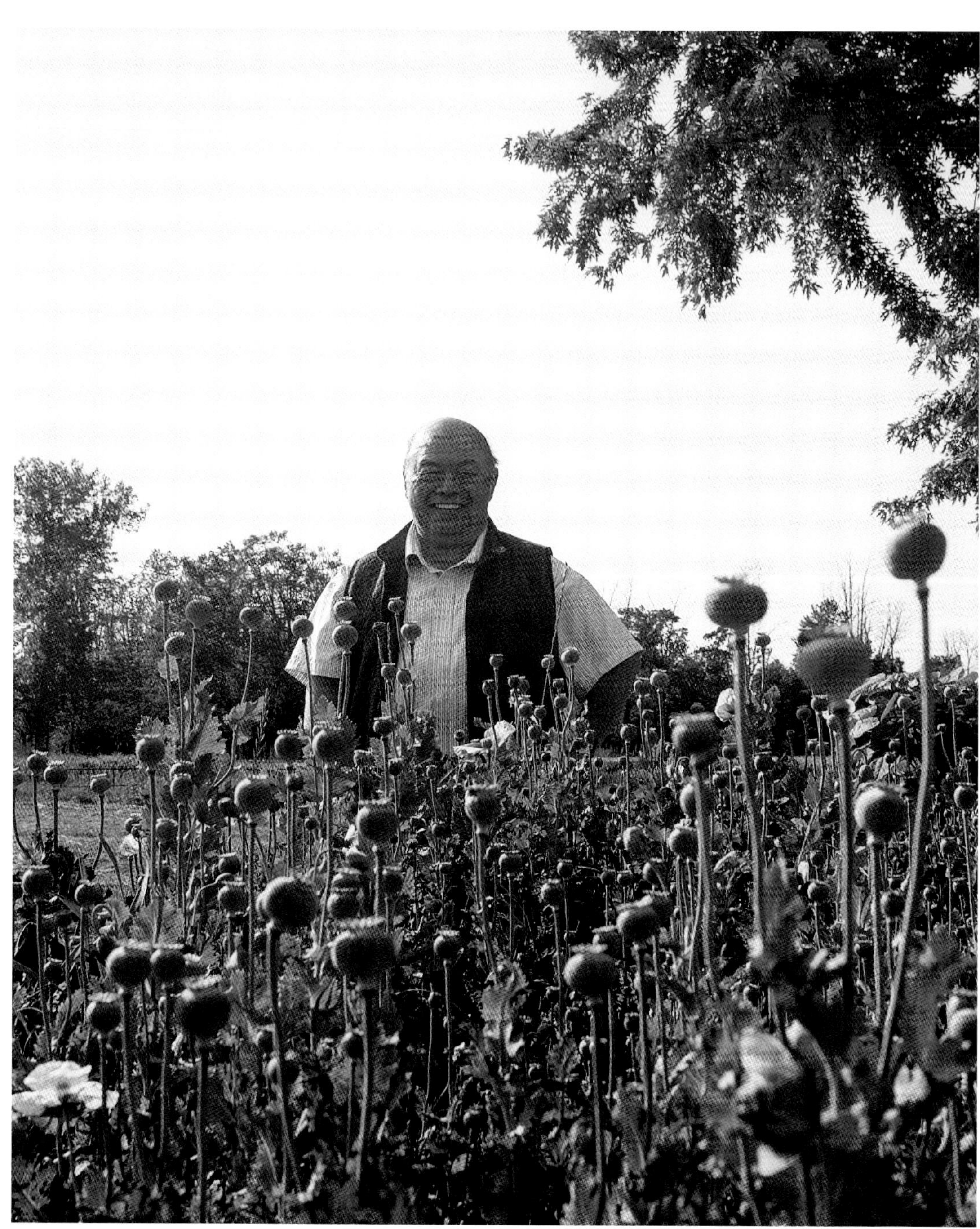

untitled (Xia Vue Yang), 2025

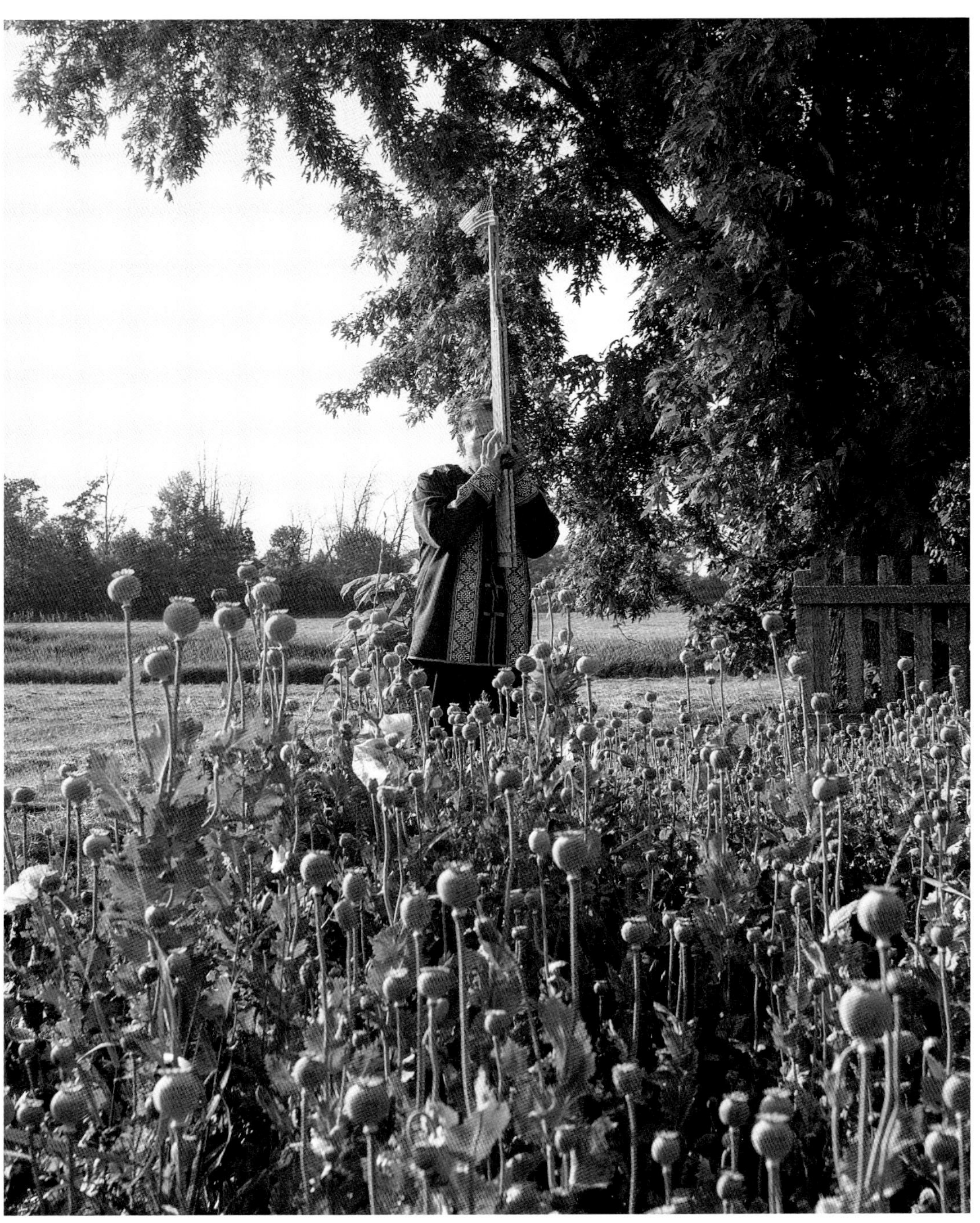

untitled (Dang Yang), 2025

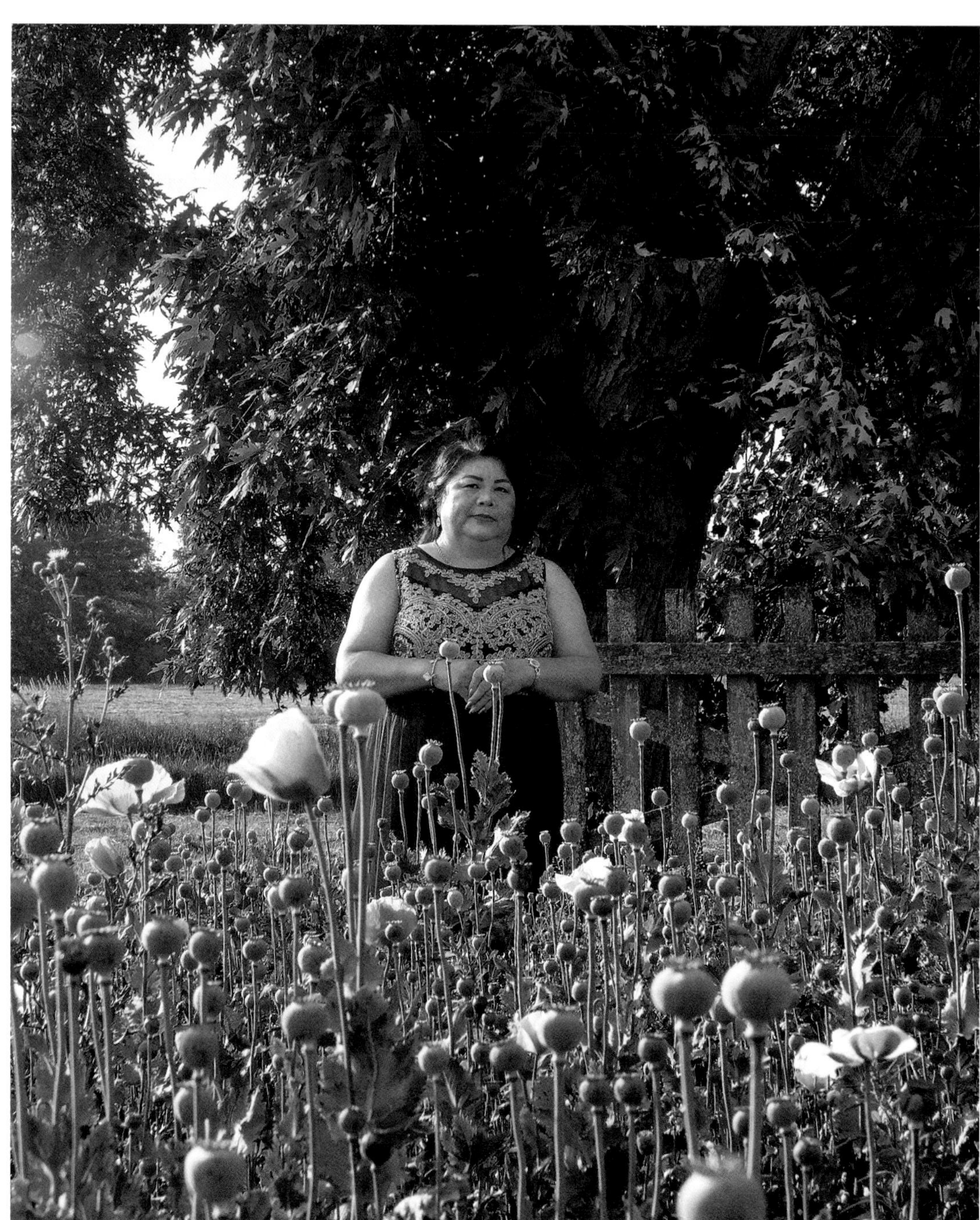

untitled (Lee Yang), 2025

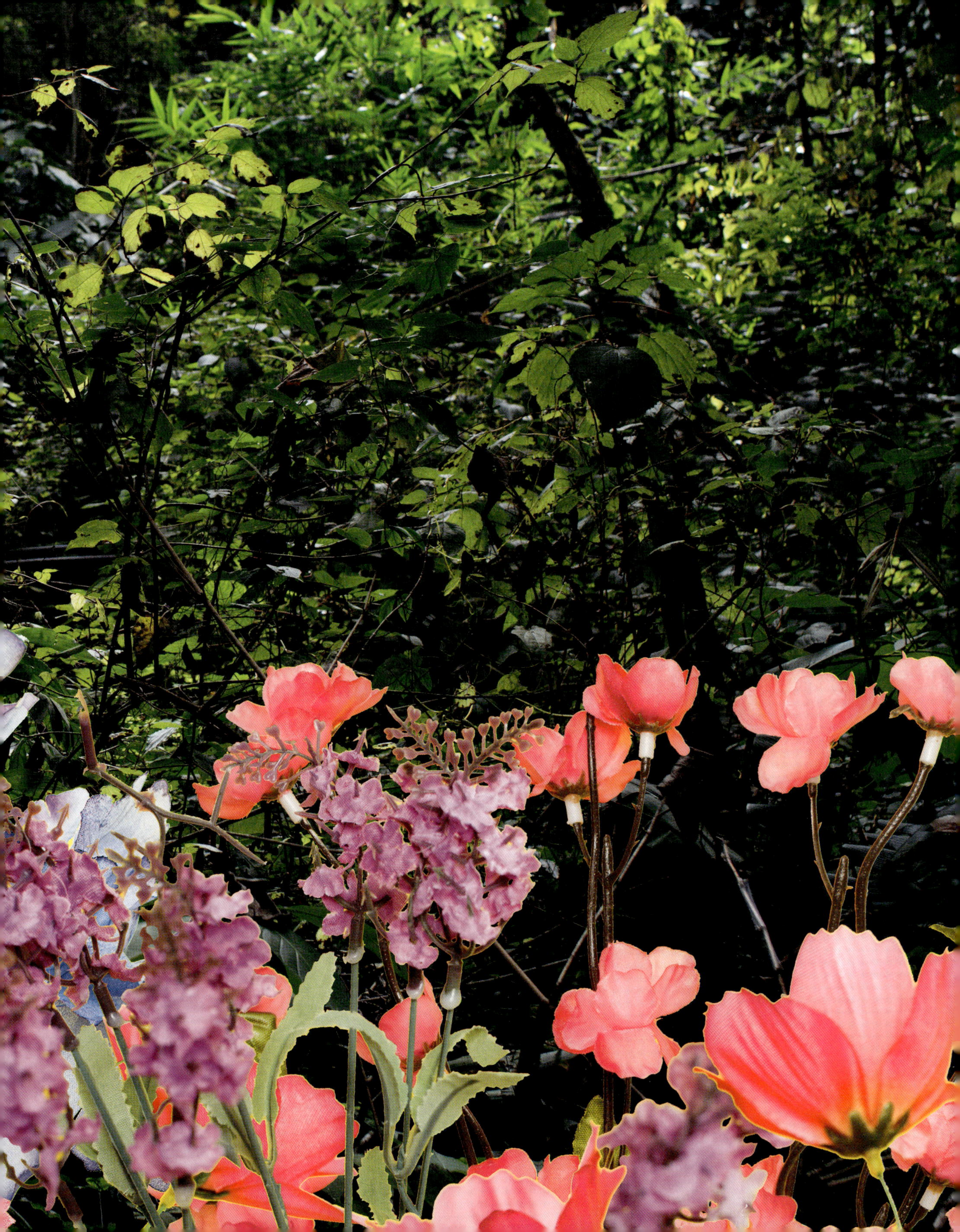

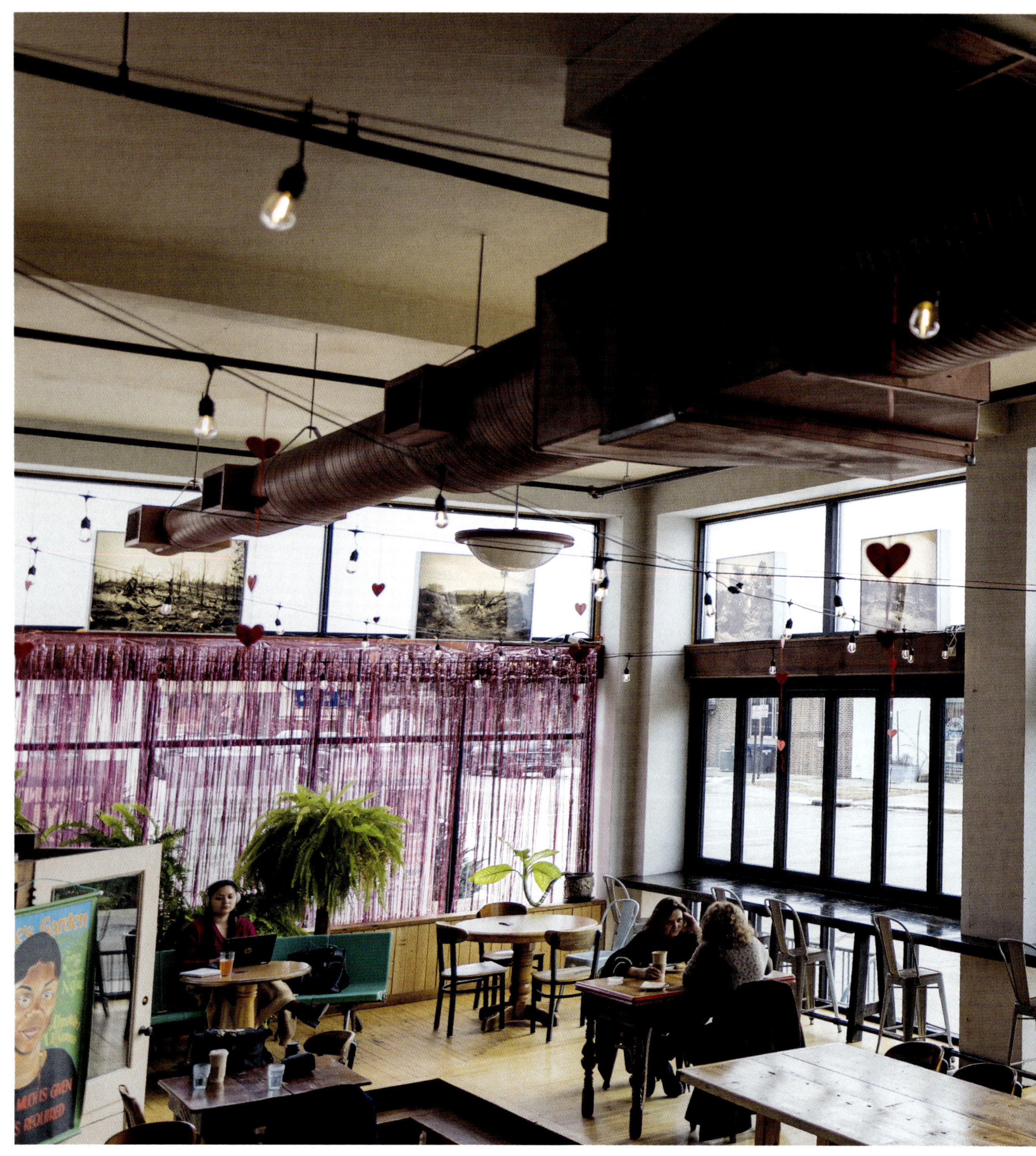

Pao Houa Her: The Imaginative Landscape, installation view at Paradigm Coffee & Music, Sheboygan, Wisconsin, 2025

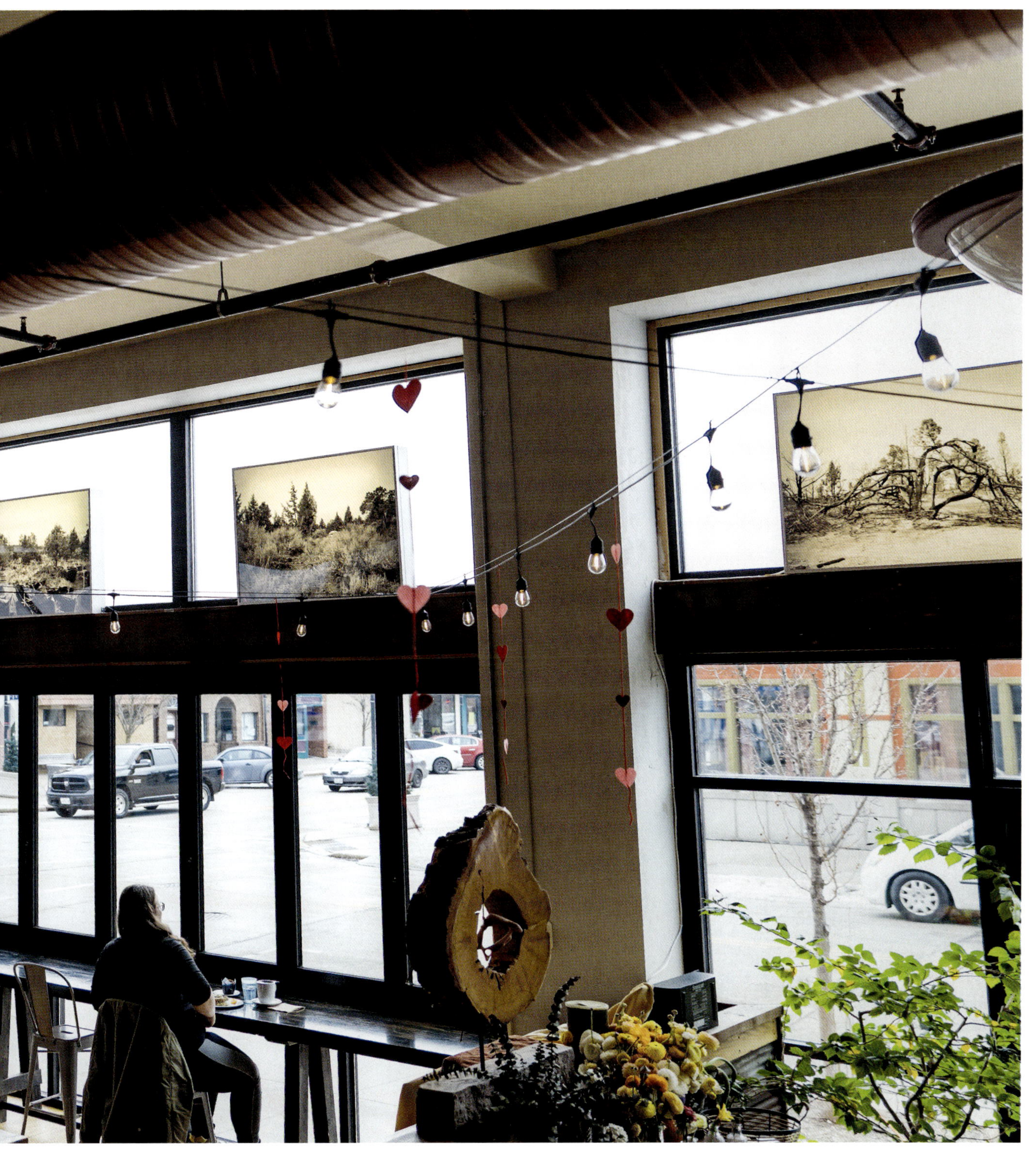

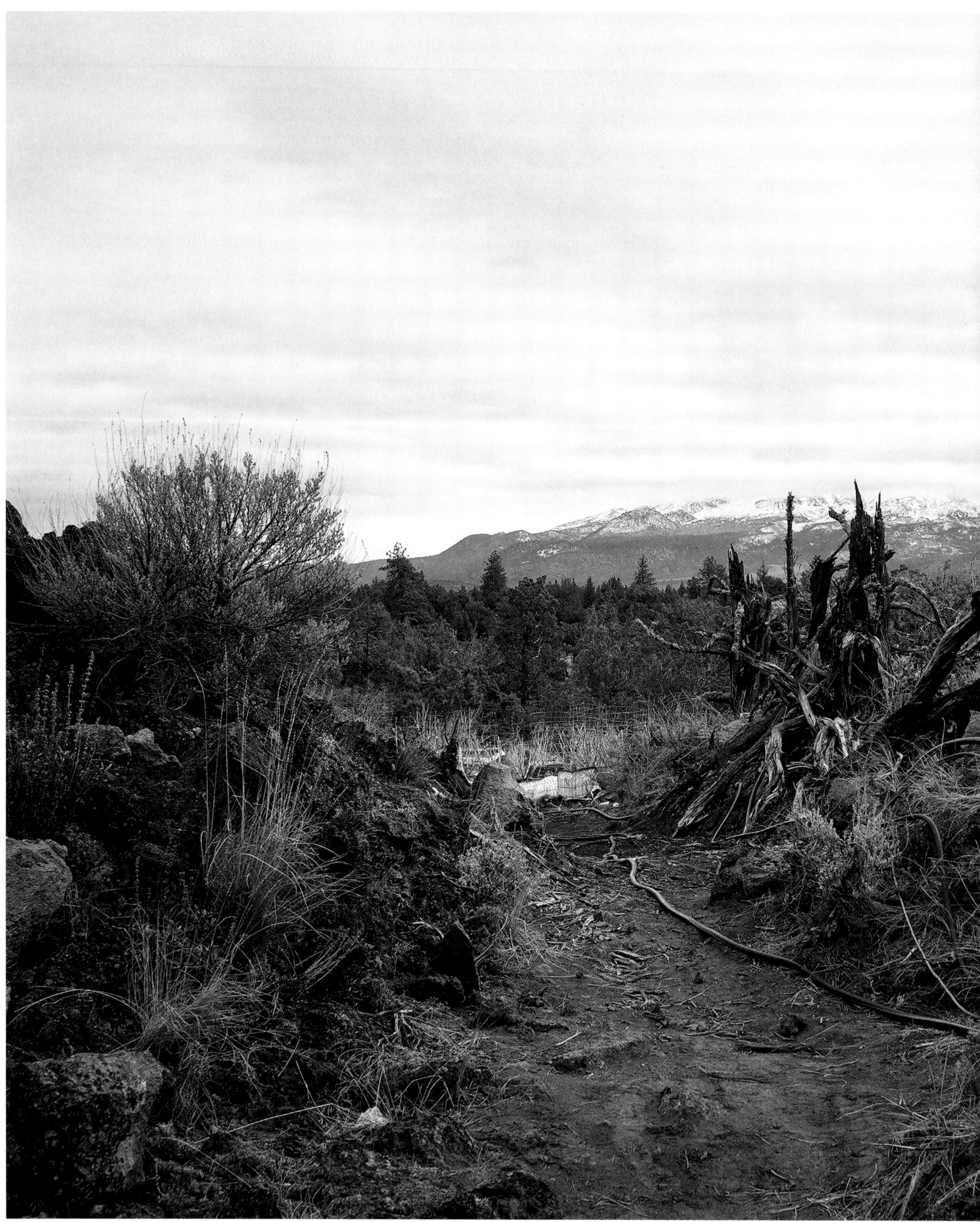

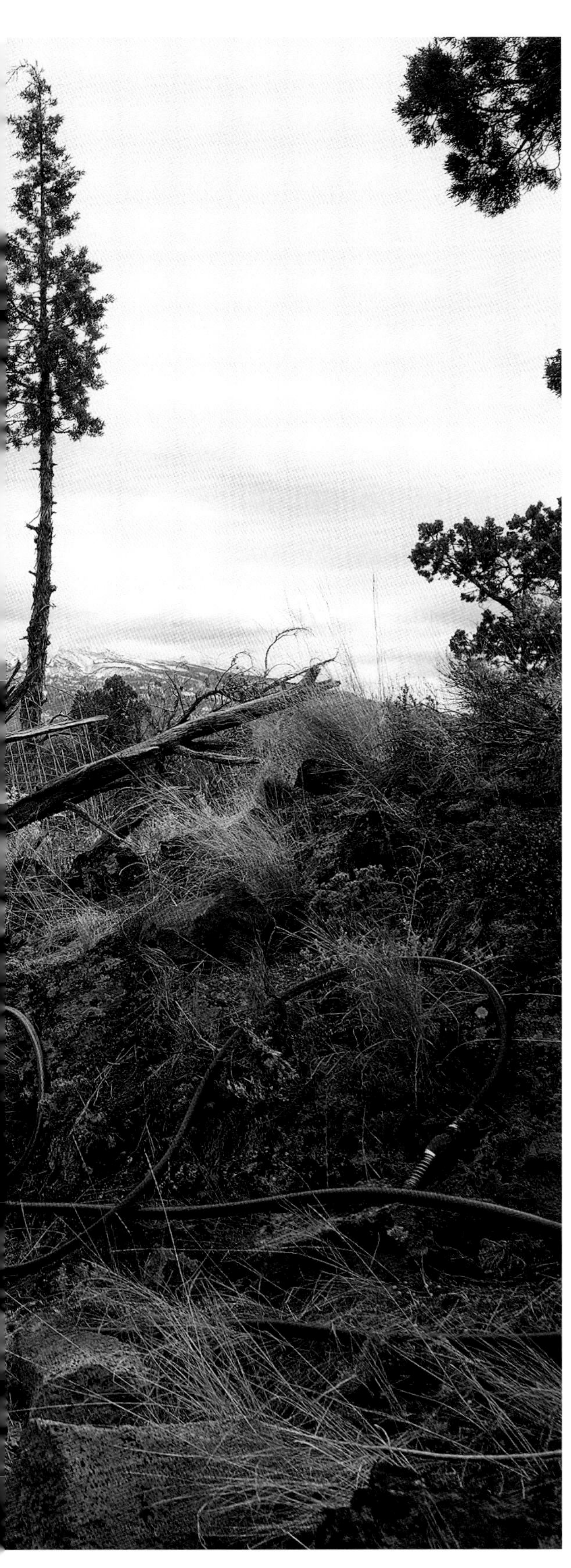

untitled, 2021–22, from the *Mt. Shasta*
series, lightbox

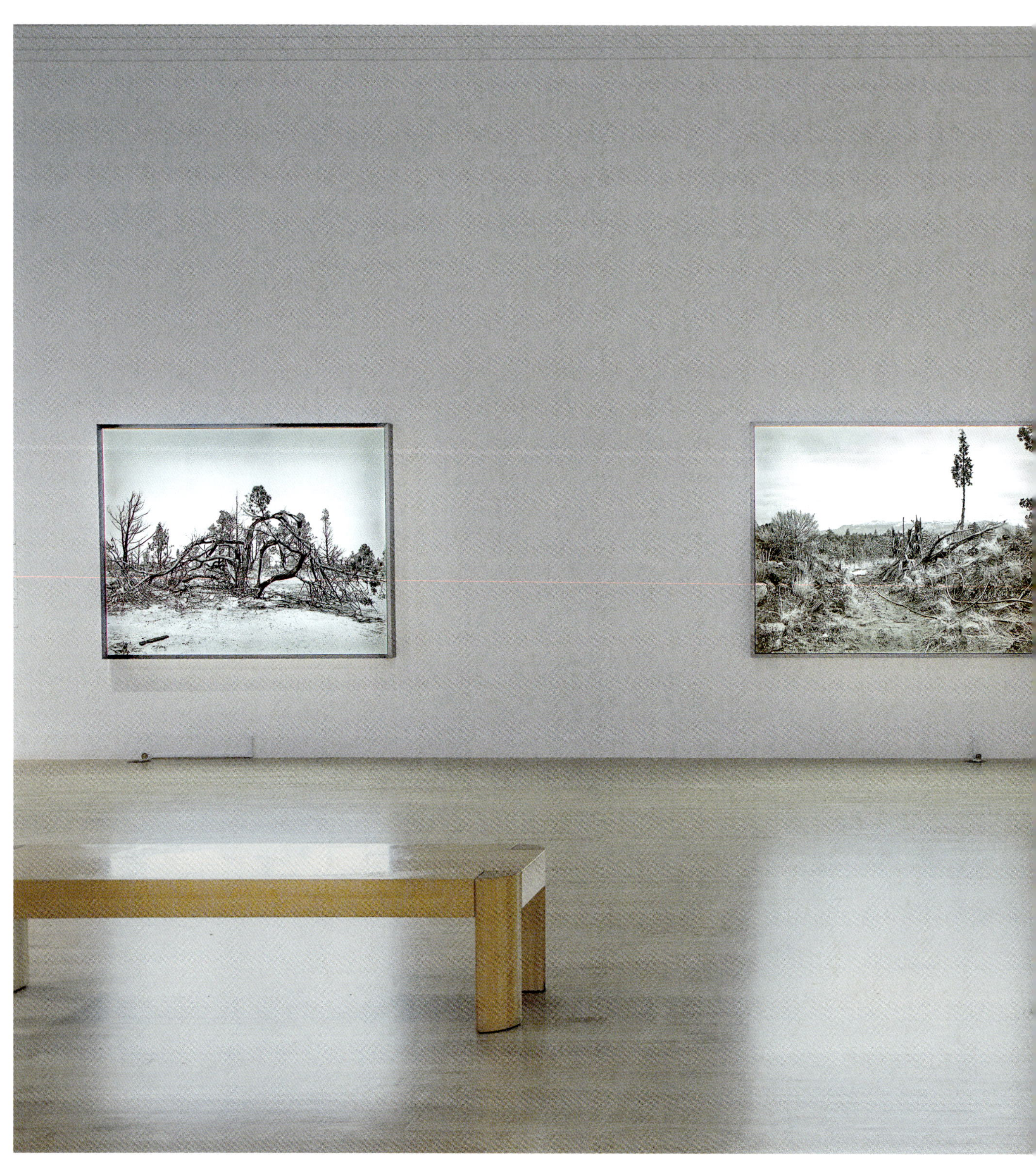

Pao Houa Her: The Imaginative Landscape, installation view
at San José Museum of Art, 2025

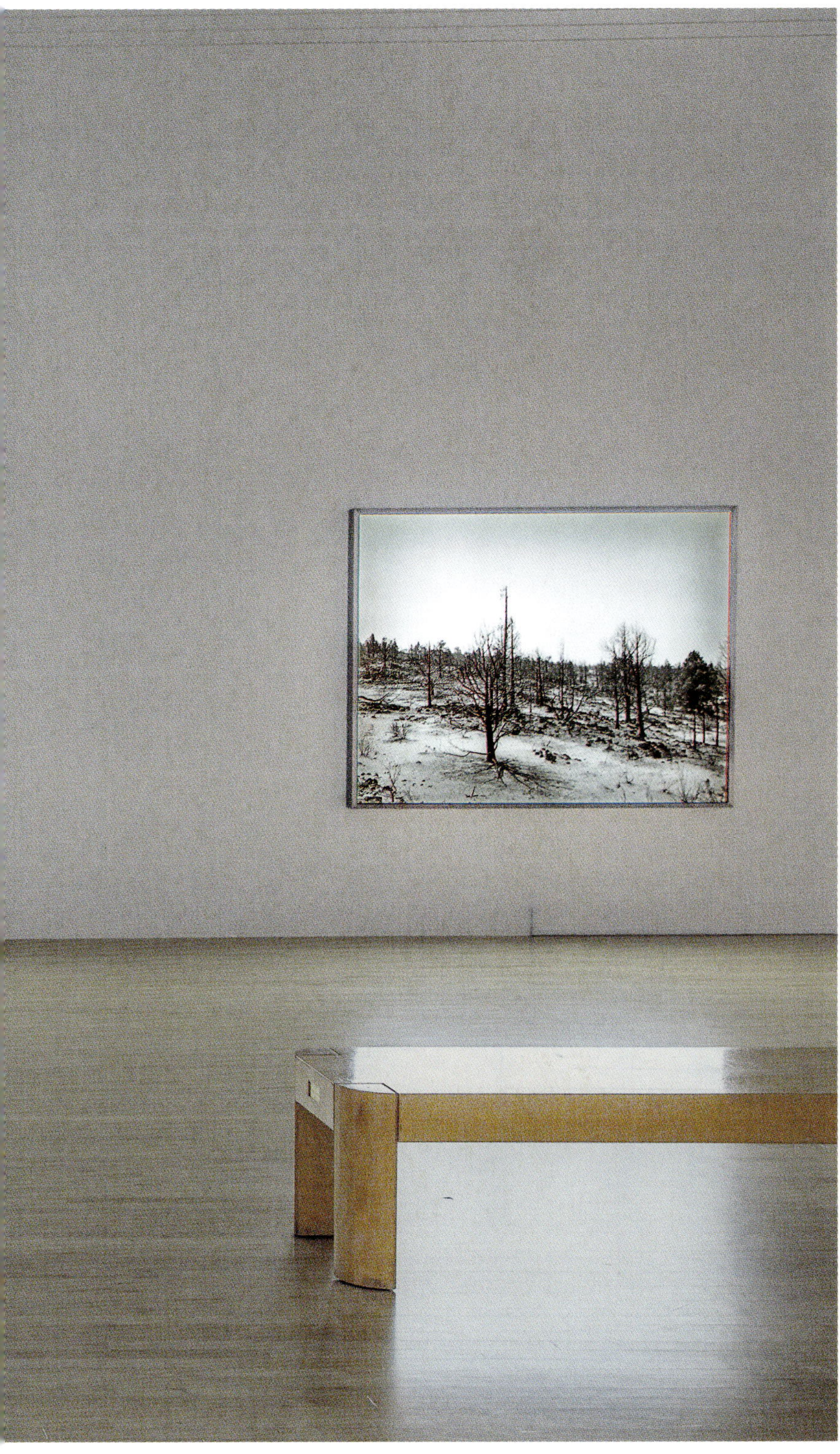

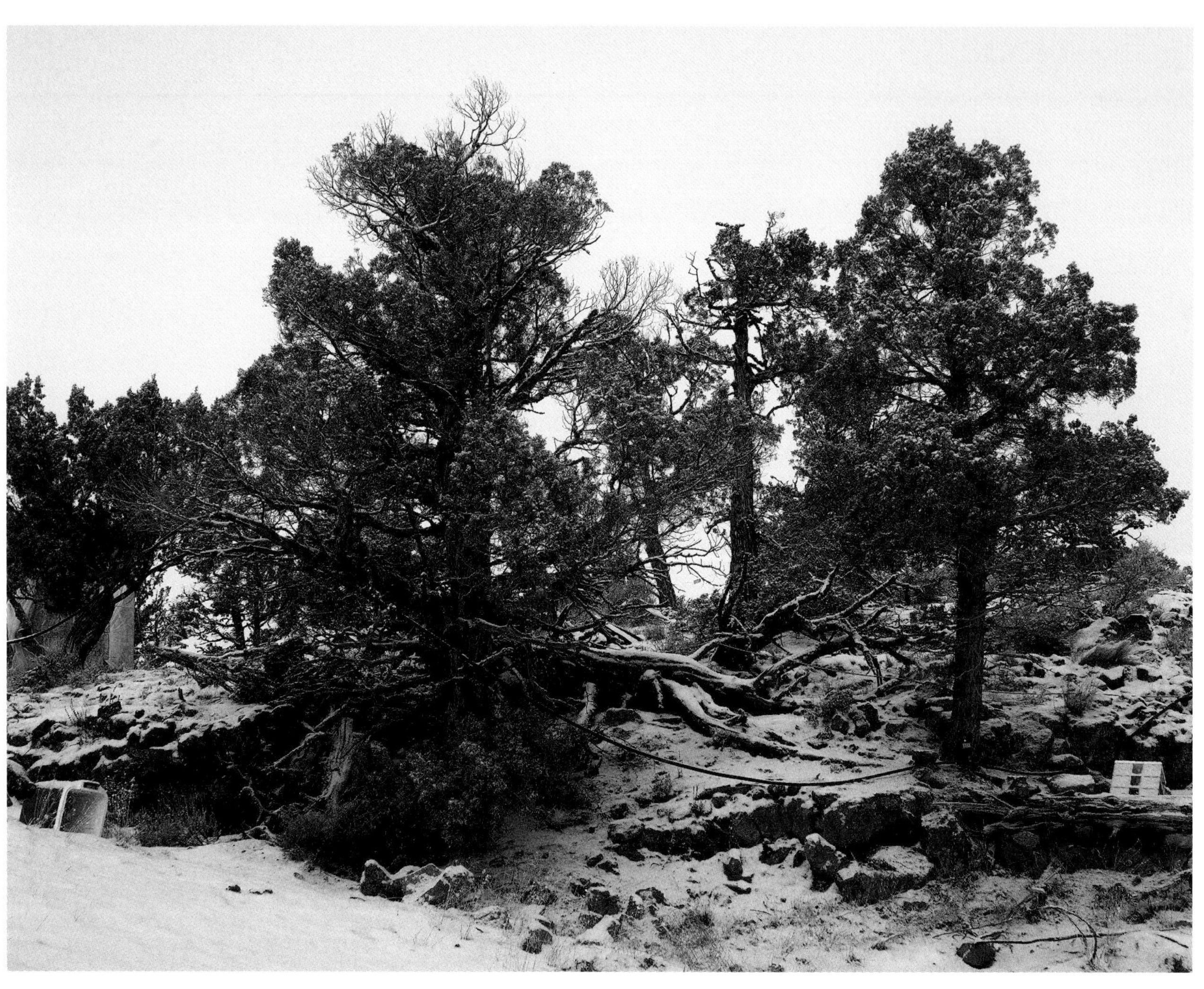

untitled, 2021–22, from the *Mt. Shasta*
series, lightbox

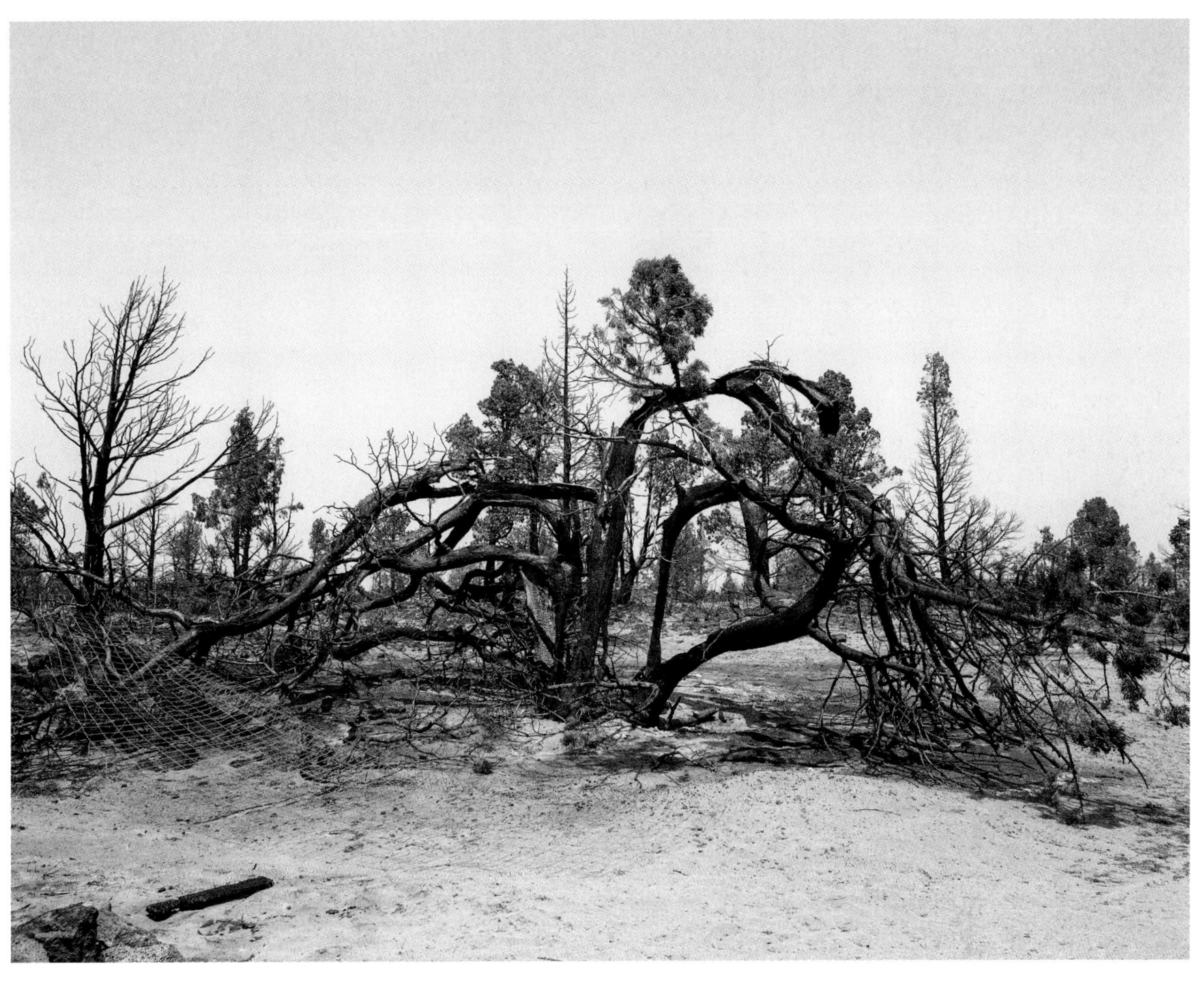

untitled, 2021–22, from the *Mt. Shasta*
series, lightbox

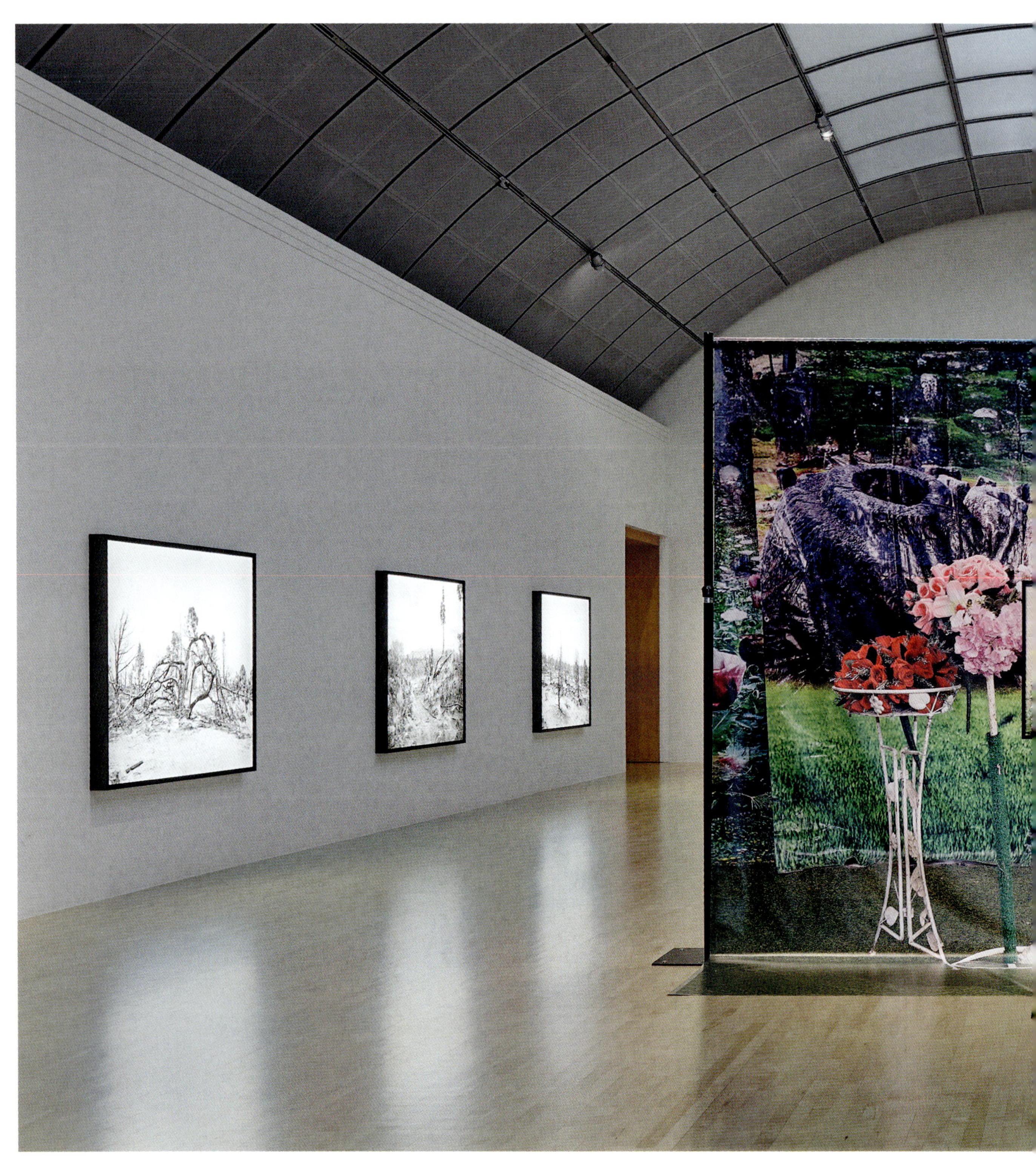

Pao Houa Her: The Imaginative Landscape, installation view at San José Museum of Art, 2025

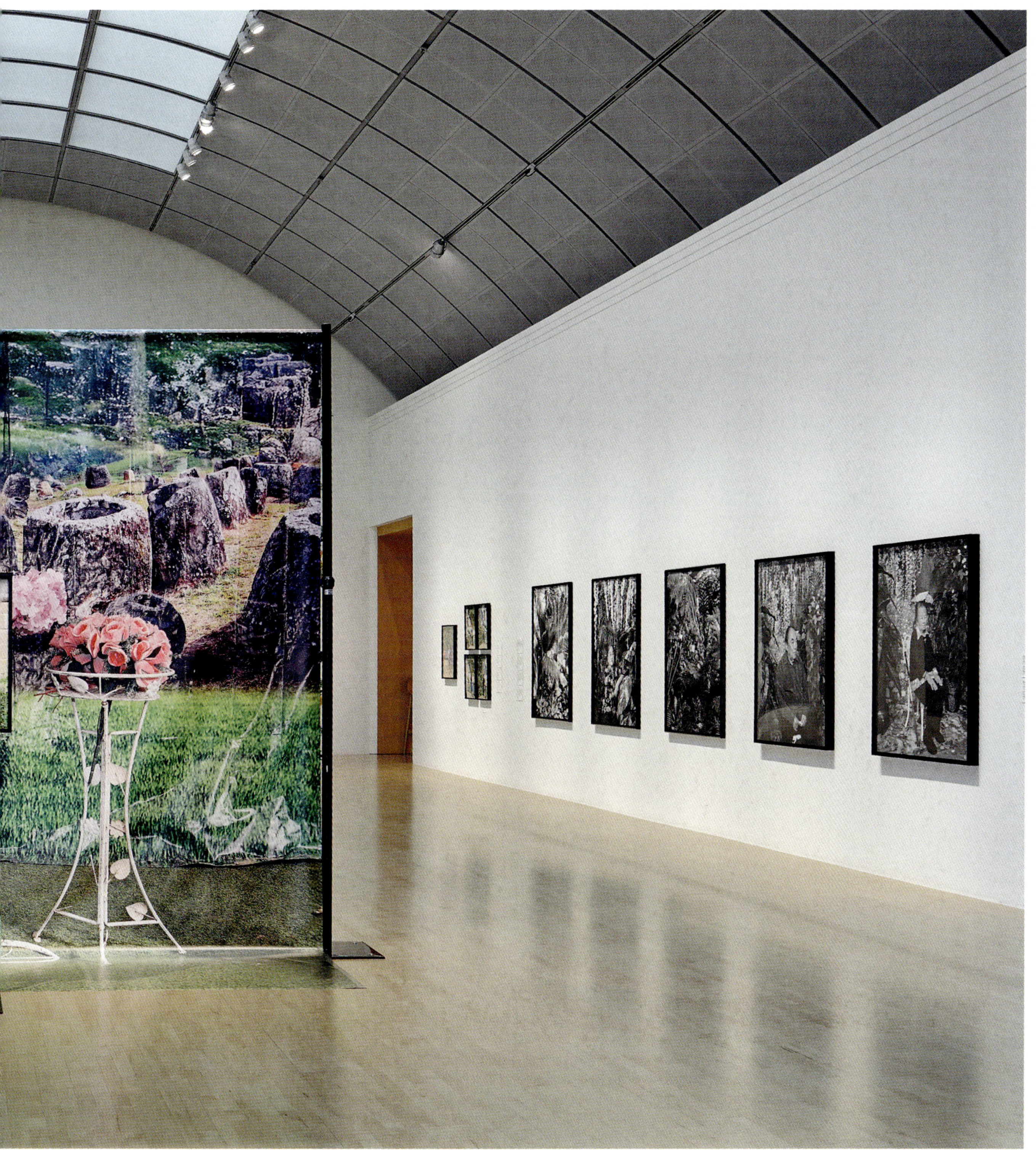

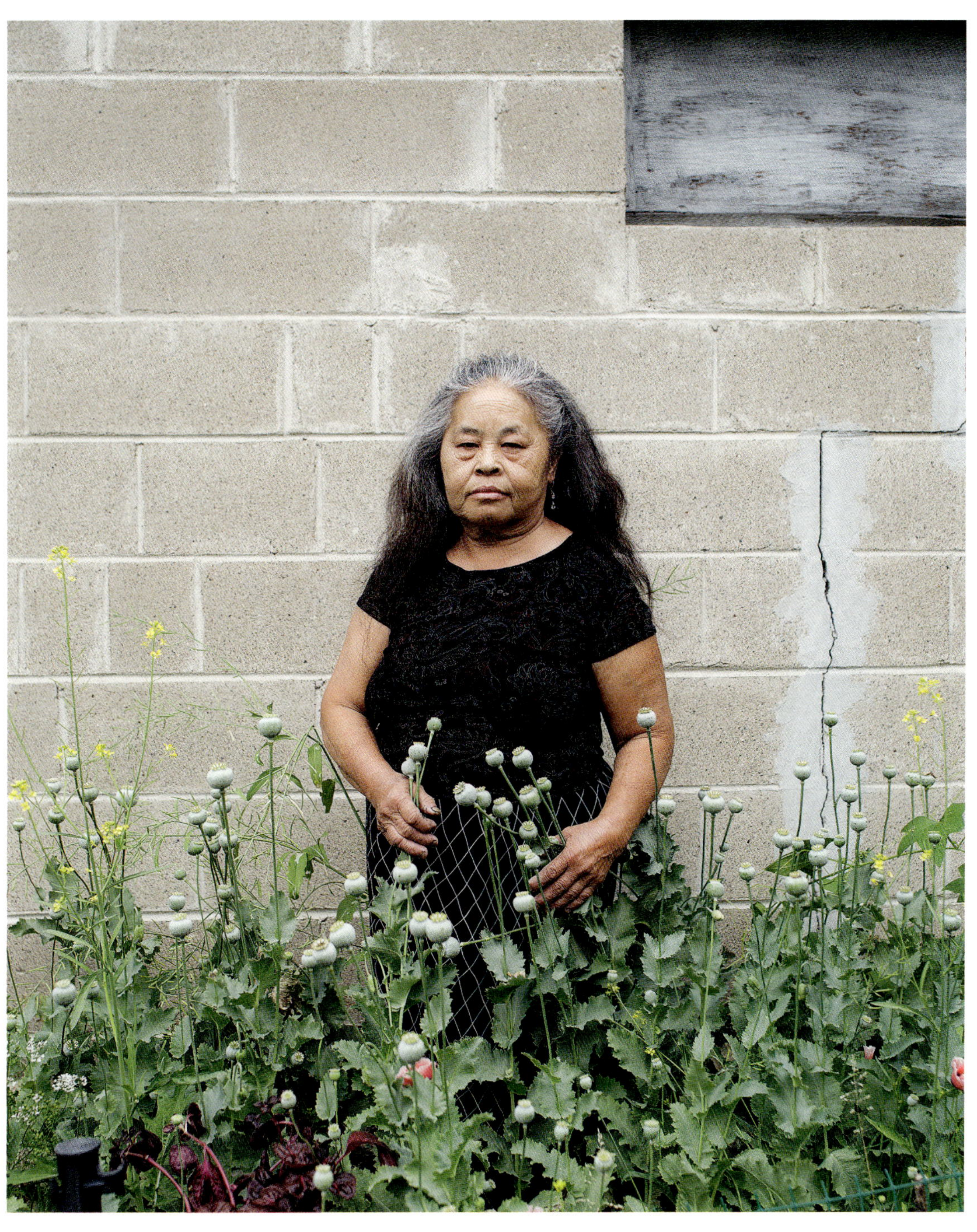

untitled (woman with poppies), 2018,
from *The Imaginative Landscape* series,
archival pigment print

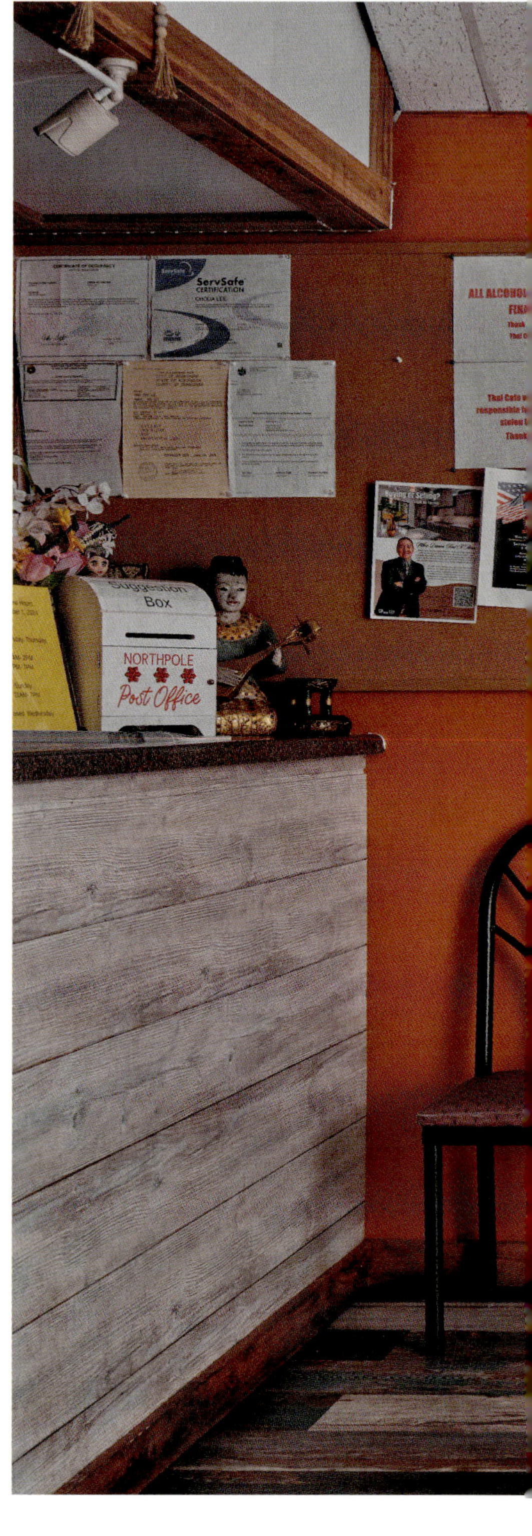

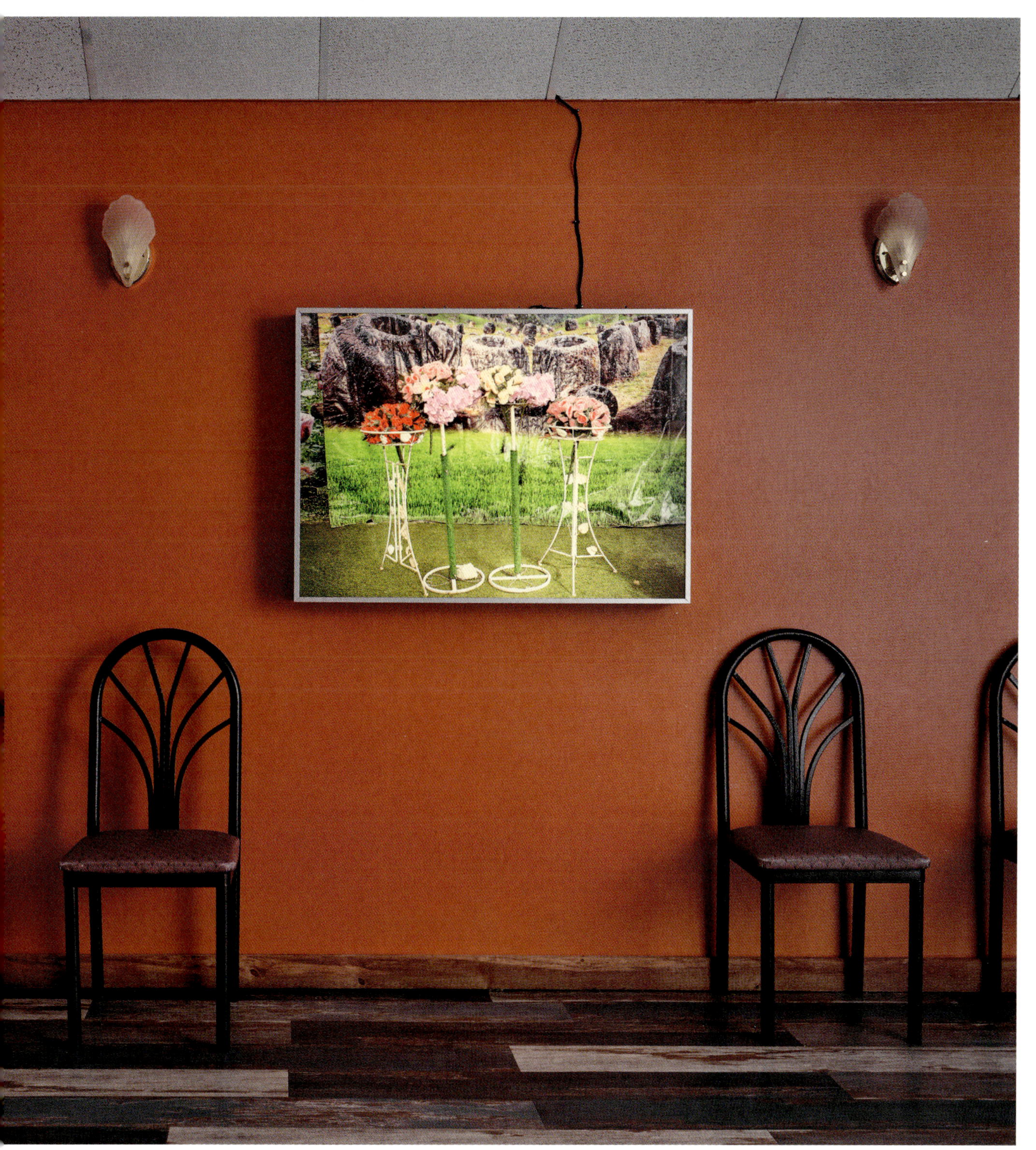

Pao Houa Her: The Imaginative Landscape,
installation view at Thai Café, Sheboygan,
Wisconsin, 2025

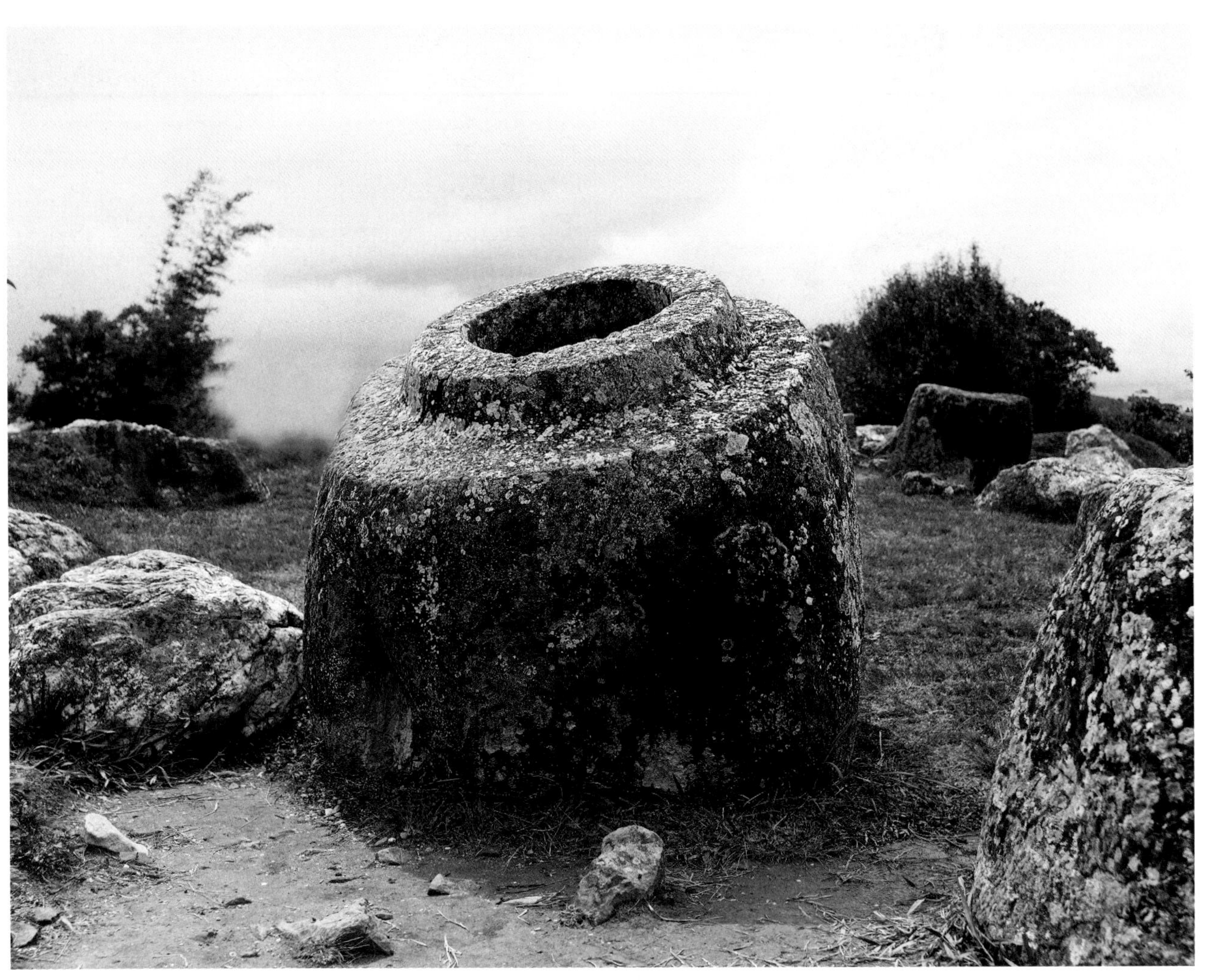

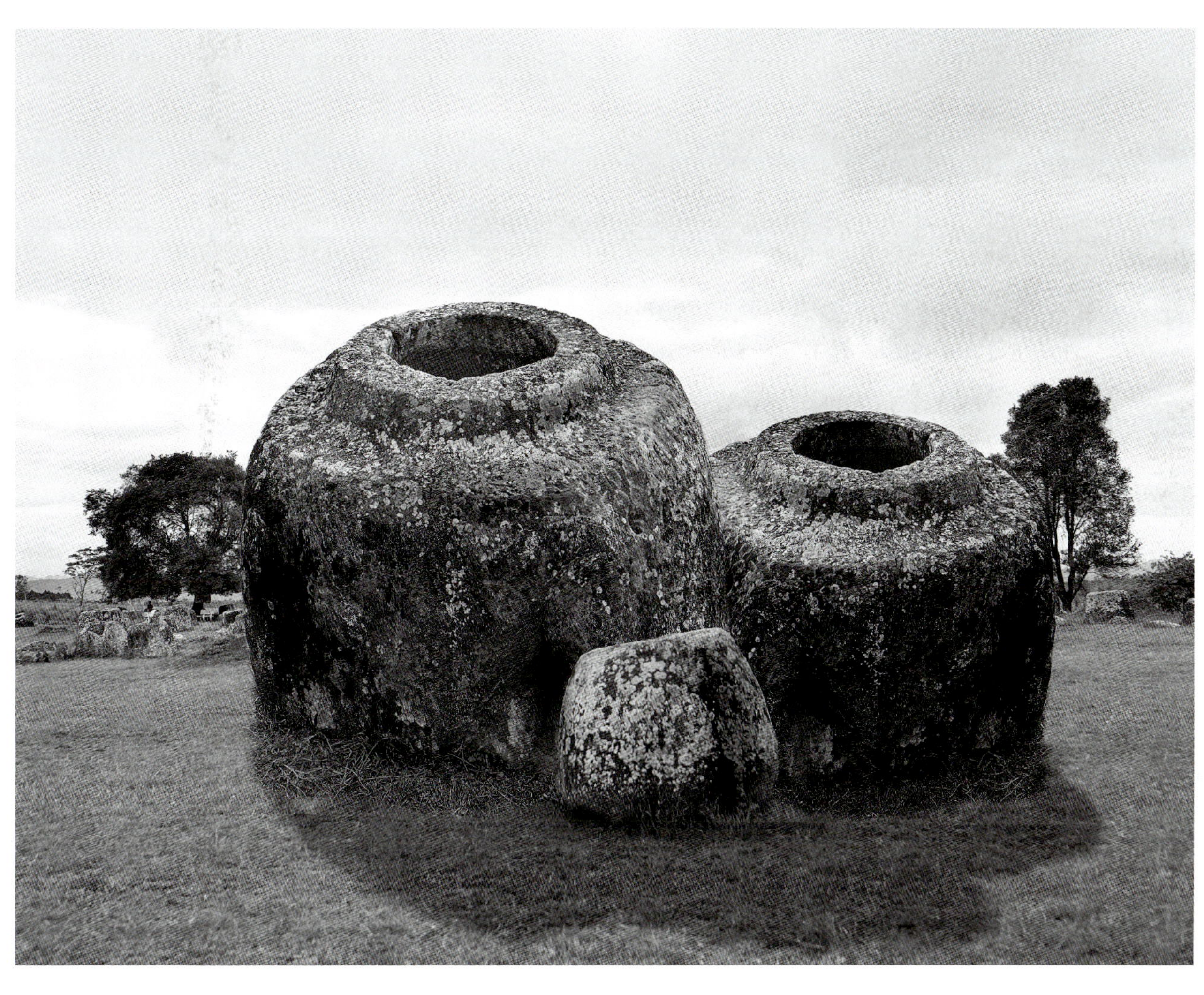

Plain of Jars, 2017, from the *My grandfather turned into a tiger* series, diptych, 3D lenticular prints

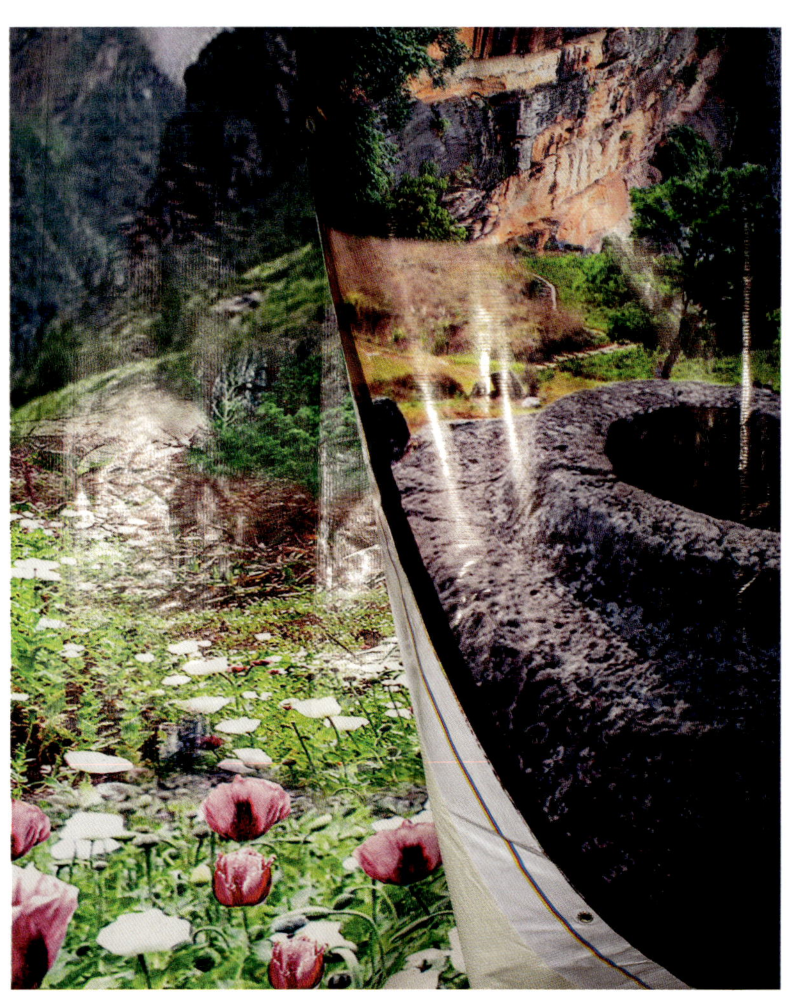

*untitled (backdrop of plain of jars and
poppy field)*, 2019, from *The Imaginative
Landscape* series, archival pigment print

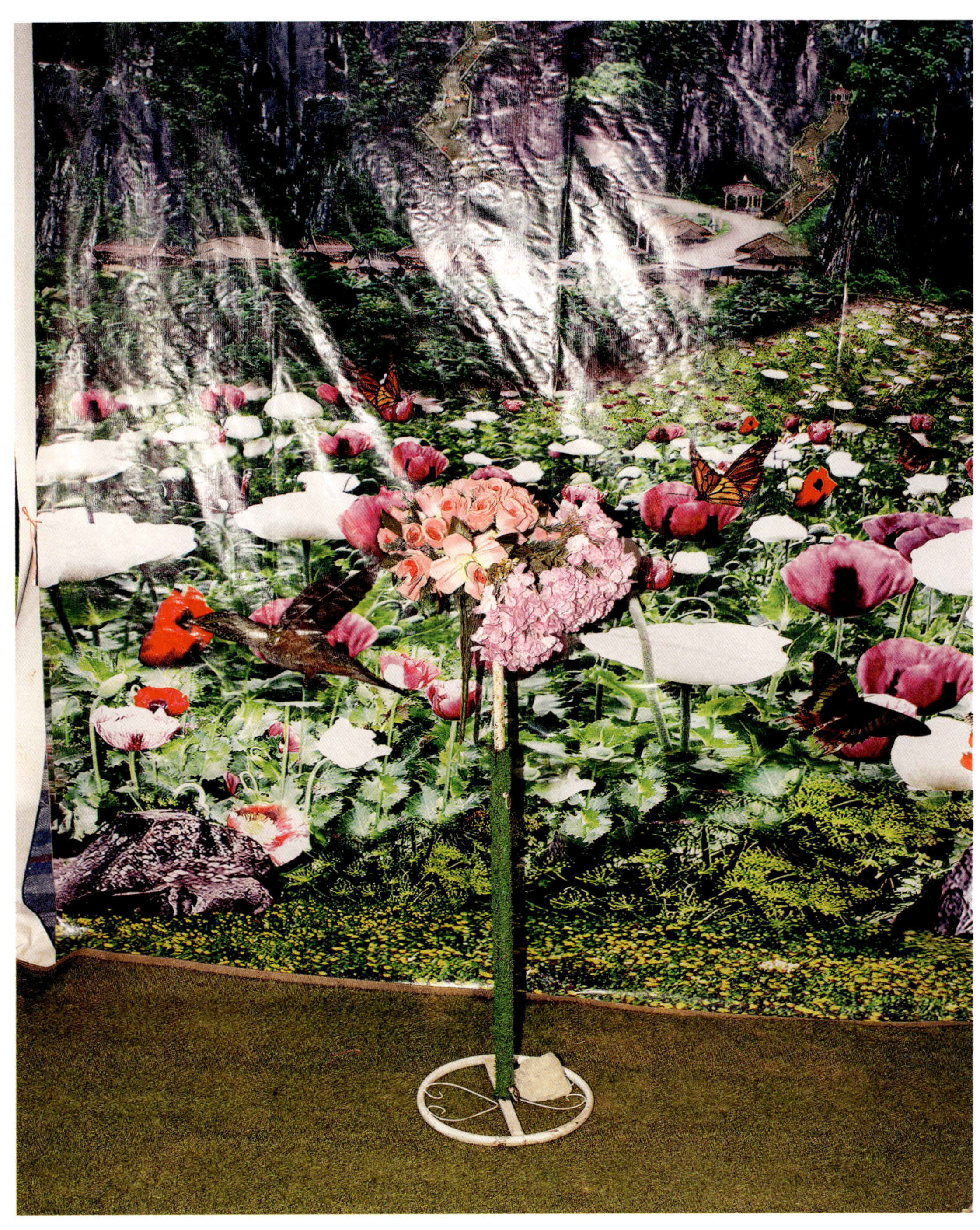

untitled (flower bouquet with backdrop),
2019, from *The Imaginative Landscape*
series, archival pigment print

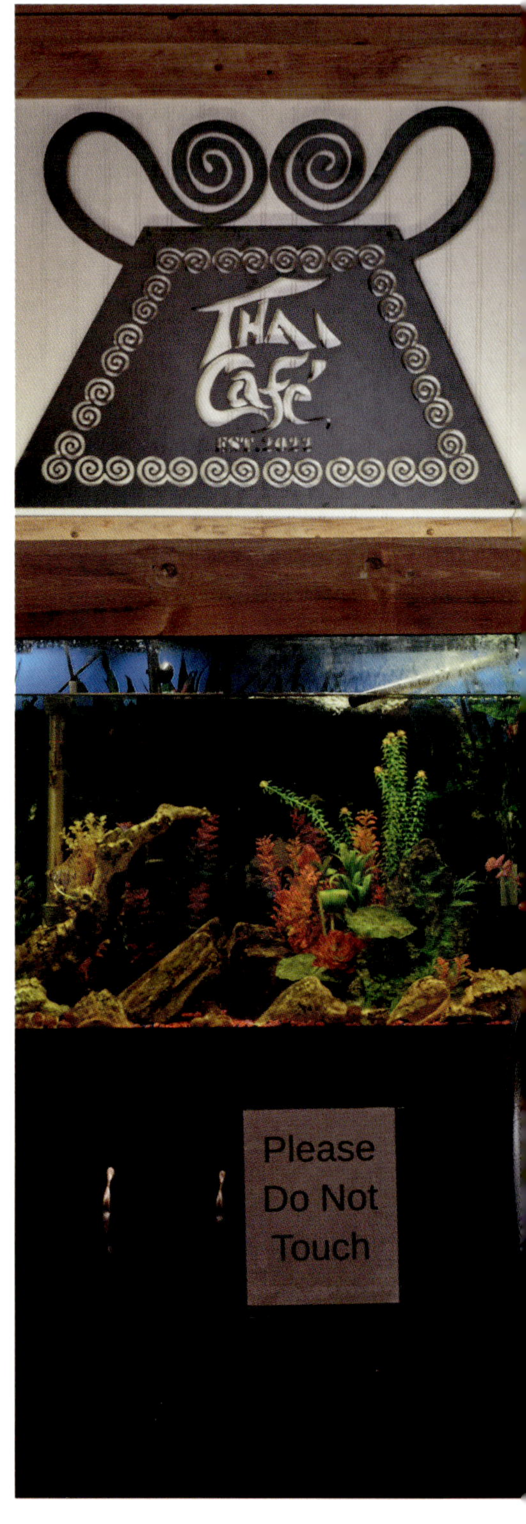
Thai
Cafe'
EST. 2022
Please
Do Not
Touch

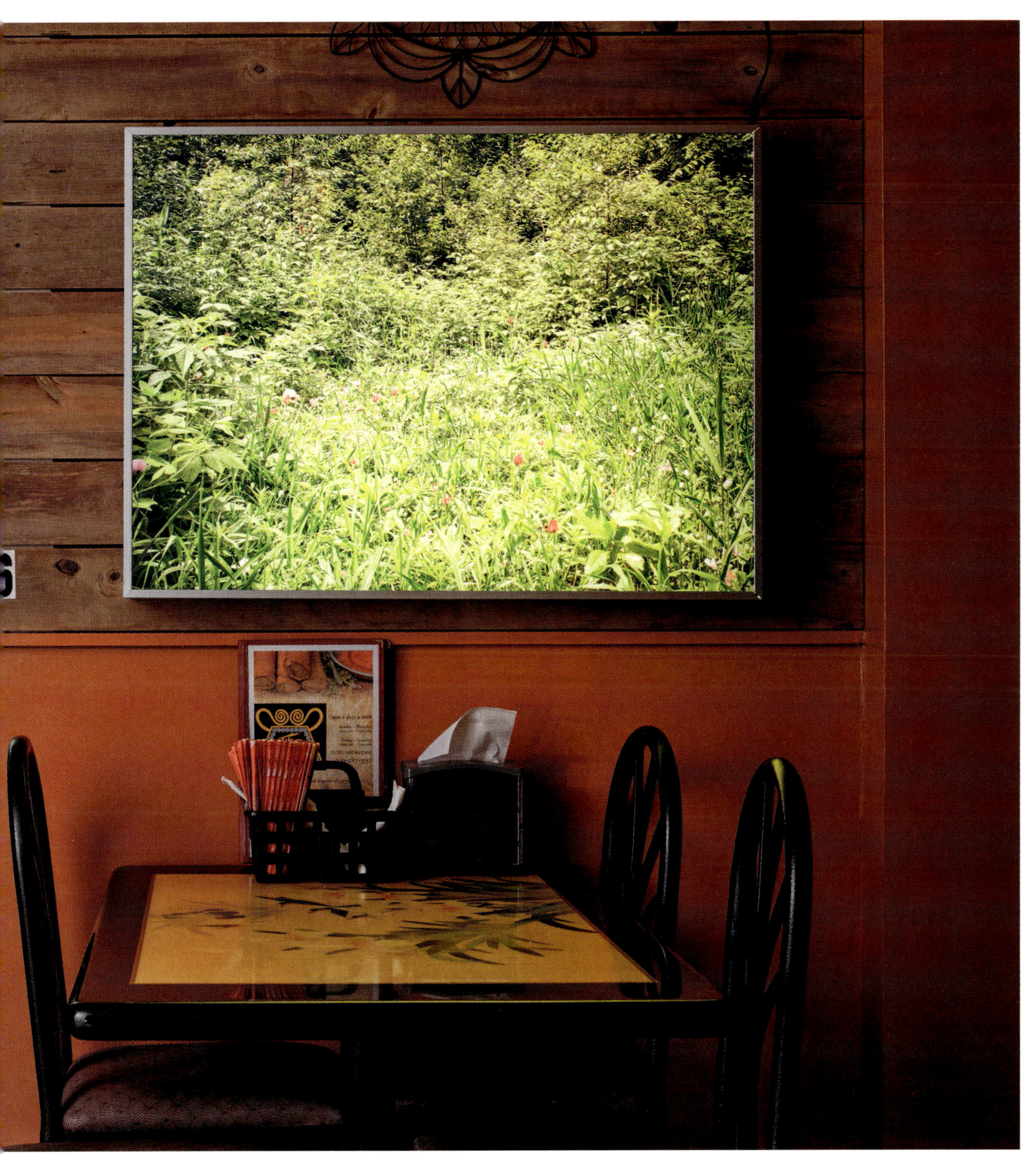

Pao Houa Her: The Imaginative Landscape,
installation view at the Thai Café,
Sheboygan, Wisconsin, 2025

117

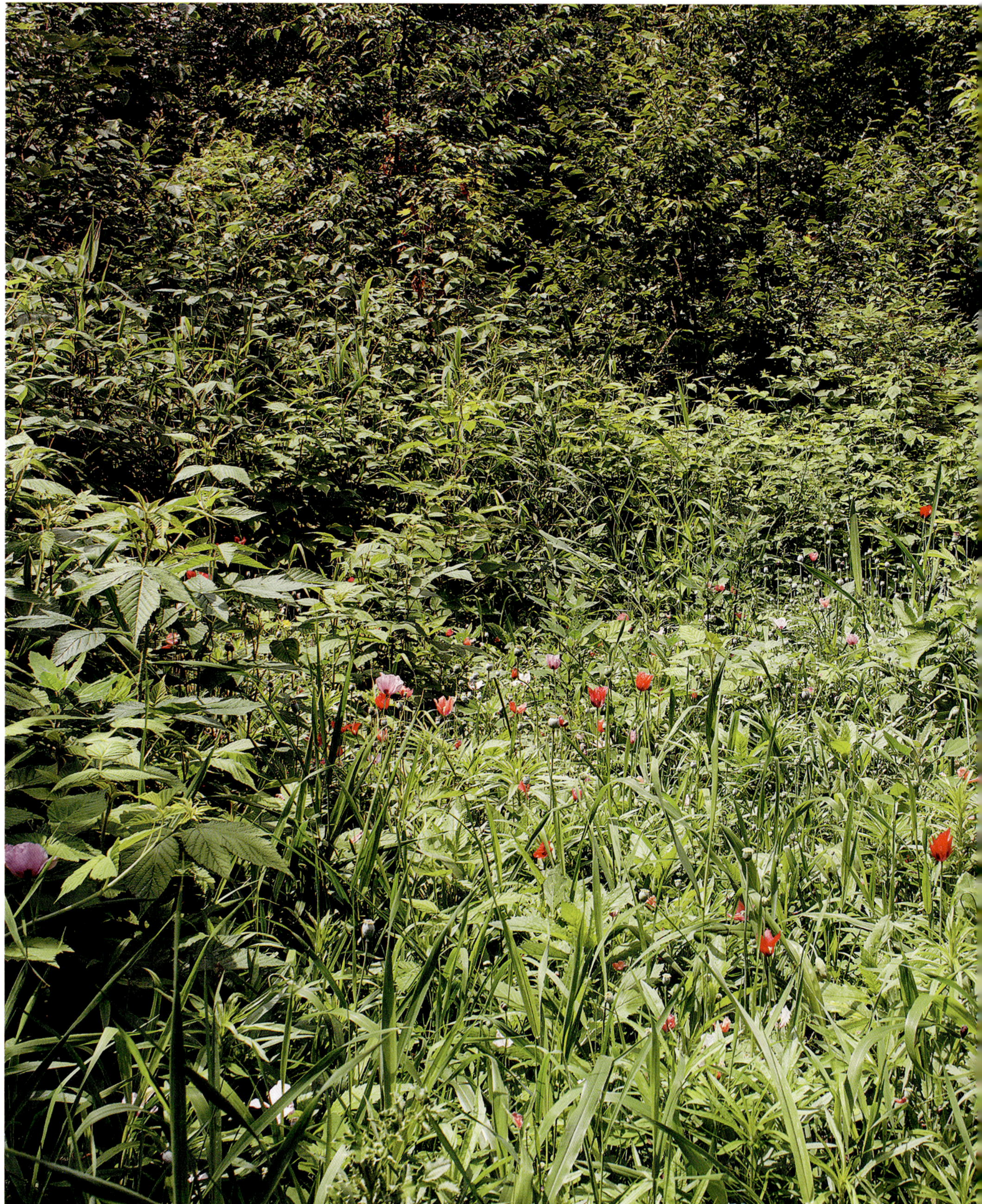

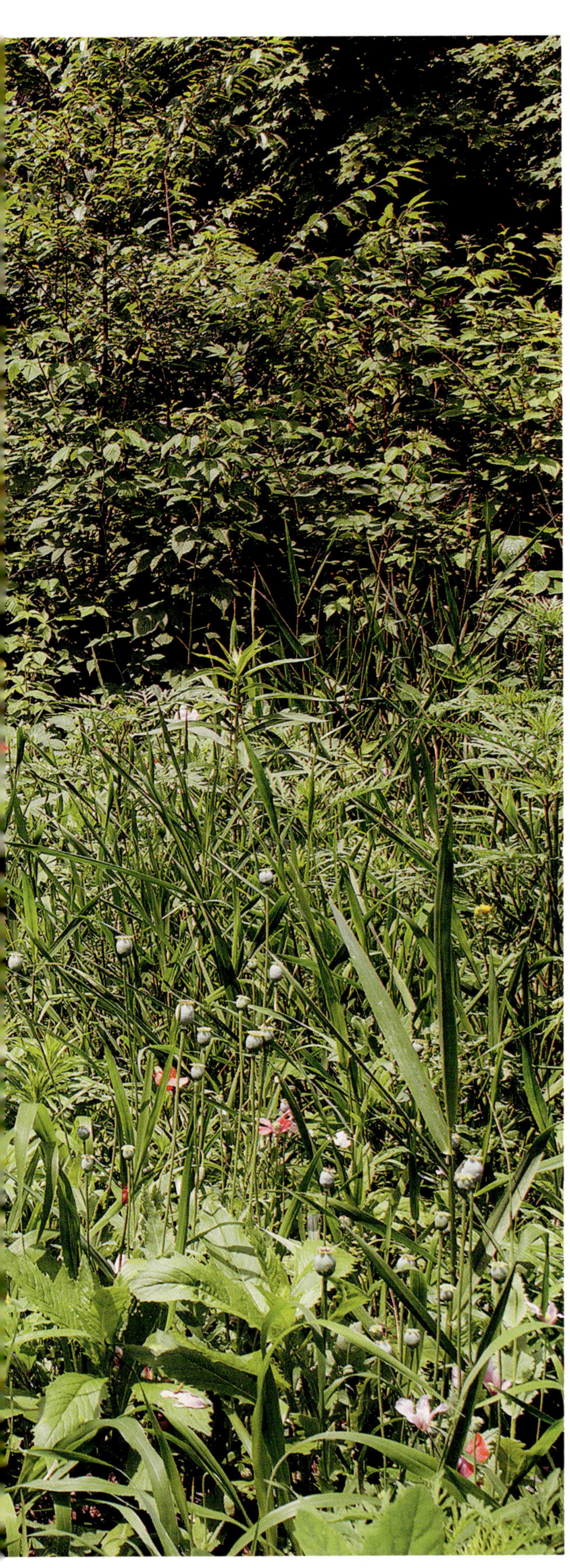

untitled (poppy field in Minnesota), 2019,
from *The Imaginative Landscape* series,
archival pigment print

119

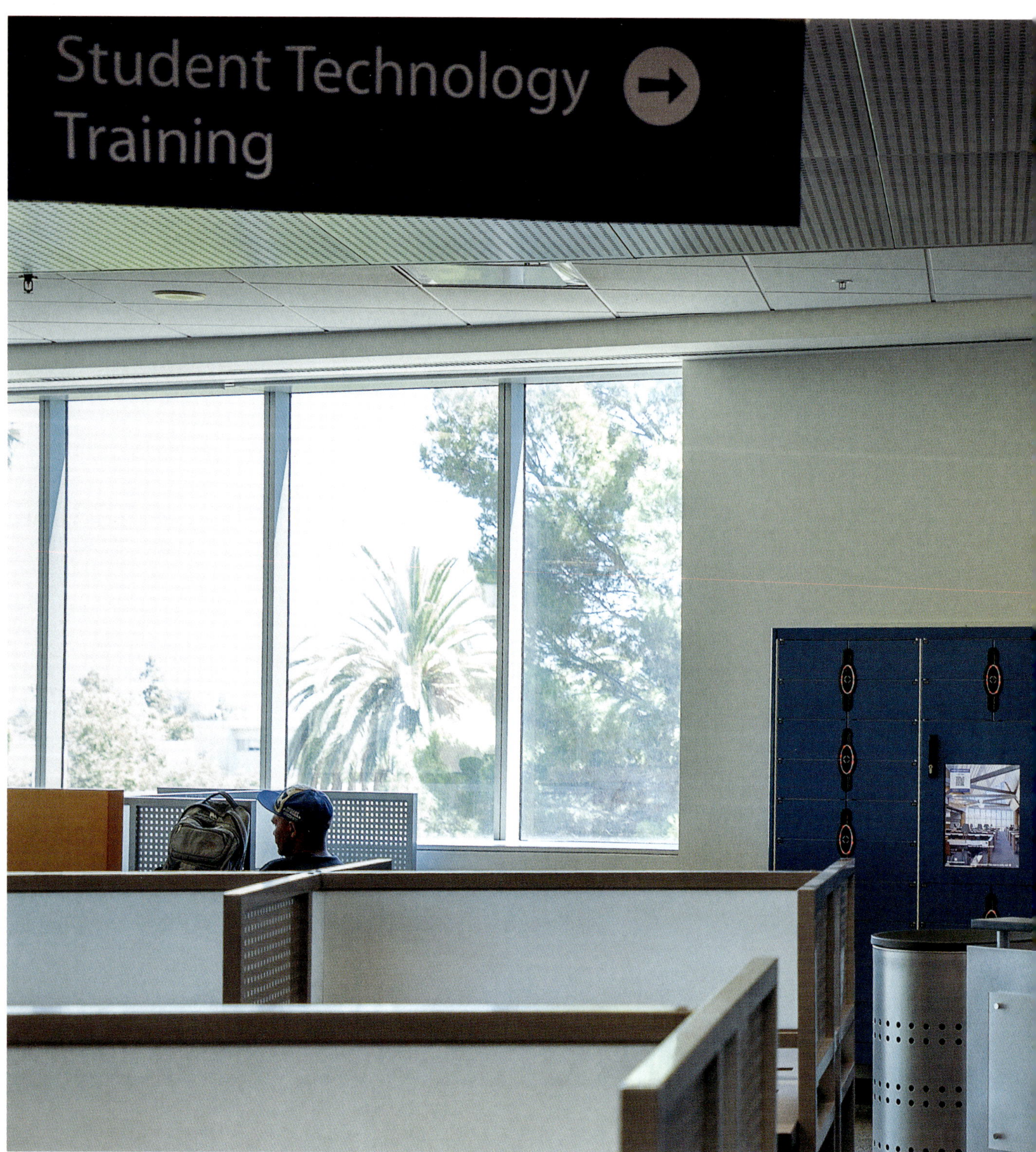

Student Technology
Training

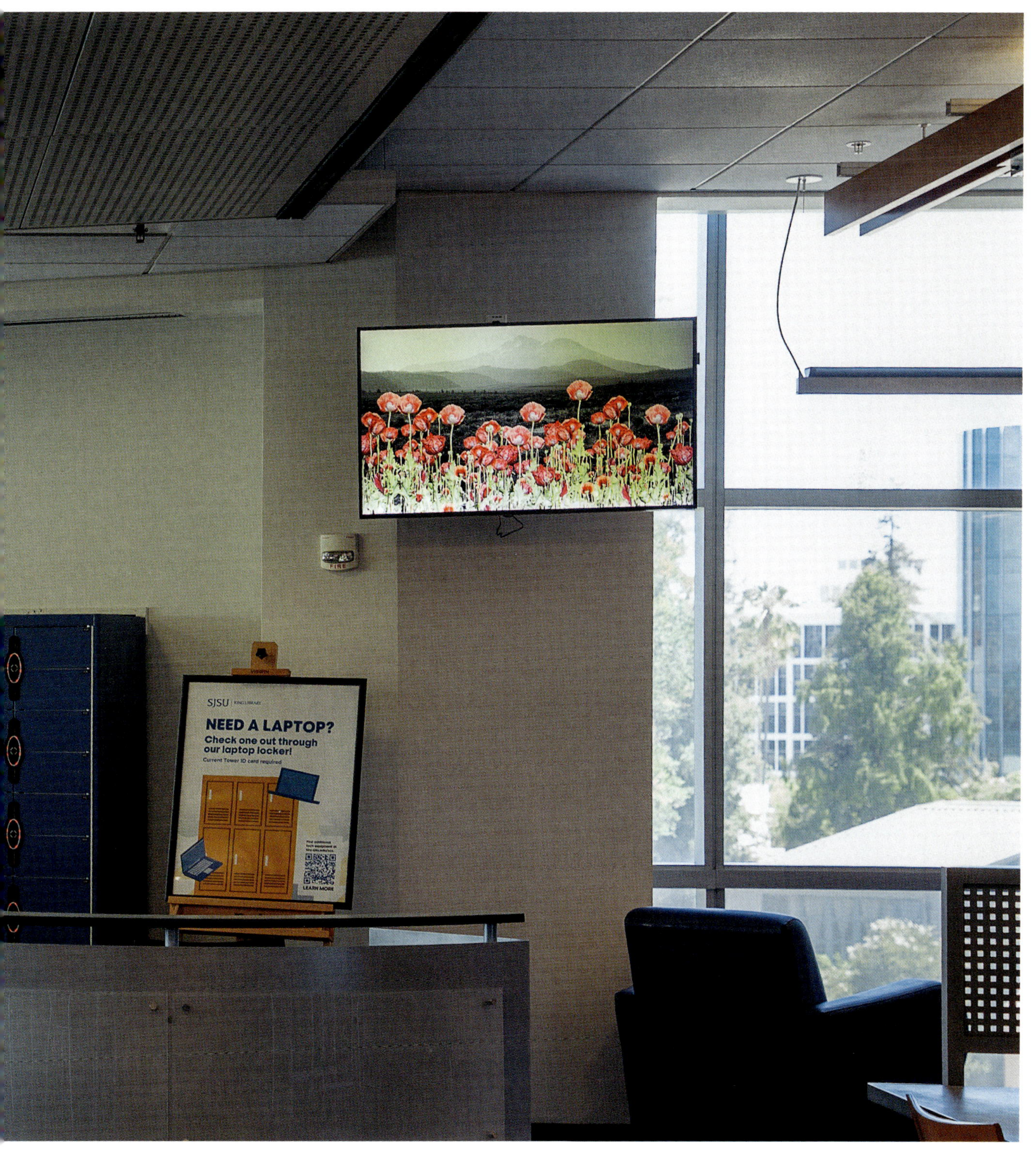

Pao Houa Her: The Imaginative Landscape,
installation view at King Library, San José
State University, San José, California, 2025

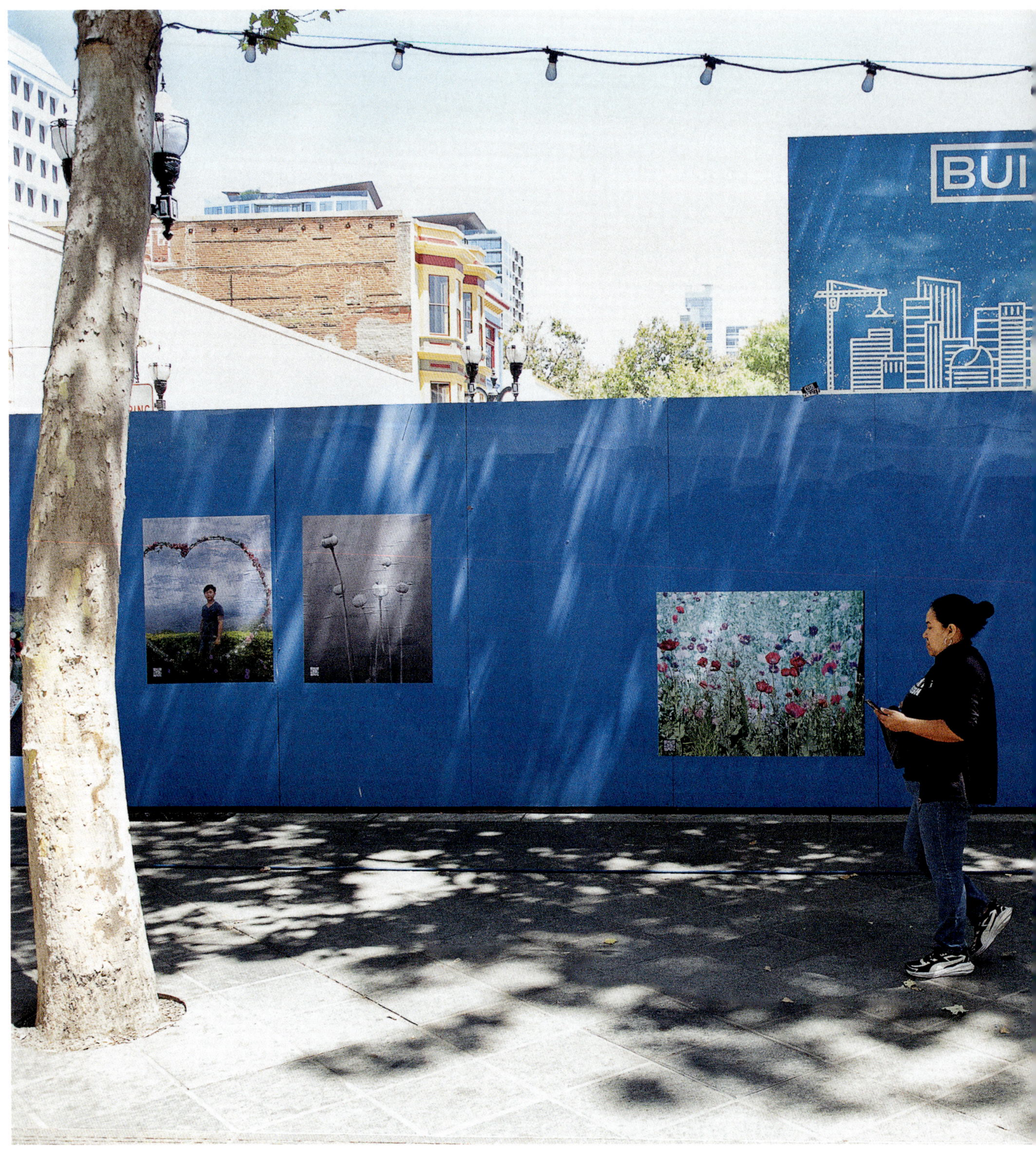

BUI

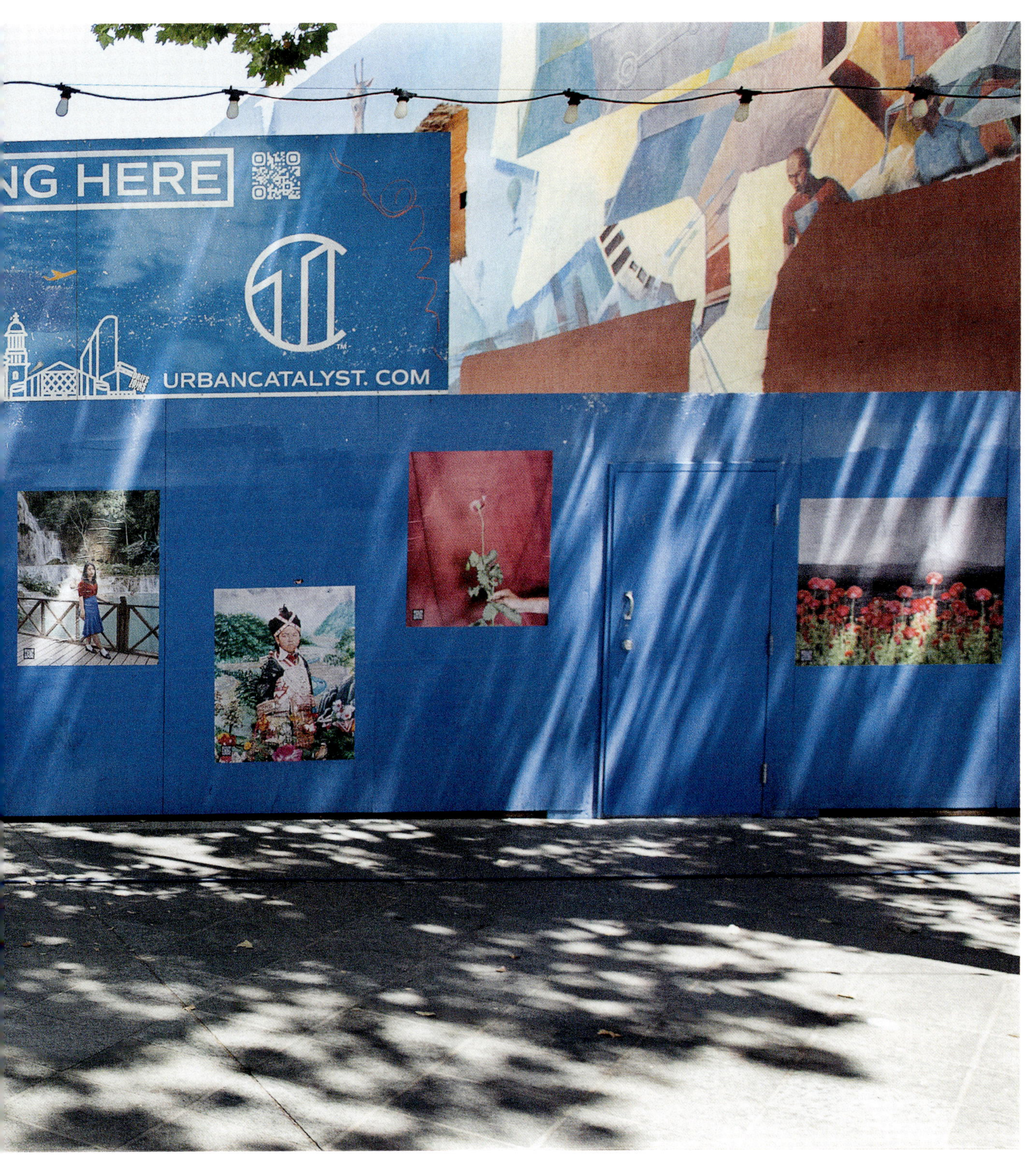

Pao Houa Her: The Imaginative Landscape,
installation view, downtown San José,
California, 2025

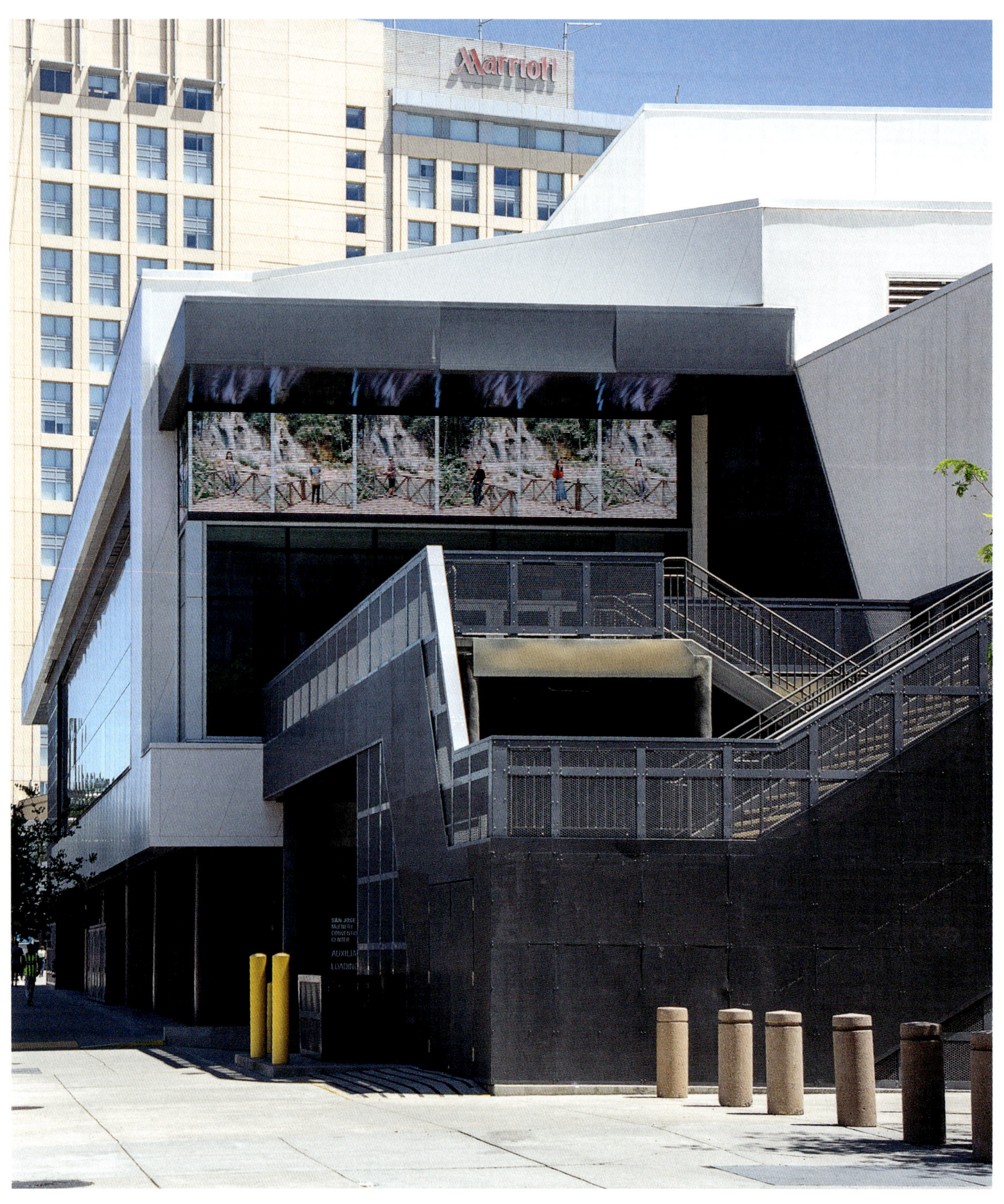

Pao Houa Her: The Imaginative Landscape,
installation view, downtown San José,
California, 2025

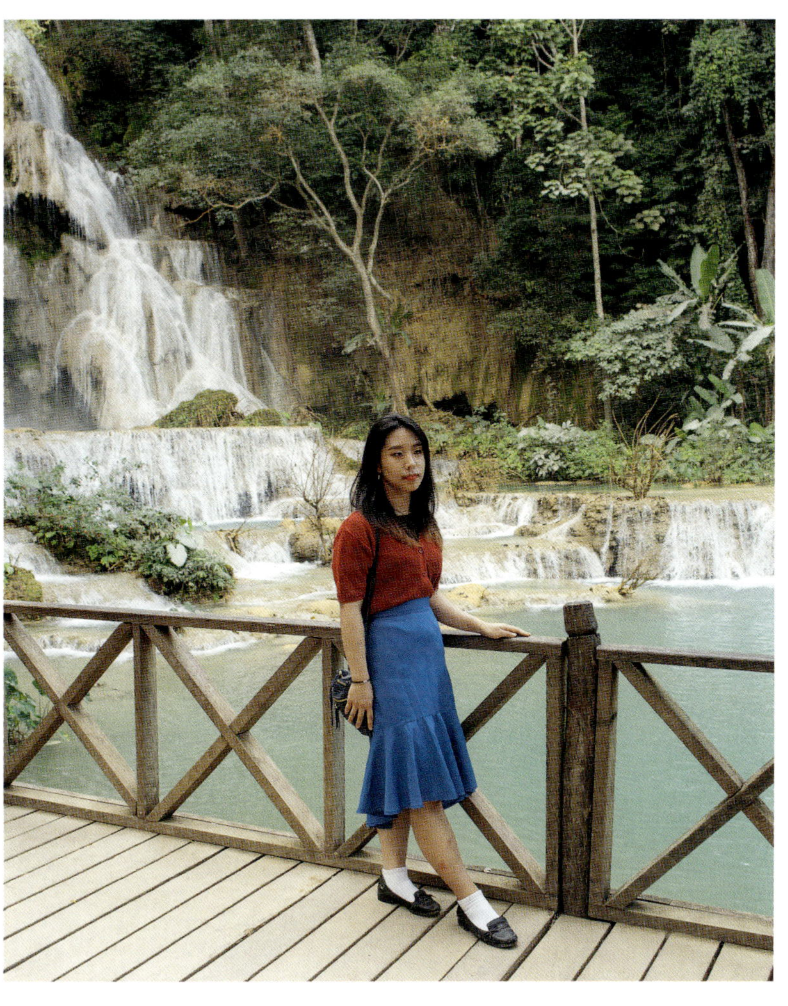

untitled (portrait of a woman in red shirt by
the waterfall), 2019, from The Imaginative
Landscape series, archival pigment print

125

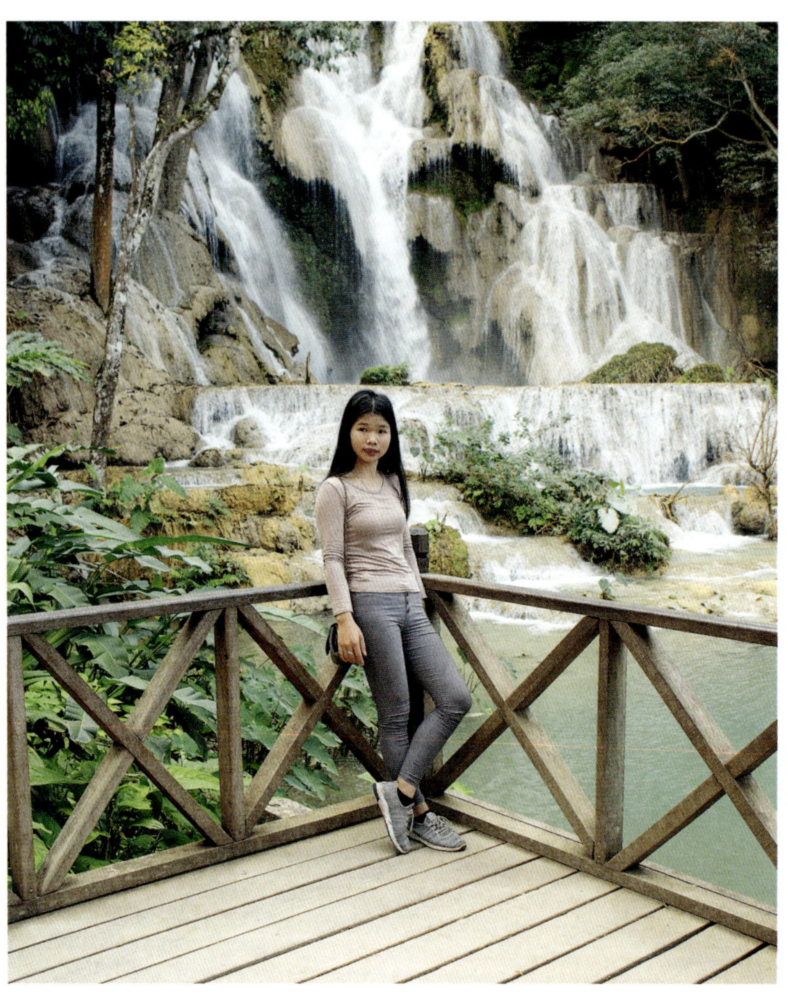

untitled (portrait of a woman in gray by the waterfall), 2019, from *The Imaginative Landscape* series, archival pigment print

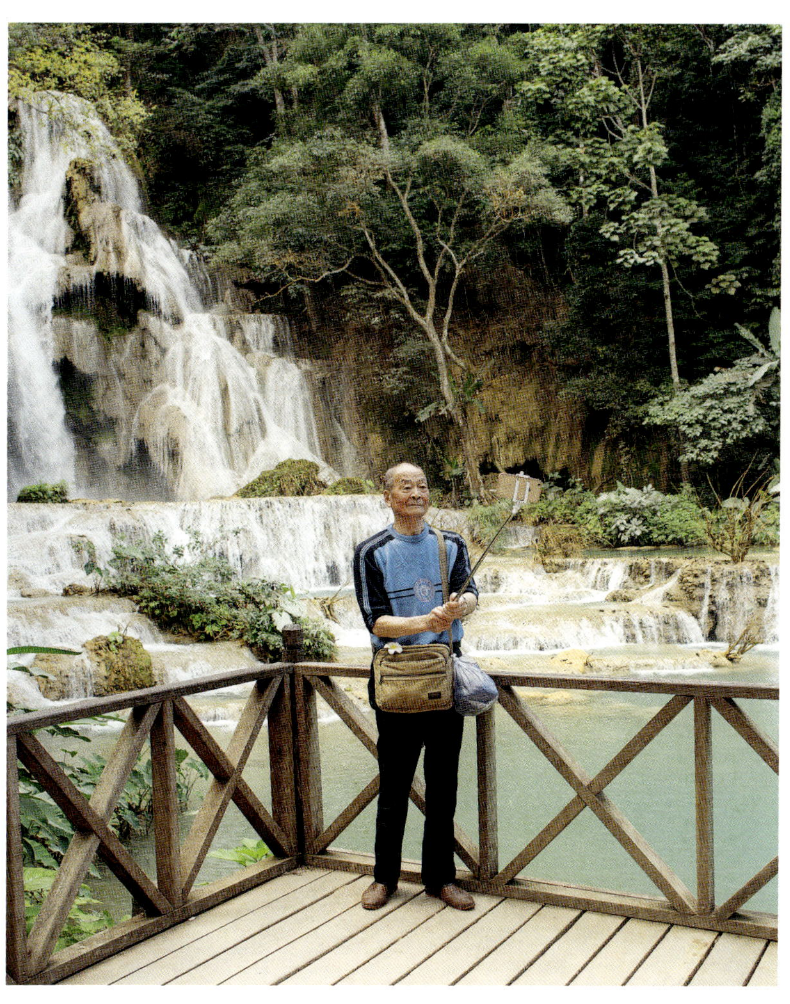

untitled, 2019, archival pigment print

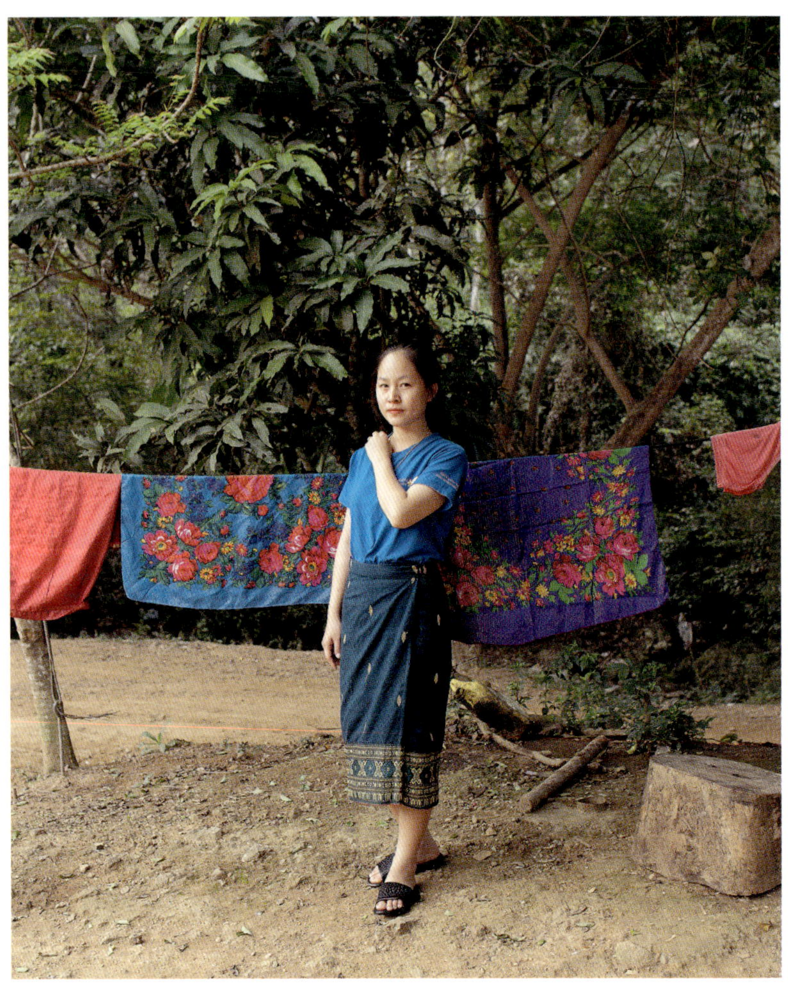

untitled (girl in the blue shirt), 2019,
from *The Imaginative Landscape*
series, archival pigment print

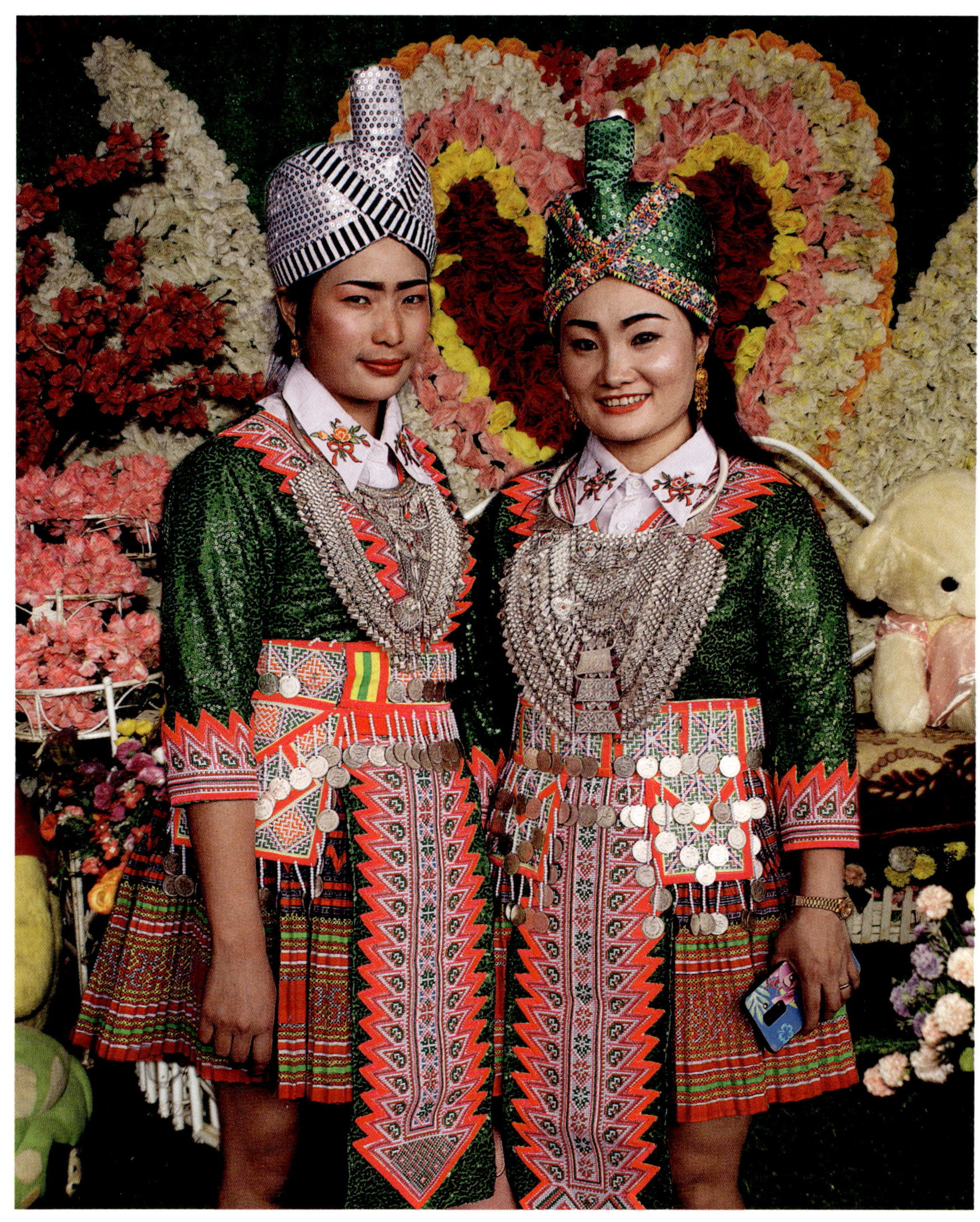

untitled (women in traditional outfits), 2019,
from *The Imaginative Landscape* series,
archival pigment print

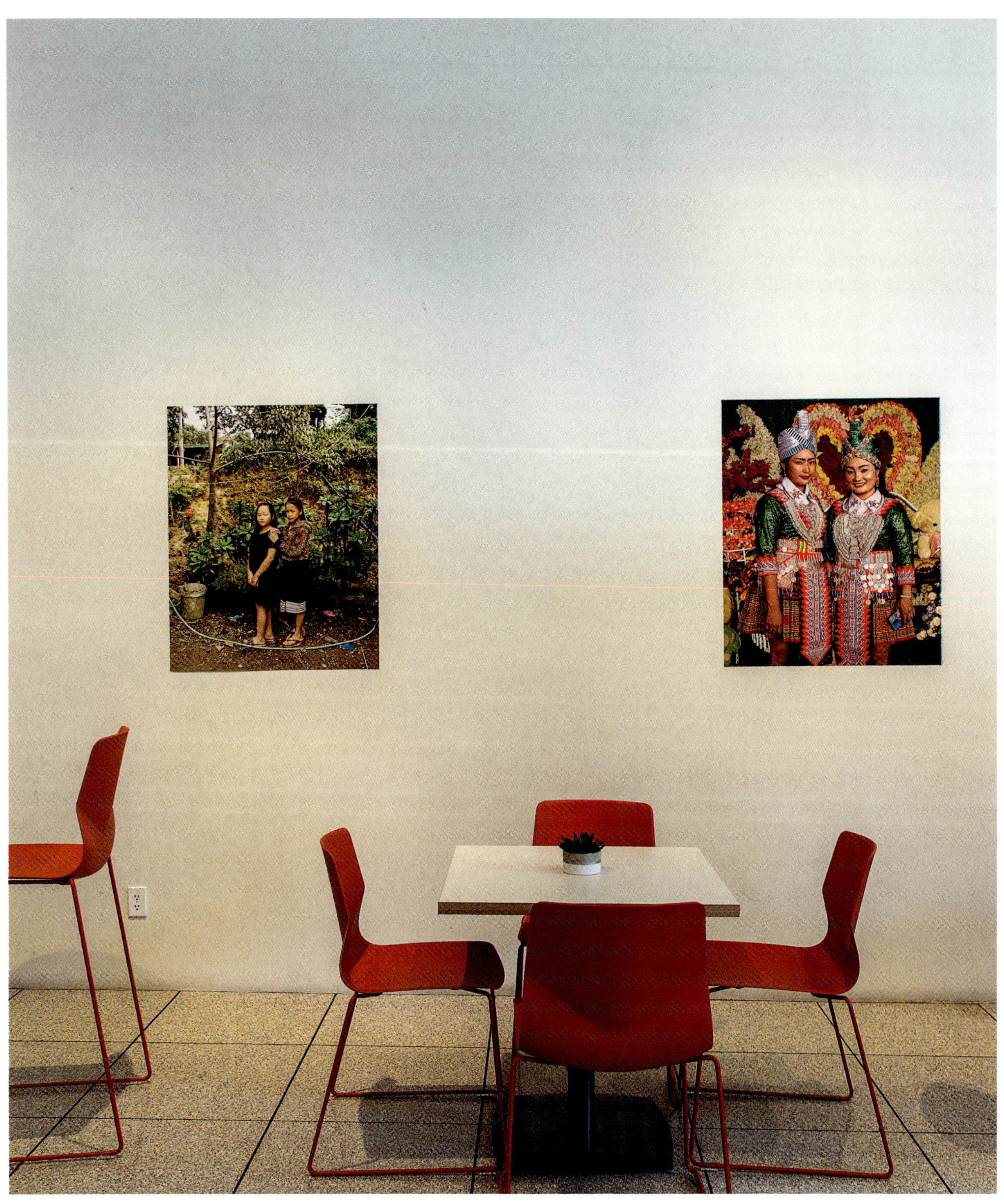

Pao Houa Her: The Imaginative Landscape, installation view
at San José Museum of Art, 2025

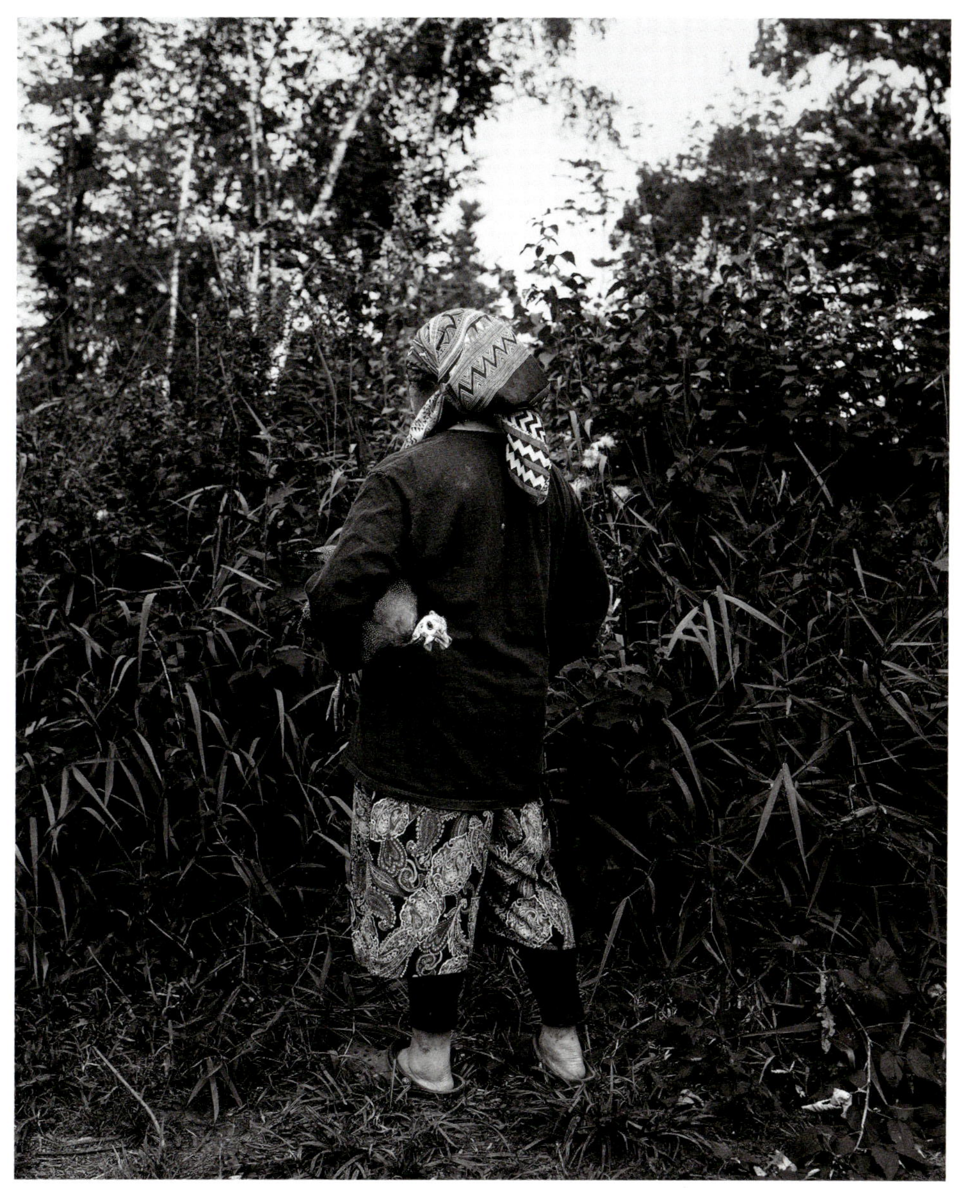

untitled (woman with guinea fowl), 2019,
from *The Imaginative Landscape* series,
archival pigment print

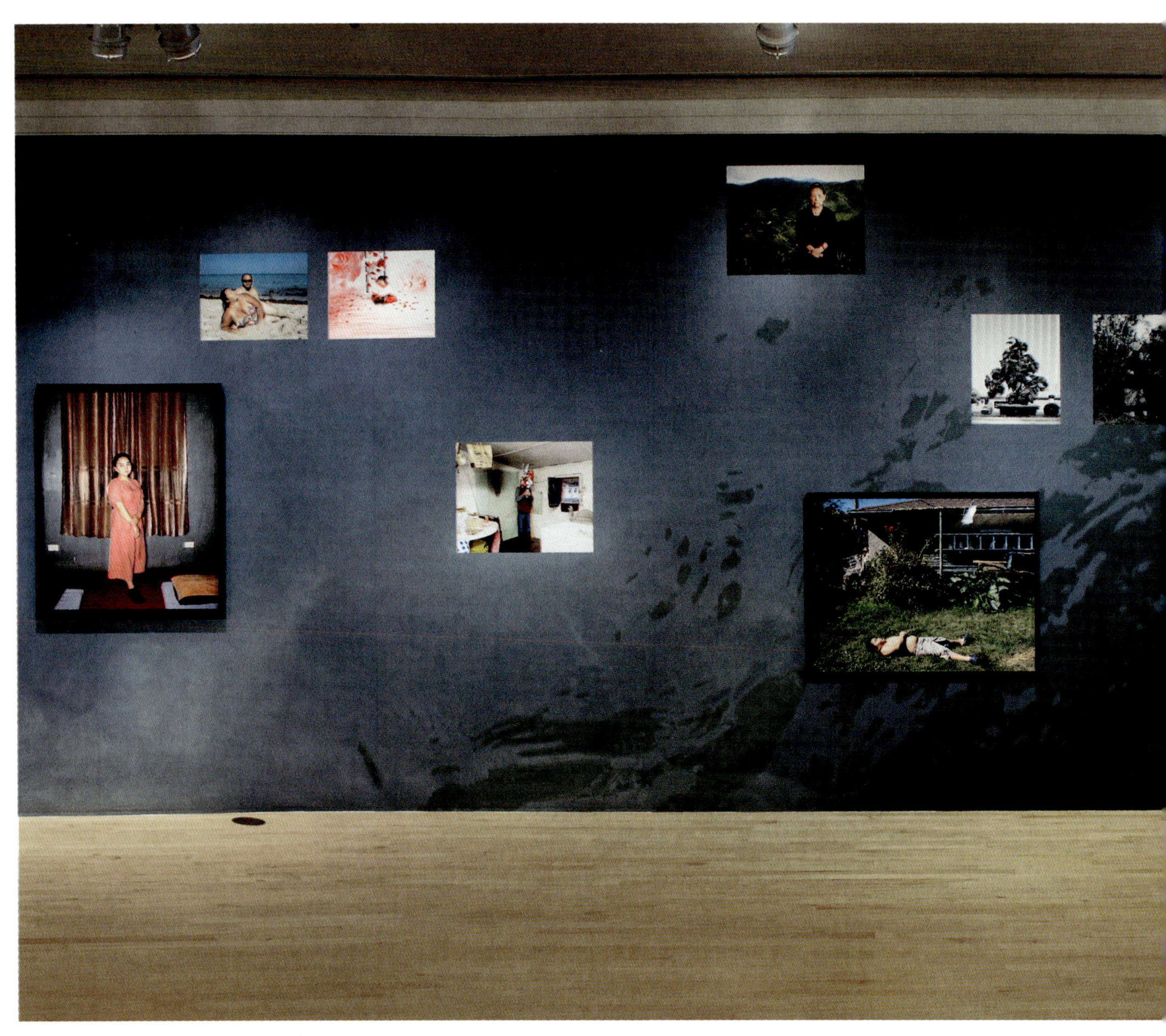

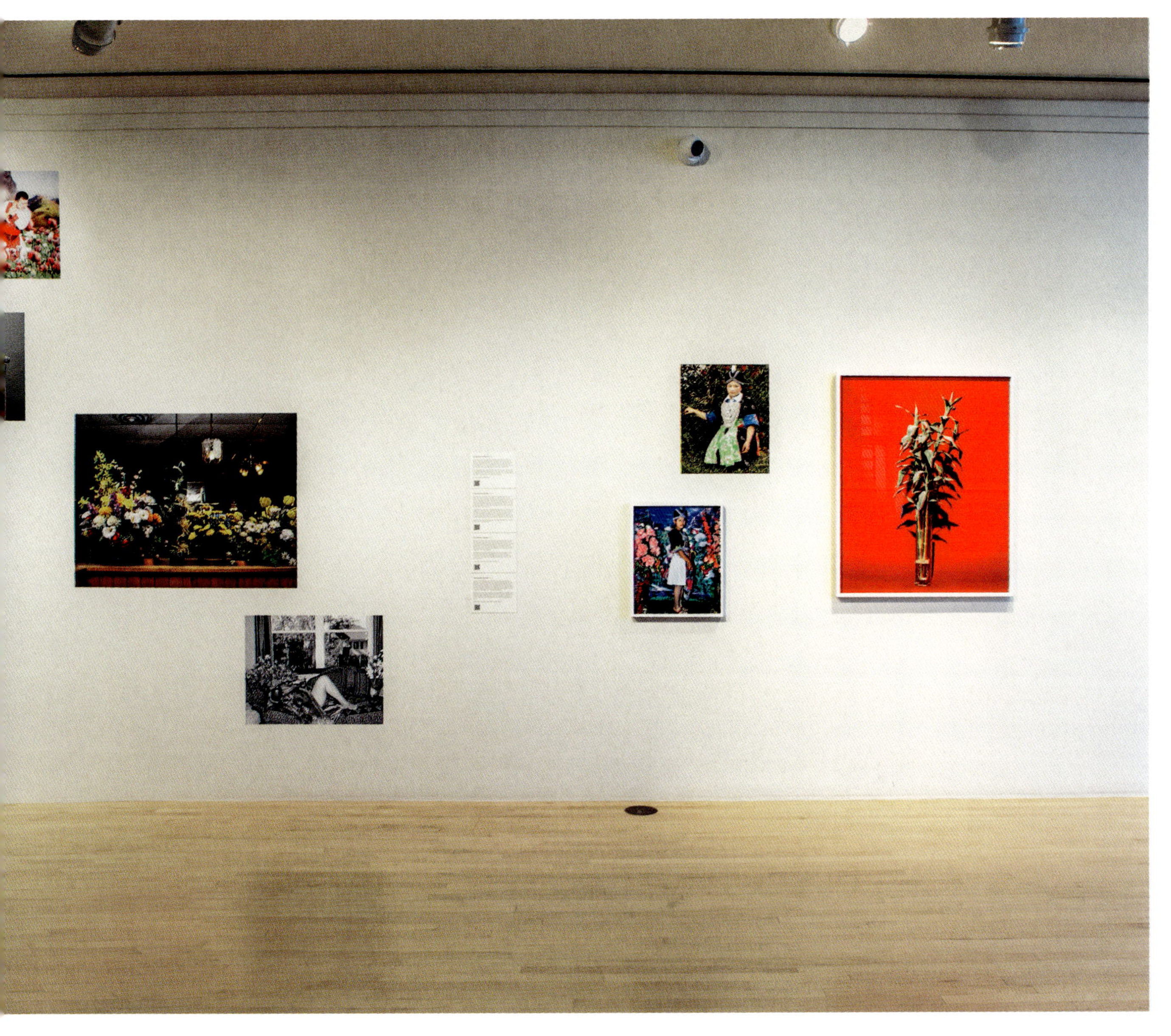

Pao Houa Her: The Imaginative Landscape, installation view
at San José Museum of Art, 2025

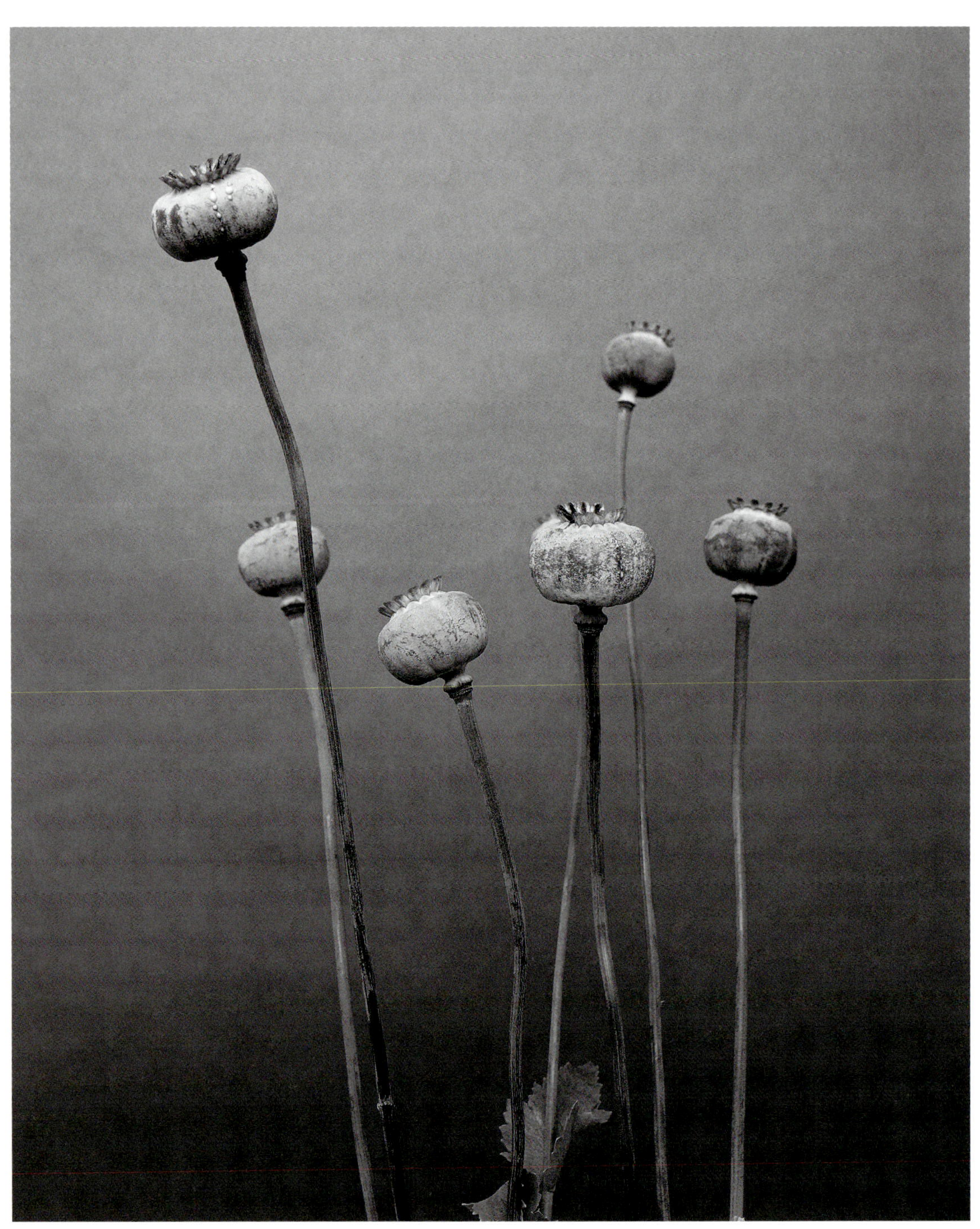

untitled (black and white dried poppies),
2019, from *The Imaginative Landscape*
series, archival pigment print

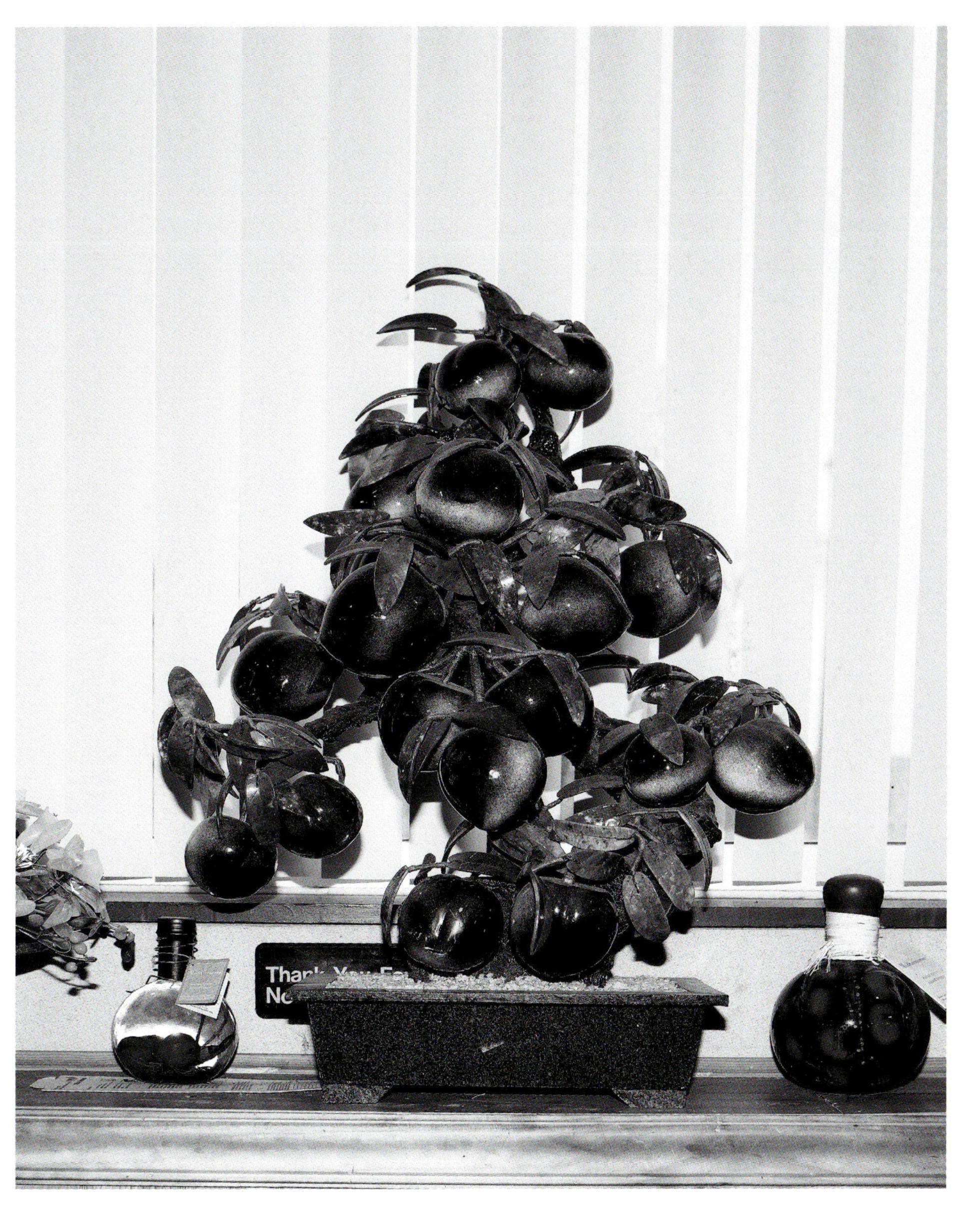

untitled (glass oranges), 2019, from
The Imaginative Landscape series,
archival pigment print   135

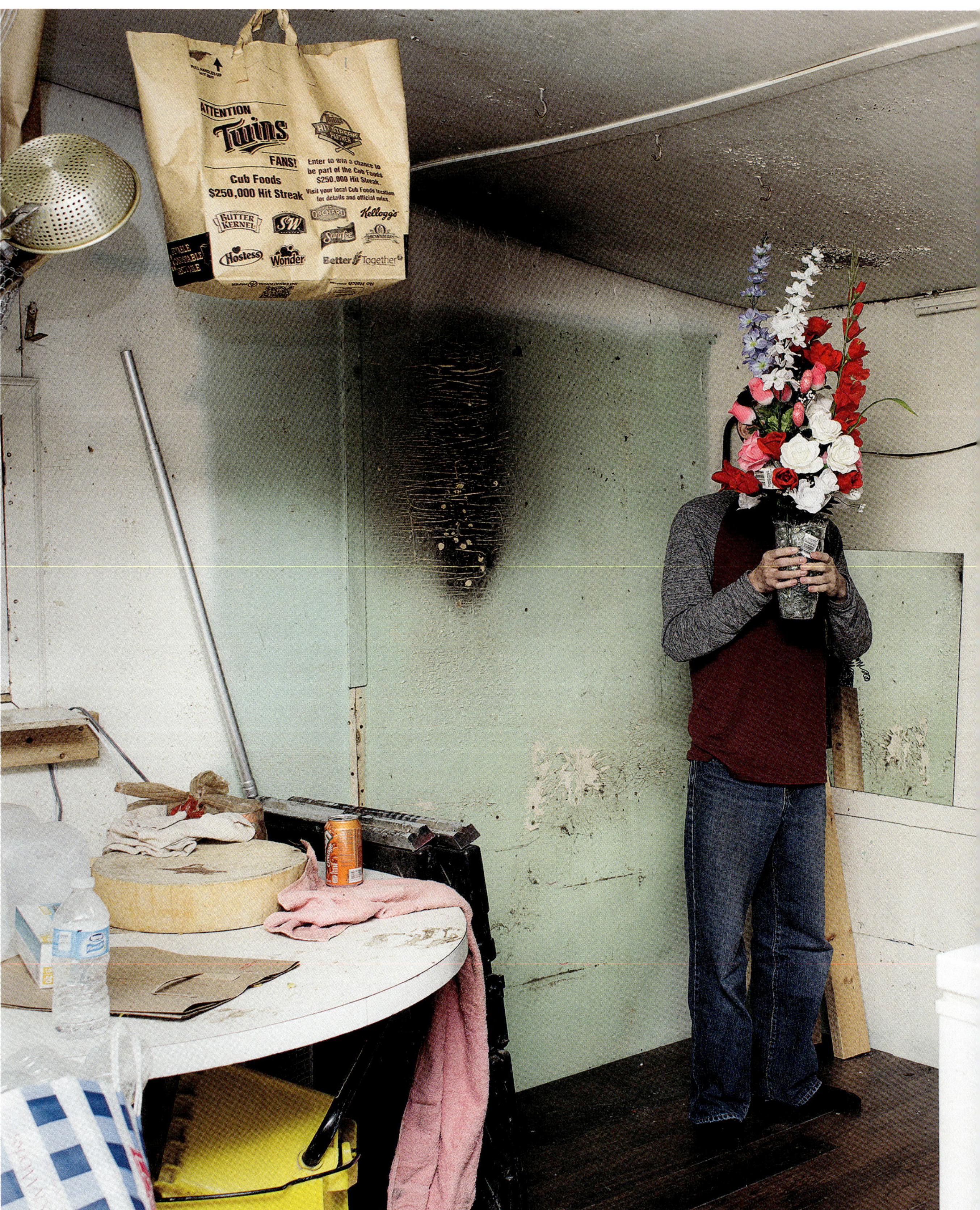

ATTENTION
Twins
FANS!
Cub Foods
$250,000 Hit Streak
Enter to win a chance to
be part of the Cub Foods
$250,000 Hit Streak.
Visit your local Cub Foods location
for details and official rules.
BUTTER KERNEL
S&W
ORCHARD
Kellogg's
Hostess
Wonder
Sara Lee
Better Together

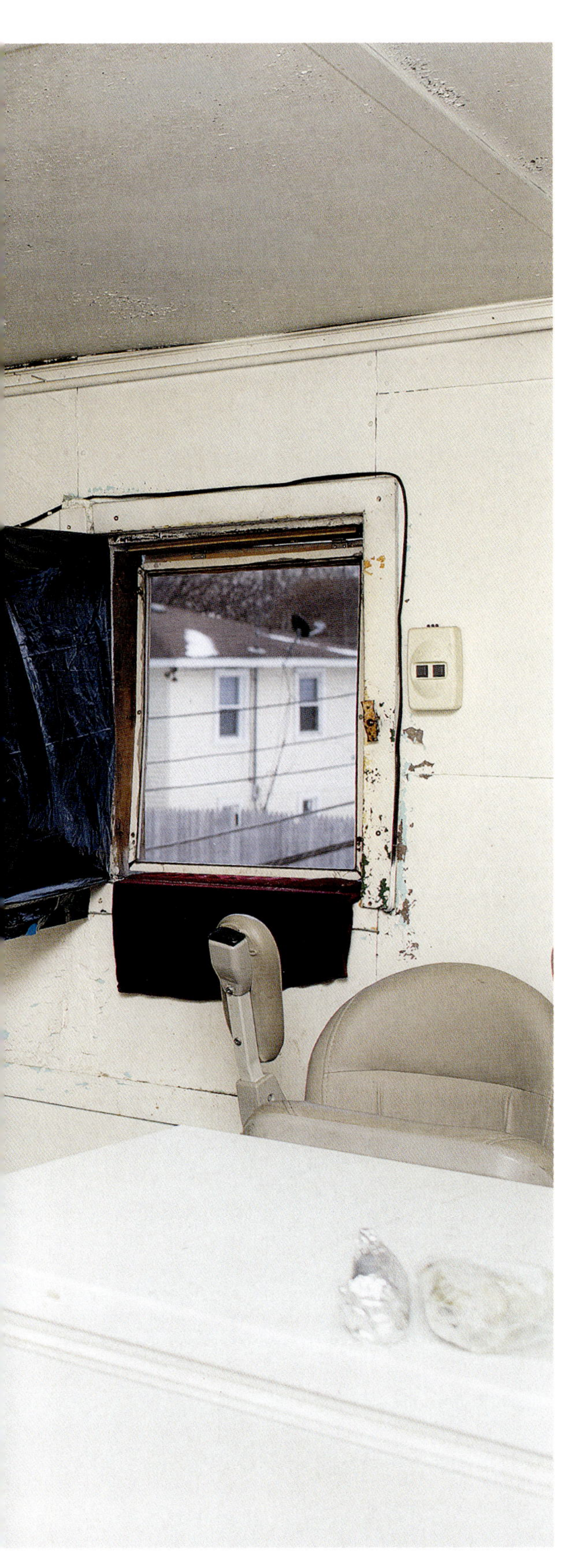

untitled (Brian with fake flowers standing
near the burn), 2019, from The Imaginative
Landscape series, archival pigment print   137

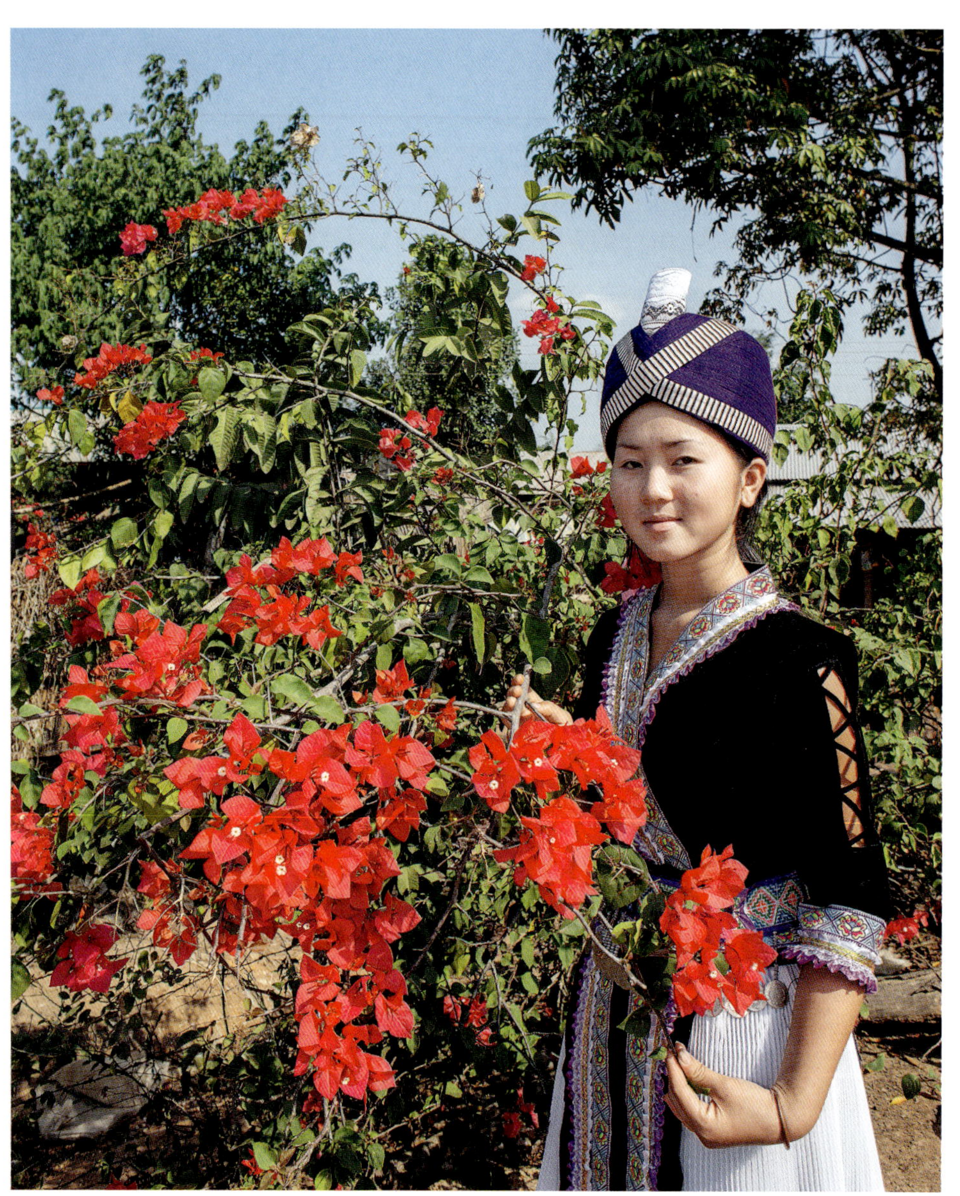

Untitled (nyab with red flowers),
2018, archival pigment print

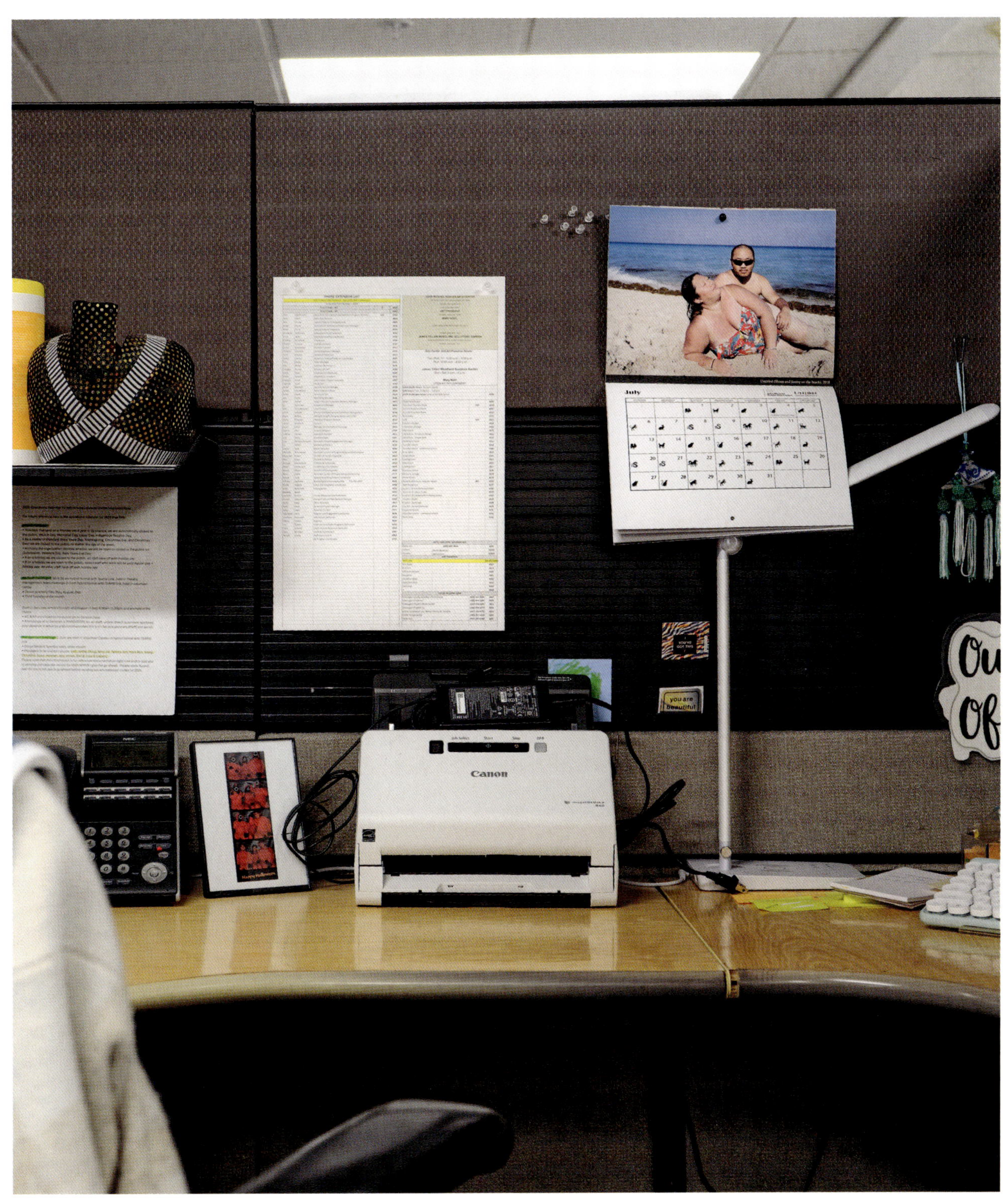

Pao Houa Her: The Imaginative Landscape,
installed calendar at the John Michael Kohler
Arts Center, Sheboygan, Wisconsin, 2025

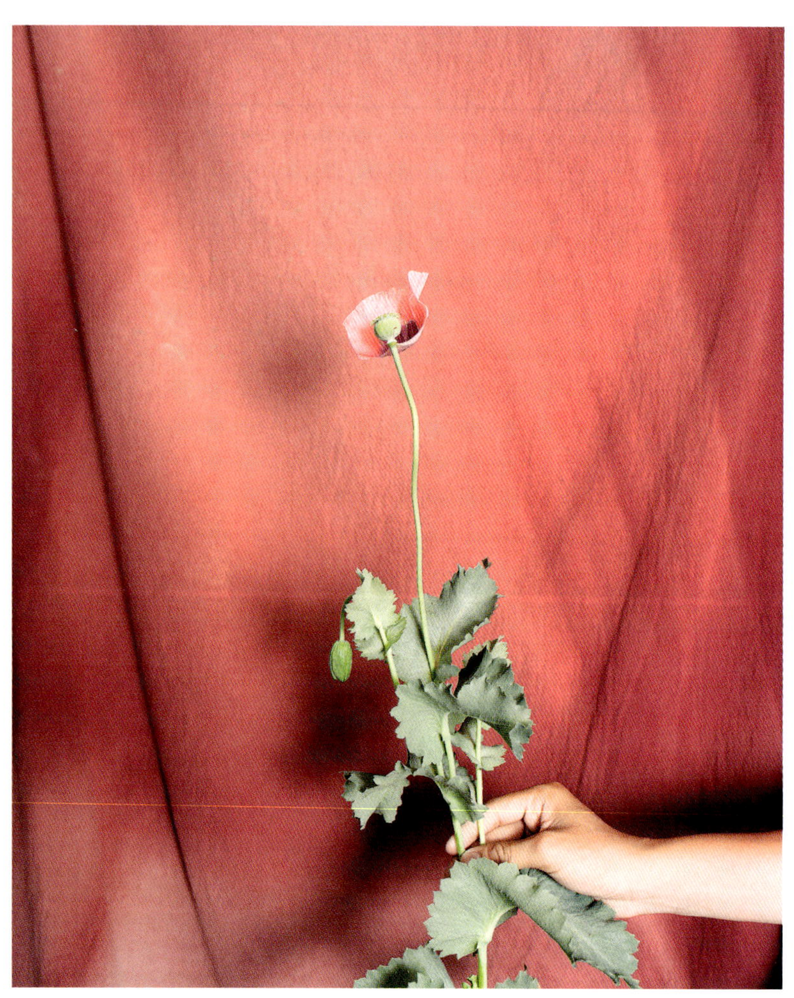

untitled (opium flower with pink fabric),
2019, from *The Imaginative Landscape*
series, archival pigment print

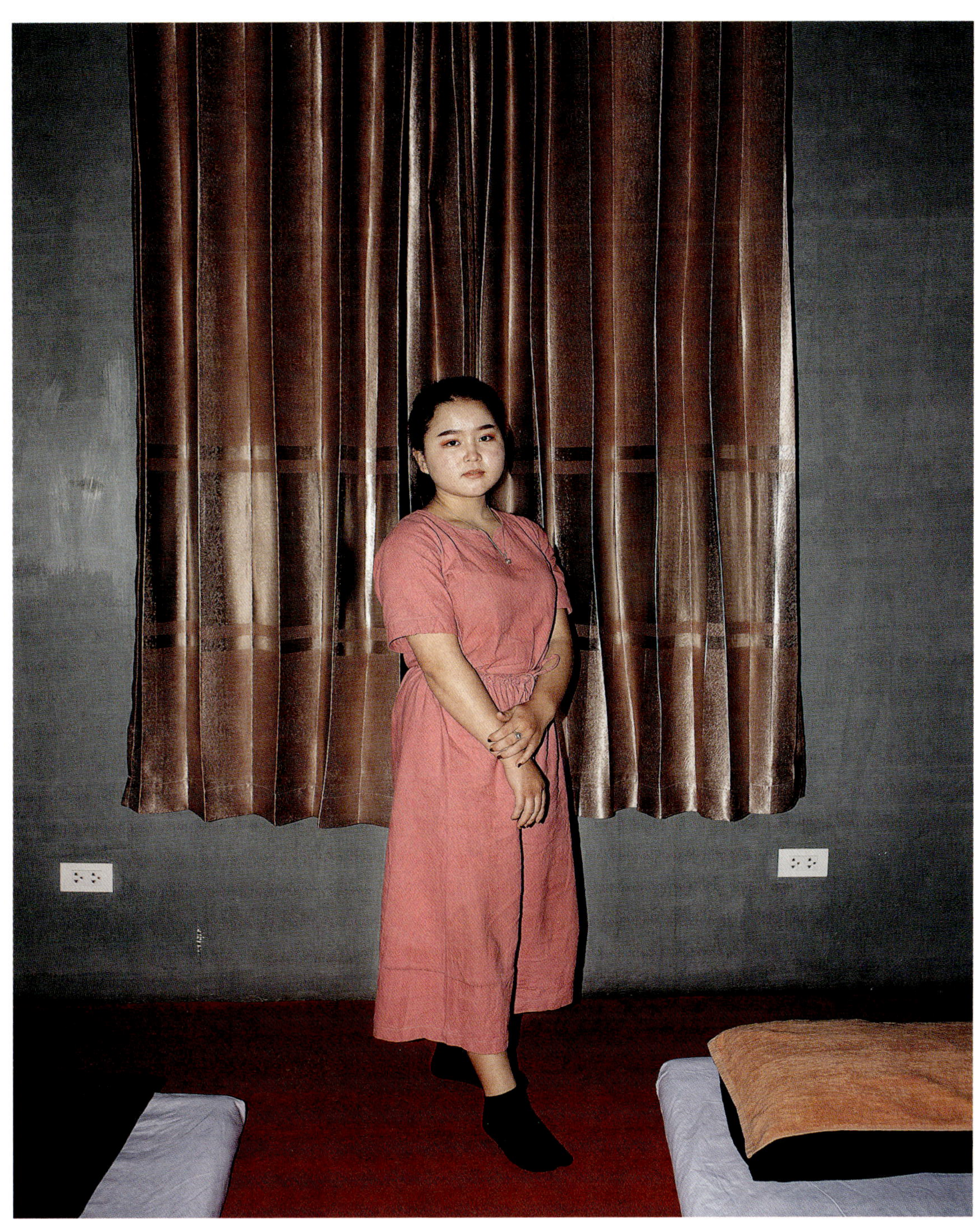

untitled (woman in pink), 2019,
from *The Imaginative Landscape*
series, archival pigment print

141

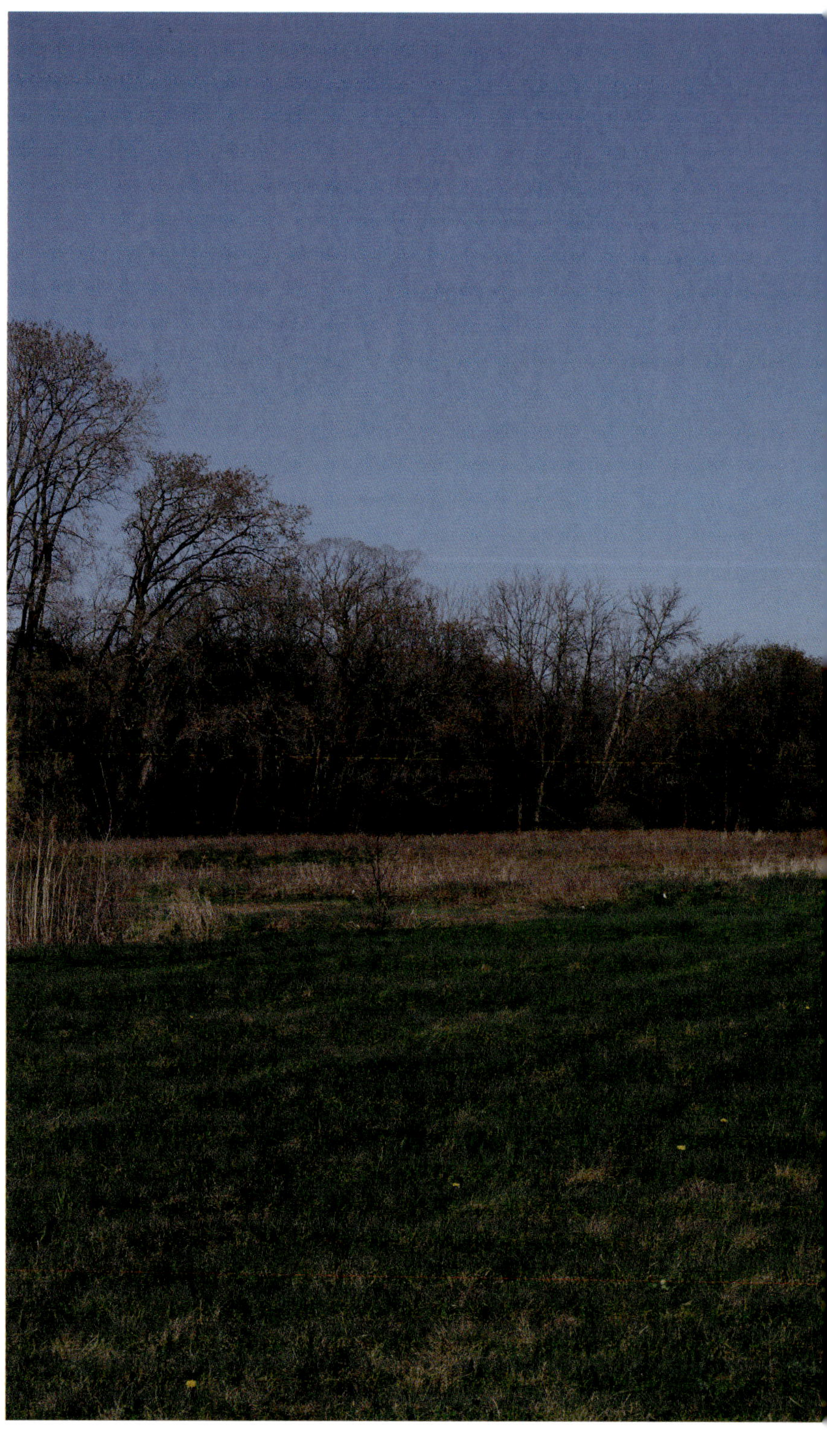

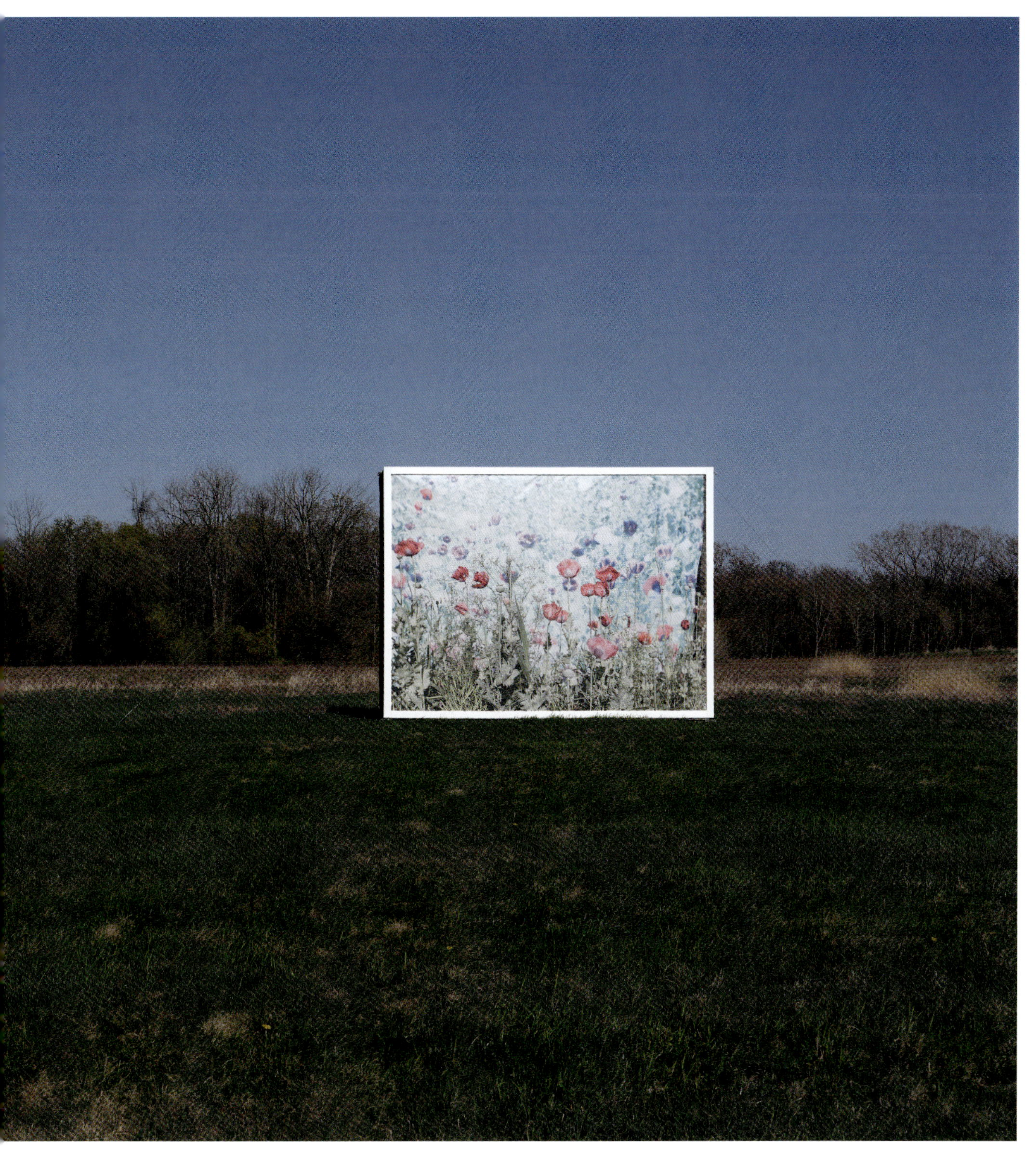

Pao Houa Her: The Imaginative Landscape,
installation view at the John Michael Kohler
Art Preserve, Sheboygan, Wisconsin, 2025

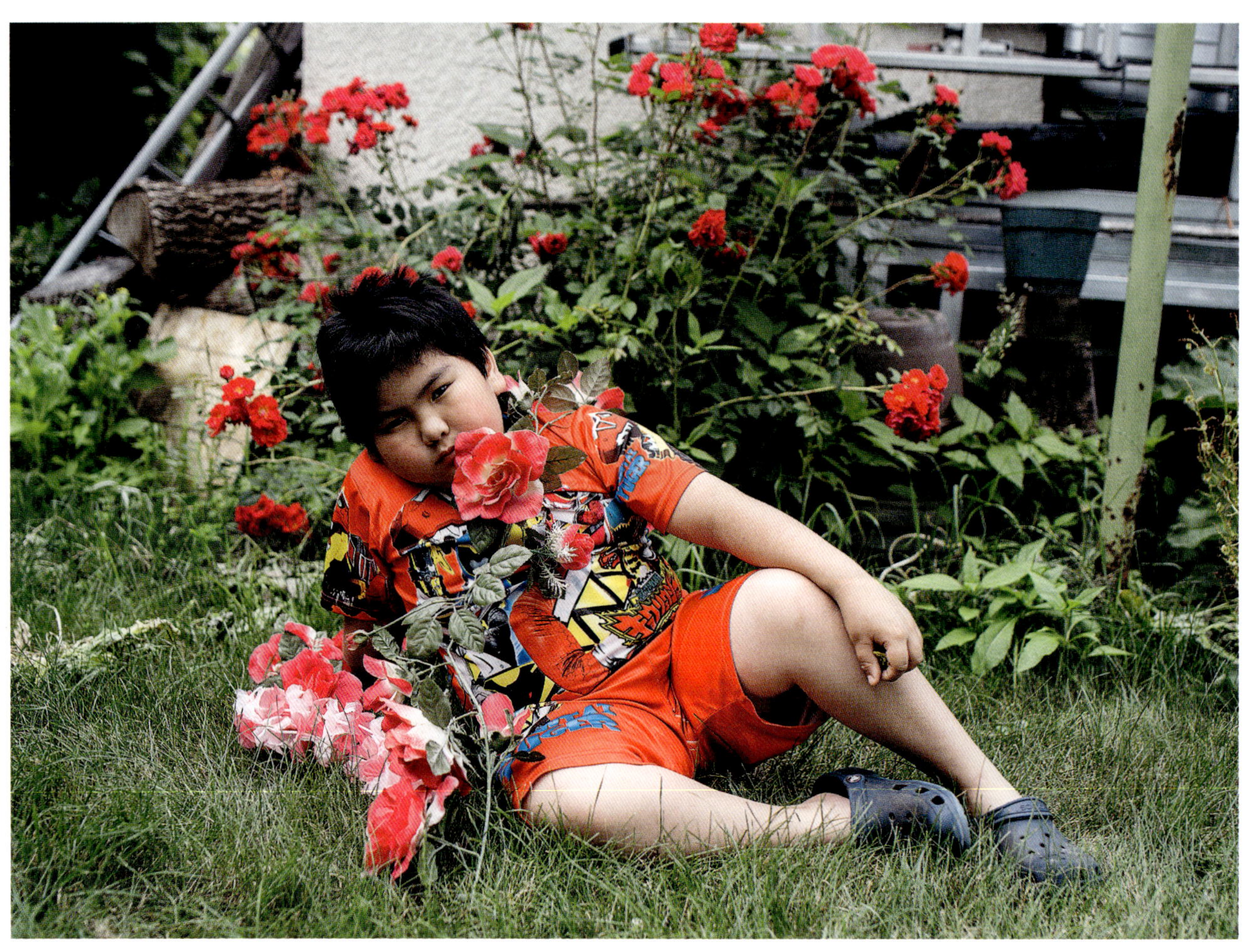

Untitled (Erik in the back yard), 2018,
archival pigment print

OTHERING STUDIO PORTRAITURE TRADITIONS IN COLONIAL SOUTHEAST ASIA

ALEXANDER SUPARTONO

Amid the infinite digital circulation on the internet, is the photograph on the following page, captioned *Phuam siv ceeb, Phaum Txoob saub*. In Hmongic, it is a description of the subject's headcloth: turban (*phuam*) and striped turban band (*siv ceeb*), and the long piece of fabric wrapped around her head and adorned by another piece of striped fabric *(phaum txoob saub)*. Fully dressed in traditional Hmong attire, the young lady stands against a plain sheet of fabric—a makeshift backdrop commonly employed in outdoor studio settings during photography expeditions to the colony's interior. Her lips are sealed but her posture is relaxed, with both hands resting at her sides nonchalantly. Her stare, however, is arresting. It is likely that she took some direction from the photographer but her gaze was beyond anybody's control but her own. In that moment, she decided to not merely stare back at the camera but engage with future viewers of her portrait. Her pose and gaze, rather than appearing submissive or challenging, suggests she was presenting herself with a considerable degree of agency. Perhaps she was a family member of local gentry, born with and raised to have an innate dignity. But the more likely scenario was that she had the opportunity to prepare for the sitting, as she was only one of many locals who participated in the photo session, indicated by the number on the bottom right-hand corner of the image (typical of the registering system employed by the photographers or photo studio for archival or commercial purposes).

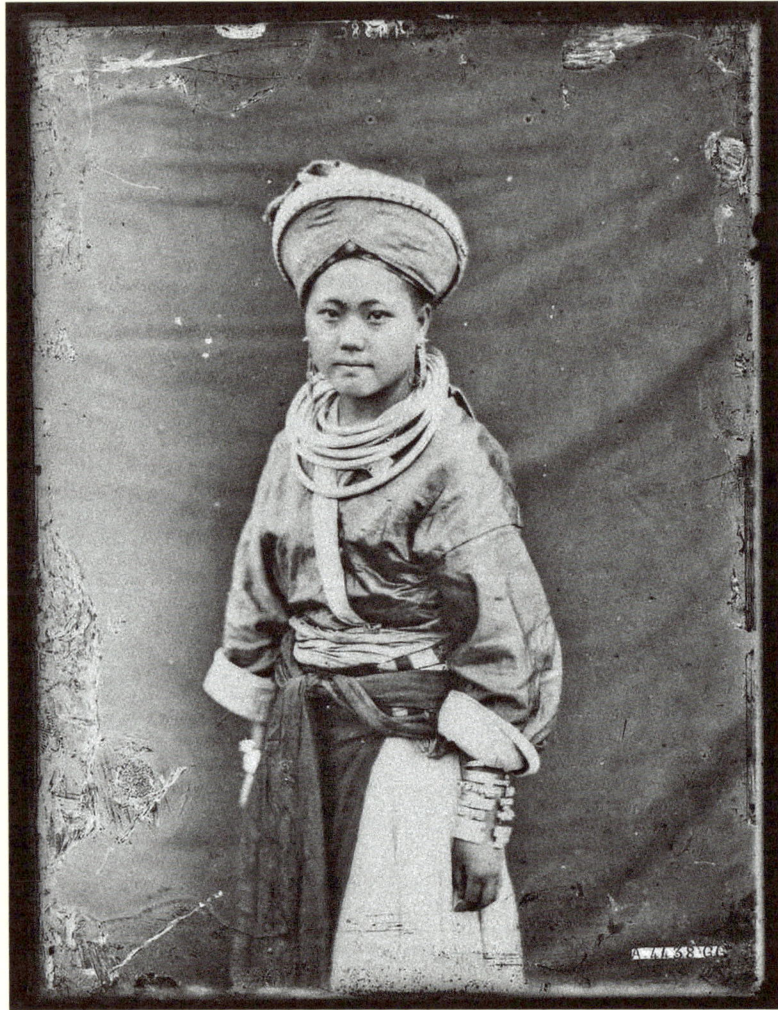

Unknown, *Untitled* (Phuam siv ceeb, Phaum Txoob saub), ca. 1880s–1920s, printed from glass negative

We may never know more about her beyond what is visible before our eyes. Her outfit betrays her ethnicity, which in turn points to the approximate geographical location where her portrait was taken, even if her surrounding was concealed by the backdrop. The image was made from a glass plate negative, a photographic process widely used from the 1850s to 1920s because of its economic, artistic, and practical qualities. Despite the mark from the glass plate holder on the edges, the photograph retains a soft, grainy look and clarity of detail. The photograph is slightly torn and there is some evidence that someone tried to remove stains or inscriptions

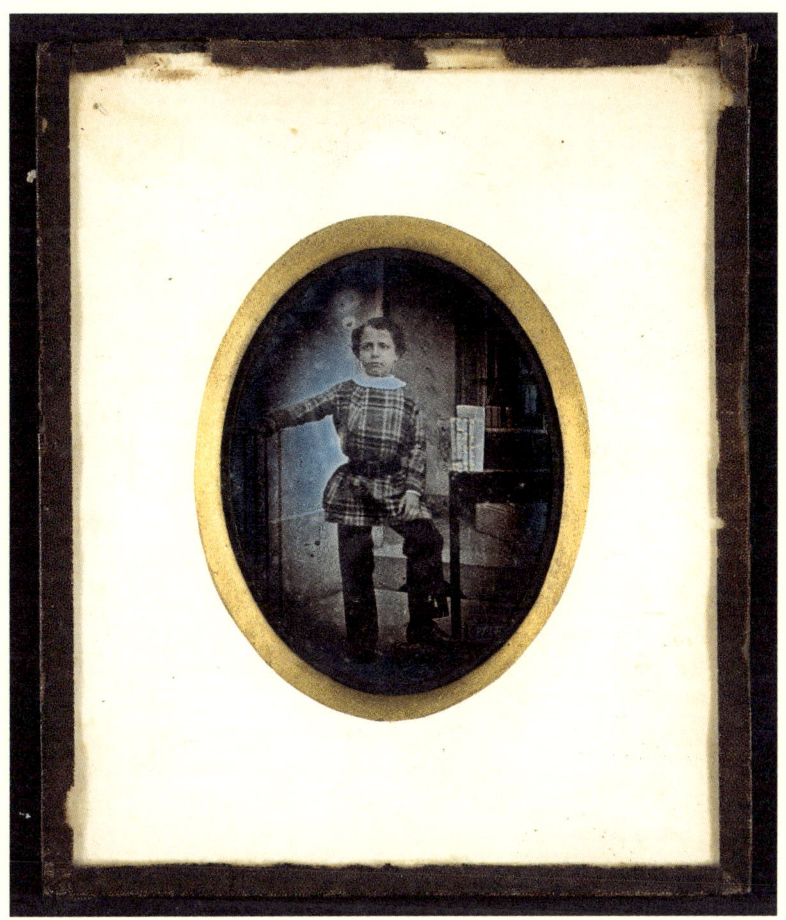

from the lower left-hand side, which suggests the photograph may have changed hands.

The portrait exemplifies the work of photographers and photographic studios in Southeast Asia at the turn of the twentieth century. The photographic process, her pose, and the dissemination of her portrait reflect a long history of photography in the region. Daguerreotype arrived in the area as early as 1840, less than a year after the public announcement of its invention in Paris in the summer 1839, when a Dutch health and army officer, Juriaan Munnich, carried a camera to Jakarta, Indonesia, for archaeological purposes but the daguerreotype equipment failed to operate due to the high tropical humidity. Five years later, Adolph Schaefer, who was known for his daguerreotype portrait studio in The Hague, produced the first daguerreotype series depicting objects from Javanese antiquity.[1] In his memoir, *Hikayat Abdullah* (Stories of Abdullah; 1849), the Malay scholar Abdullah bin Abdul Kadir Munsyi recounted his meeting in 1841 with Dr. Wright, a junior doctor on board the American ship USS *Constellation*, who took a photograph of Singapore from Fort Canning. Encountering a copper plate on which the detail of Singapore settlement was imprinted, Abdullah wrote: "without deviation even by so much as the breadth of a hair."[2] On December 7, 1843, the *Singapore Free Press and Mercantile Advertiser* published the earliest photographic service advertisement for a "daguerreotype portrait" by French portrait painter Gaston Dutronquoy. Whereas the oldest surviving photographic image of Southeast Asia was a daguerreotype titled *Boat Quay and the Singapore River* (1844), taken by French custom officer Jules Itier during his official visit to Singapore, Borneo, and the Philippines between 1843–45.[3]

The expansion of shipping routes in the nineteenth century ushered in daguerreotype's circulation to metropolitan port cities in Southeast Asia. In the second half of the 1840s, daguerreotypes were primarily employed for official or scientific purposes, often capturing landscapes and archaeological subjects, as with Schaefer and Itier. By the 1850s, however, they had become more commercial in nature, focusing on portraiture. During this period, itinerant daguerreotypists stayed in hotels, built temporary portrait studios, and announced their portraiture services in the local press. Although advertisements in Singapore and Jakarta documented lively activities of these mid-nineteenth-century nomad entrepreneurs, their works, as far as we know, remain unknown.[4] Perhaps unsurprisingly, it was the work of resident daguerreotypists with studios whose work survived.

Portrait of C. J. Sayers is one of the oldest known daguerreotype portraits produced by a resident studio in colonial Southeast Asia. It was taken between 1852 and 1857 by the Grivel & Co. studio in Semarang, one of the main port cities of the Dutch East Indies (now Indonesia). The portrait of the young man is a typical daguerreotype that—through embellishment—turned a lackluster image into a precious photographic object, and at the same time met the clientele's aspiration as an elite member of colonial society. Mounted on a passepartout with golden border and protected behind glass in a metal frame, these material elements enhanced the

1   See Alexander Supartono, "'The Silent Waiting': Javanese Antiquity and 19th-Century Photography in the Dutch East Indies," in Charmaine Toh, ed., *Living Pictures: Photography in Southeast Asia* (National Gallery of Singapore, 2022), 306–11.

2   As quoted in Janice Loo, "Daguerreotypes to Dry Plates: Photography in 19th-Century Singapore," in *BiblioAsia* (Oct.–Dec., 2019): 8.

3   Gilles Massot, "Jules Itier and the Lagrené Mission," in *History of Photography* 39, no. 43 (2015): 319–47.

4   See for example Robert Lenz & Co. and Saurman advertisements in *Singapore Strait Times*, July 10, 1896 and May 1, 1855, respectively.

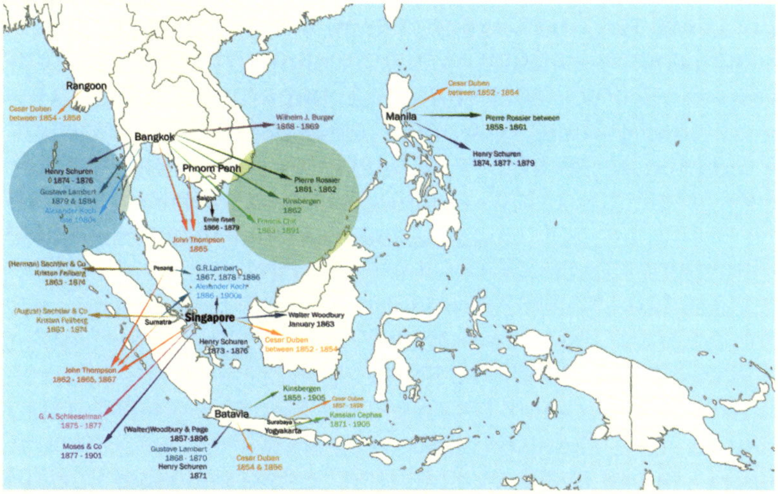

Map of photographers' activities in nineteenth-century Southeast Asia

5   Although paper negatives from calotype, which also allowed reproduction, was invented in 1840, this process is unknown in Southeast Asia.

6   The scene was also punctuated by amateur photographers, scientists, missionaries, travelers, and colonial government and military officers visiting or living in the colonies who owned a camera. For example, Dutch amateur enthusiast and wealthy traveler Gerrit Vershuur would present a letter from the Dutch Ministry of colonies to gain access to and photograph the kingdoms of Siam and Vietnam, and the Sultanates of Solo and Yogyakarta. See A. Groeneveld, and S. Wachlin, *From Bombay to Shanghai: Historical Photograph in South and Southeast Asia* (Stichting Fragment Foto, 1994), 7–9. Another example is John Lamprey's well-known anthropometric 1860s photograph *Front and Profile View of a Malayan Male* inspired similar endeavors in the region as exemplified in the 1885 album *Philippinen-Typen* by the Austrian A. B. Meyer. See Linda Roodenburg ed., *Anceaux's Glasses: Anthropological Photography since 1860* (Waanders Uitgevers, 2002).

7   See, for example, an Indonesian case, which is comparable anywhere else in Southeast Asia, Anneke Groeneveld and Steven Wachlin, "Commercial Photography til 1870," in Paul Faber, ed., *Toekang Potret: 100 years of Photography in the Dutch East Indies* (Fragment Uitgeverij, 1989).

subject's characterization and stature. The sitter, a young Charles Jacques Sayer, would become the general manager of a sugar factory in Java, the largest and most profitable agricultural industry in colonial Indonesia. Sayer exemplified the demographic of clientele drawn to early studio photography, which was principally made up of elite members of society: high ranking officers, industrialists, and local beau monde.

The advancement of photographic technologies and techniques in the 1850s, principally the wet collodion negative process combined with the albumen print positive process, allowed not only easier and cheaper production but also *re*production, which replaced the unique and costly daguerreotype plate.[5] The paper printing process rapidly spread photography beyond Southeast Asian port cities. The scope of clientele expanded to the colonial middle class. At the same time, the array of photographic products expanded to include stereographs, bound albums, and small portraits. Portraits of locals and their customs also became increasingly common and readily available in studios for general purchase. Photographers began to travel to interior Southeast Asia in search of new clients and to collect principal views and portraits of locals.[6] Owing to bourgeoning industry and trade across the region that provided steady and ever-growing clientele, commercial photo studios started to blossom.[7]

Singapore and Bangkok played important roles in the early development of photographic industry and culture in Southeast Asia. Singapore became a hub, serving as a meeting place where photographers from the West would set up temporary bases while collecting photography supplies or stop on their way back to Europe. Many of them stayed for much longer—setting up shop permanently and sometimes becoming residents.[8] Thailand's royals exhibited much enthusiasm toward the medium and turned Bangkok into a photography magnet where countless photographers plied their trades and aspired to the title of court photographer.[9] Jakarta-based Dutch photographer Isidore van Kinsbergen, for example, made portraits of members of royal families and locals when he visited Bangkok, in 1862, as part of Dutch official delegation.[10] An ambitious Scottish photographer named John Thomson, who worked in Singapore for four years, moved to Bangkok in 1865 before traveling onward to the continental part of the region, Cambodia.[11] Many of Thomson's contemporaries and the generations after shared his trajectory. Dutch, German, British, and French photographers crisscrossed colonial borders, disregarding their own nationalities.[12] The regional scope of commercial and artistic activities would characterize the photographic representation of Southeast Asia.

British duo Woodbury and Page was active in the Dutch colony of Indonesia and comprised the earliest photo studio to market and sell portraits of Malay and Chinese people as well as members of Javanese sultanates and other local gentries from late 1850s to the West. "We shall visit the Princes' Lands where all the native princes live, and all the magnificent ancient temples are,"[13] wrote Walter Bentley Woodbury to his mother in England in September 1857. The Mancunian photographer traveled east from Jakarta with over twenty indentured laborers carrying the cumbersome equipment required for the wet collodion process, which he had adapted to the tropical climate with great commercial success. This was, arguably, one of the earliest commercial productions of "type and custom" photography of communities in Southeast Asia. The studio collaborated with London-based photo agency Negretti and Zambra to market their photographs in Europe and America. In the same year, after ending his employment with Negretti and Zambra to make stereo views in China, Japan, and the Philippines, Pierre Rosier traveled to Bangkok where he made "ethnographic studies" and stayed for about four years.[14] The increased demand from the international market encouraged Philip Klier to open a studio in Rangoon,

8   Jason Toh, *Singapore Through 19th Century Photographs* (Editions Didier Millet, 2009).

9   Joachim K. Bautze, *Unseen Siam: Early Photography 1860–1910* (River Books, 2016).

10   Gerda Theuns-de Boer and Saskia Asser, *Isidore van Kinsbergen 1821–1905: Photo Pioneer and Theatre Maker in the Dutch East Indies* (Uitgevereij Aprilis, 2005).

11   Joel Montague and Jim Mizerski, *John Thomson, the Early Years – In Search of the Orient* (White Lotus Press, 2014).

12   There was also significant activity by Chinese, Japanese, and local photographers, and photo studios across Southeast Asia although their operational scope was not regional in nature.

13   As quoted in Steven Wachlin, *Woodbury and Page: Photographers in Java* (KITLV Press, 1994), 15.

14   Bautze, 45–71, and Terry Bennett, "Pierre Joseph Rossier (1829–1886) – Pioneer Photographer in Asia," accessed February 20, 2025, https://oldasiaphotography.com/pdf/researches/article-rossier-2022.pdf.

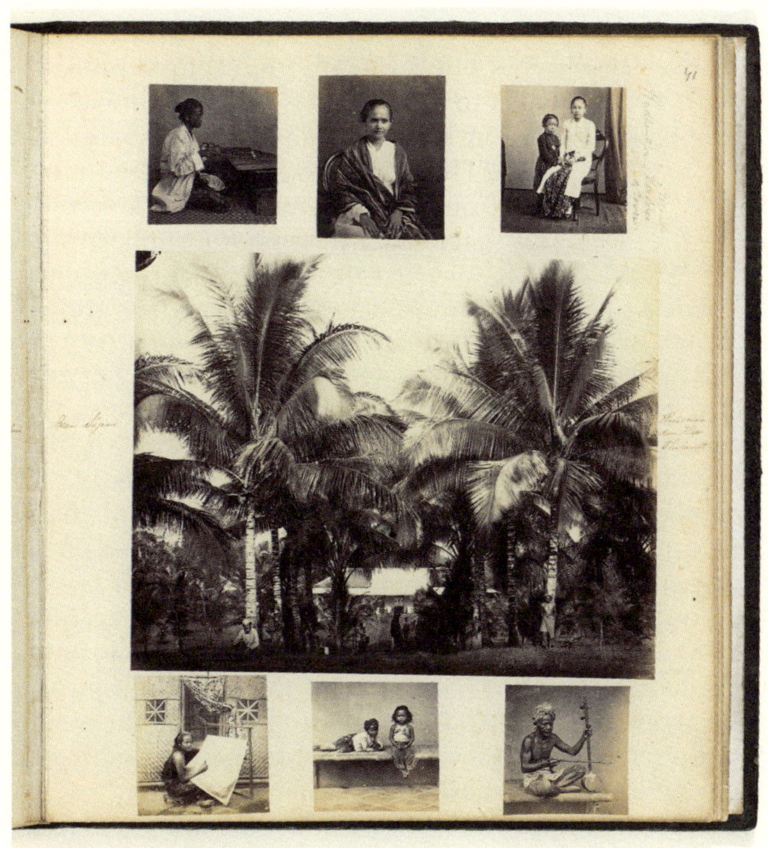

Woodbury and Page Studio, page from the album *Vues de Java* (Views of Java), 1863–66, Rijksmuseum, Amsterdam

15   Noel F Singer, *Burma A Photographic Journey 1855–1925* (Paul Straham-Kicadale Ltd, 1993).

Myanmar, in 1871, which produced extensive and high-quality works that further consolidated the market for photographic imagery of faraway lands and unfamiliar faces.[15] These resident photographers successfully marketed architectural and landscape views, as well as portraits and depictions of local customs. Their works were available for general purchase as individual photographs or in album format. These scenic views and studio-based "customs" would illustrate travel albums and travel books of turn-of-the-century global trotters.

A photo album called *Vues de Java* (Views of Java) is one of the earliest examples of the commodification of "view, type, and custom" photographs from colonial outposts that were collected into souvenir photographic albums. Now part of the Rijksmuseum collection, the original owner of the album was the Specht-Grijp family who had established a successful pharmaceutical business in Jakarta. Bound in green leather with gilt lettering, the album serves as a testament to their memories in the colony—a souvenir to share with family and friends in the Netherlands that offered a glimpse into the family's life in the tropics. The album page illustrated here describes the local "view, type, and custom." In the middle the page is a view of a garden with its tropical insignia: coconut trees swaying in the wind above everyday domestic scenes. Across the top is a row of three studio portraits featuring women in *kebaya*: one playing a wooden *gambang* from the gamelan orchestra, another seated on a chair with her gaze averted from the camera, and another accompanied by a child, both dressed in the attire of the Javanese gentry. At the bottom, from left to right: a Javanese woman crafting batik, two toddlers in batik cloths posing on a bamboo bench, and a bare-chested man wearing a headcloth, playing the *rebab*—a string instrument, also from the gamelan orchestra.

The meticulously crafted and orchestrated portraits of local inhabitants—the selection of subjects, their clothing, and specific activities—combined with the carefully composed arrangement of the seven photographs on the album page is a testament to the studio's astute understanding of both what its clientele desired and what they "ought" to see. Woodbury and Page's prescience in establishing a market for exotic photographs from the Orient is demonstrated in the inclusion of, for example, some of the traditional musical instruments of *gambang* and *rebab*. It would be another twenty years before the rise in popularity of Javanese gamelan music in the West, which followed its introduction at the 1889 Exposition Universelle in Paris. Such astute business vision, I argue, was shared among photographers and resident photo studios operating across Southeast Asia from the 1860s onward. They were responsible for the transformation of the region into a dynamic photographic scene at the turn of the twentieth century. They catered to their clientele with enticing formats such as stereographs, and widened their market with modestly priced *cartes de visites,* which were particularly popular locally.

The commercial success of photographers and photo studios in nineteenth- and early twentieth-century Southeast Asia was not only based on the ability to establish international market. More importantly, it was about cultivating a domestic market. As illustrated by *Vues de Java*, their immediate

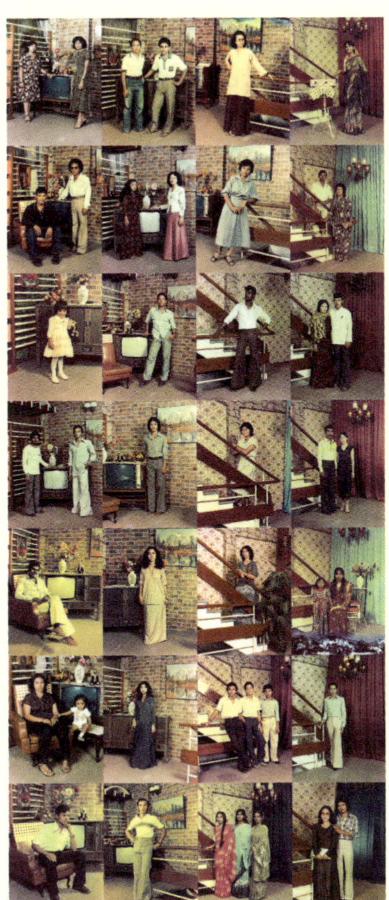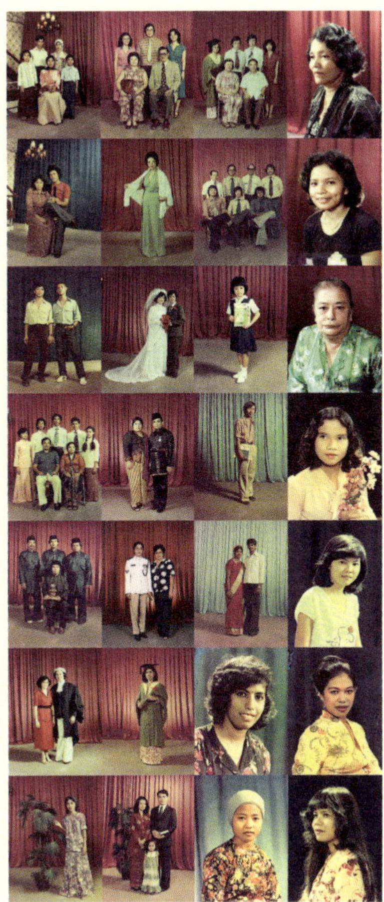

customers were the local elites, who sought photographic chronicles of their life and work in the colony, preferably structured and bound in lavishly decorated albums. This supply-and-demand dynamic fueled the industrialization of photography in Southeast Asia, along with establishing photography culture in the colonies. Within this industrial and cultural craze, the pictorial commonplace of Southeast Asia photographic representation was formulated. It enabled photographers to travel extensively across the region, capturing panoramic views and portraits to supply the growing market. From this production at industrial scale, we begin to see the development of patterns and motif, whether it be Javanese women with long hair dressed in *kebaya* and batik sarongs, Burmese women holding cigarettes, or Hmong women in turbans. The camera, in this case, offered technological and visual links that unified different Southeast Asian visual traditions in their photographic expression, reflected the region's shared political, economic, and social conditions of colonial relations.

POSTCOLONIAL POSTSCRIPT

The well-established colonial photography industry in Southeast Asia collapsed following the region's long decolonization process from the mid-1940s to the '70s. Western (and a few Japanese) photographers and photo studios closed, and the majority of their traditional clientele left the liberated colonies. Against this historical backdrop the growing numbers of Chinese commercial photographic studios across the region (and a small numbers of native photographers) bridged the photographic tradition from the colonial to the postcolonial era. Their continuing practices therefore were an adaptation and adoption of colonial convention in order to forge new national visual idioms in many Southeast Asian countries. They became part and parcel of the national identity project in their respective newly independent countries.[16] In this light, the photo studio serves as a lens through which to examine how the photographic tradition that developed during the colonial era influenced tradition and practices in the postcolonial era. What are the continuities, commonalities, synergies, or points of departure between them?

The so-called archival impulse in the 1990s and archive digitization in the following decade provided momentum for Southeast Asian artists to engage not only with colonial photographic material in established institutions such as the British Library or Amsterdam's Tropenmuseum, but also with local archives.[17] Malaysian artist Yee I-Lann, for example, repurposed the archive of Pakard Photo Studio, established by Chinese photographers Tam Hong Liam and Foong Han, in Melaka, in 1959. Their commercial activities documented generations of Chinese communities in Malay society. In her *Malaysiana* series (2002) I-Lann presented hundreds of studio portraits from Pakard's archive in a grid and created an immersive environment for audience to experience the multicultural society of Malaysia. These studio portraits chronicled milestones of family histories from birthdays and graduations

16   Karen Strassler, *Refracted Visions: Popular Photography and National Modernity in Java* (Duke University Press, 2010); Gael Newton, "Toward a History of the Asian Photographer at Home and Abroad: Case Studies of Southeast Asian Pioneers Francis Chit, Kassian Céphas and Yu Chong," in Patrick Flores and Sze Wee Low, *Charting Thought: Essays on Art in Southeast Asia* (National Gallery Singapore, 2018), 78–89.

17   Alexander Supartono and Alexandra Moschovi, "Contesting colonial (hi)stories: (Post)colonial imagining of Southeast Asia," *Journal of Southeast Asian Studies* 51, no. 3 (2020): 343–71.

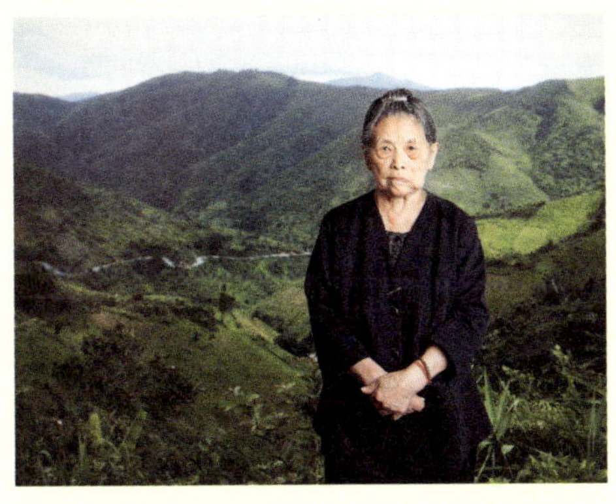

untitled, 2011–12, from the *Laos via Google* series, archival pigment print

to weddings. Observed at scale in an artistic repurposing, those humble studio portraits revealed the notion of sameness and otherness within Malaysian society, as seen in the racial and class identities of the sitters. The roots of this commercial portraiture typology can be traced in colonial practice. Critical comments on this tradition by contemporary Southeast Asian artists disclose and elaborate on different aspects of colonial power relation, while still operating within existing iconographies and visual idioms. The photo studio tradition in colonial Southeast Asia has endured through the postcolonial era.

Pao Houa Her's *Laos via Google* series can be seen as an attempt to break out from the race-based colonial photo studio typological tradition by devising technical convergence between the ubiquity of digital portraiture and real time availability of Google Images.

Untitled, from the *Laos via Google* series showcases a ubiquitous and familiar photographic genre: vernacular portraiture executed in the manner of a snapshot. An elderly woman stands against a backdrop of a picturesque tropical landscape. Her bewildered gaze contrasts with her relaxed pose. She is simultaneously at ease and bemused. She seems not to mind her portrait being taken but she doesn't understand the rationale behind it. For her, photography is far from a serious matter, a novelty. Having her portrait taken is not a special occasion anymore. In the past, she would wear her Sunday best to go to a photo studio and would pose to reveal her subjectivity. The ubiquity of photographic portraiture with the arrival of camera phones increased not only her familiarity with portraits of herself and her family and friends but also reduced the value of the occasion. A Google image of a vivid Laos landscape was digitally collaged to become a backdrop, which further enhances the vernacularity of her pose.

The generic nature of the snapshot, in which style, originality, and the agency of the photographer become irrelevant, allows Her to exercise the othering from the existing photo studio tradition. By employing a snapshot approach, literally and metaphorically, Her liberates herself from those conventions. And this is where she departs from visual idiom and iconography to create her own model—one that is informed by a long-distant nationalism and technology.

This project would not have been possible without the support and collaboration of Jodi Throckmorton, Lauren Dickens, and their dedicated teams and institutions. Thank you for believing in the vision behind my work.

To Bockley Gallery—Todd Bockley, Emily Marsolek, Nora Stewart, and Erin Robideaux Gleeson—thank you for your tireless coordination. Without you, this exhibition would not exist.

To my family—my mother, Mao Lee; my father, Neng Chou Her; Choua, Neng Her, Celina, Julie, Mai Youa, Allan, Anjelynt, and Erik—your unwavering support and encouragement make everything I do possible.

To my friends—Mee Xiong, Jenny Thao, Luci Vang, Hlee Thao, Glenda Yang, Bao Lee, Chelsey Xiong, Padee Vang, Monica Haller, and Tia Simon-Gardner thank you for keeping me grounded.

To my children—Toumeng, Brian, Matthew, Xander, Leroy, Sophia, Kailee, and Vince—everything I create is for you.

And finally, to my late husband, Ya Yang—none of this would have been possible without you.

The complexities of a project like this are numerous, as are the possibilities that emerge through meaningful community and institutional collaboration. *The Imaginative Landscape* grew from these possibilities—shaped by Pao Houa Her's vision, our curatorial kinship, and a supportive web of partners.

We are profoundly grateful to Her for her trust, brilliance, and fearless engagement with personal and political histories. It has been a privilege to work alongside her on this multifaceted exhibition and publication.

At JMKAC, we thank Chava Krivchenia, assistant curator; Jonas Sebura, director of exhibitions and collections; and Sheila Yang, community connection administrative associate— they each approached this complicated project with excitement bringing their problem-solving, open minds, good humor, and ability to keep a karaoke party rolling. To Amy Horst, executive director and Ann Brusky, deputy director of programming—thank you for developing and protecting a place where unconventional and challenging art and ideas are welcome and for your belief in this project. Also, from JMKAC, Adam Baas, Doug Brusky, Emily Duke, Brian Foree, Tanya Gayer, Charlie O'Connell, Peter Rettler, and Lisa Vihos provided crucial support. Daniel Abrahamson and Walter Lehmann provided great advice and assistance with Her's installation—thank you especially to Daniel for the years of conversations and problem solving. With deep appreciation to Zig, whose generous spirit, curious mind, and warm presence opened new possibilities for Pao's work in Sheboygan.

At SJMA, we thank Oshman Executive Director Sayre Batton and Karen Rapp, deputy director, for supporting the ambitious vision of simultaneous institutional presentations. To Robin Treen, manager of special projects and community partnerships, a special thanks for your expansive enthusiasm and finesse in bringing Her's work into the varied spaces of downtown San José. We're grateful to registrar Anamarie Alongi for her care with details, and Jonas Sebura for lending us his lenticular expertise. With heartfelt appreciation, we acknowledge the work of the SJMA exhibitions team, led by director of design and operations, Richard James Karson; Daniel Becker, associate exhibition designer; and Aaron Lee, preparator, and for the creative thinking of Jeff Bordona, director of education, and Daniel Jimenez, manager of museum experiences. Special thanks to our intrepid wheat-pasting team including Gemma Armas, Juan Omar Rodriguez, Melanie Samay, Frederick Liang, Bjorn Remo, Alma Luna, and Julian Zamora.

We are deeply grateful to Todd Bockley, Emily Marsolek, and Nora Stewart from Bockley Gallery in Minneapolis, for their support in putting this exhibition and publication together. Thank you to Chong Moua and Caroline Thao for their beautiful work translating text and Hmong song for the exhibition. We are indebted to Judith Thomas for her efforts organizing this publication—and her kind yet firm ability to keep us all on track. Thanks also to the team at Inventory Press for their beautiful book design and creative approach.

Pao Houa Her: The Imaginative Landscape received early and critical support from Teiger Foundation and The Andy Warhol Foundation for the Visual Arts, allowing it to expand and flourish. We echo the gratitude and appreciation to the exhibition and catalogue funders expressed in the directors' foreword.

Pao Houa Her:
The Imaginative Landscape
is published by
Inventory Press
2305 Hyperion Ave
Los Angeles, CA 90027
inventorypress.com
&
John Michael Kohler Arts Center
608 New York Ave
Sheboygan, WI 53081
jmkac.org
&
San José Museum of Art
110 S Market St
San José, CA 95113
sanjosemuseumofart.org

© 2025 Inventory Press, Los Angeles,
John Michael Kohler Arts Center,
Sheboygan, San José Museum
of Art, San José, and the authors.
All artworks © Pao Houa Her.

Unless otherwise stated all images
courtesy of the artist and Bockley
Gallery, Minneapolis, Minnesota

p. 16: ©Collection T. Dworzak/
Magnum Photos; p. 18: ©Atelier
Thomas Struth

Photography courtesy Frederick
Liang: pp. 43, 54, 74, 94–95, 112–16,
122, 124–25, back endpapers; Glen
Cheriton: pp. 45, 47, 84–85, 98–99;
Erin Little: pp. 27, 33, 35, 36, 38,
40, 49, 51, 56, 61, 65, 70, 73, 77, 78,
80, 86, 103, 109, 131, 135, 136, front
endpapers; Michael Huibregtse:
pp. 30, 63; Samer Ghani: p. 90.

Distributed by
ARTBOOK | D.A.P.
75 Broad St, Suite 630
New York, NY 10004
artbook.com

ISBN: 978-1-941753-83-5
LCCN: 2025945727

Publication Coordination
Zoe Kauder Nalebuff
Judith Thomas

Copyediting and Proofreading
Eugenia Bell

Lithography
Marjeta Morinc

Design
IN-FO.CO
(Adam Michaels, Ella Gold)

Printed and bound in Lithuania
by Balto

Front endpapers:
untitled, 2023–24, from the *Pictures
of paradise* series, 3D lenticular print

*untitled (Hmong elder in Hmong
clothes)*, 2018, from *The Imaginative
Landscape* series, archival pigment
print

Back endpapers:
*Pao Houa Her: The Imaginative
Landscape*, installation at Mezcal
Restaurant, San José, 2025

*Pao Houa Her: The Imaginative
Landscape*, installation view at
3 Sheeps Brewing, Sheboygan,
Wisconsin, 2025

This book is published in conjunction
with the exhibition *Pao Houa Her:
The Imaginative Landscape*,
co-organized by the John Michael
Kohler Arts Center, Sheboygan,
Wisconsin and San José Museum
of Art, California.

John Michael Kohler Arts Center
March 15–August 31, 2025

San José Museum of Art
July 11, 2025–February 22, 2026

This publication has been made
possible by Teiger Foundation and
The Andy Warhol Foundation for
the Visual Arts. The John Michael
Kohler Arts Center presentation is
made possible by the Kohler Trust
for Arts and Education, Ruth
Foundation for the Arts, the Mellon
Foundation, the Frederic Cornell
Kohler Charitable Trust, Kohler
Foundation Inc., the Wisconsin
Arts Board with funds from the State
of Wisconsin and the National
Endowment for the Arts, and from
the generous support of our members
and donors. The San José Museum
of Art presentation is made possible
by the SJMA Exhibitions Fund,
with generous support from the
E. Rhodes and Leona B. Carpenter
Foundation, Brook Hartzell and
Tad Freese, Wanda Kownacki,
and Mary Mocas and Marv Tseu.